MARK TWAIN
IN ERUPTION

Books by
MARK TWAIN

The Innocents Abroad
Roughing It
The Gilded Age
A Tramp Abroad
Following the Equator
Pudd'nhead Wilson
Sketches New and Old
The American Claimant
Christian Science
A Connecticut Yankee in King Arthur's Court
The Adventures of Huckleberry Finn
Personal Recollections of Joan of Arc
Life on the Mississippi
The Man That Corrupted Hadleyburg
The Prince and the Pauper
The $30,000 Bequest
The Adventures of Tom Sawyer
Tom Sawyer Abroad
What Is Man?
The Mysterious Stranger
In Defense of Harriet Shelley and Other Essays

Europe and Elsewhere
Mark Twain's Letters
Mark Twain's Speeches
The Autobiography of Mark Twain
Mark Twain's Notebook
Mark Twain in Eruption
St. Joan of Arc
Capt. Stormfield's Visit to Heaven
Concerning the Jews
The Private Life of Adam and Eve
Slovenly Peter
Adam's Diary
A Dog's Tale
A Double-Barreled Detective Story
Editorial Wild Oats
Eve's Diary
Is Shakespeare Dead?
A Horse's Tale
The Jumping Frog
The £1,000,000 Bank-Note
Travels at Home
Travels in History

HARPER & BROTHERS
PUBLISHERS

Always do right. This will gratify some people, & astonish the rest.

Truly Yours

Mark Twain

New York, Feb. 16, 1901.

MARK TWAIN
IN ERUPTION

Hitherto Unpublished Pages about
Men and Events

by

MARK TWAIN [pseud.]
Samuel Clemens

EDITED
AND WITH AN INTRODUCTION
BY
BERNARD DeVOTO

HARPER & BROTHERS PUBLISHERS

NEW YORK AND LONDON

CONTENTS

INTRODUCTION

I

When Albert Bigelow Paine published his two-volume edition of Mark Twain's *Autobiography* in 1924, he used something less than half of the typescript in which everything that Mark wanted in his memoirs had been brought together. This book uses about half of the remainder. It has been selected, rearranged, and to some extent edited. The man who ventures to edit Mark Twain must account for himself to the public, and I ask leave to describe what I have done.

I have prepared the book as an agent of the Mark Twain Estate and of Harper & Brothers, who asked me to read the unpublished Mark Twain Papers and to determine which of them, in my judgment, were worth publishing. It soon became clear that unpublished portions of the *Autobiography* contained many things that should see print. But it was also clear that if the book were to interest more than a small group of students and collectors, some surgery must be done on the text. If I should follow the plan of my predecessor, Mr. Paine, which was to publish selections in the arrangement Mark Twain originally gave them, interspersed as they were with trivialities, irrelevancies, newspaper clippings, and unimportant letters—disconnected and without plan—then I should come out with something as shapeless as the published portion, which had always seemed to me an annoying book. It would be more unsatisfactory, in fact, for Mr. Paine had published most of the longer sequences that would stand on their own feet. On the other hand, by omitting trivialities and joining together things that belonged together, I could make a book which, I thought, would interest many people and add much that was characteristic and something that was new to our picture of Mark Twain.

What is printed here is printed in Mark Twain's own words. I have modernized the punctuation by deleting thousands of commas and dashes, and probably should have deleted hundreds more. I have corrected several obviously inadvertent slips in grammar; to have let them stand would have been absurd. And perhaps a dozen times I have broken up sentences that had got intolerably long because Mark was lounging in bed and talking with such comfort that he forgot the shortness of a reader's breath. Most readers will probably wish that I had broken up others like them. For the rest, I have done nothing except to change a pronoun to the name of a person or a book where such a change was necessary because I had omitted something that went before.

None of those omissions has been made in the interest of decency. The rumor will not down that the unpublished Papers are full of obscenities. Well, there are a few satirical pieces which some people who have read them at my request profess to find shocking, though it seems to me that the shock must be of an antique kind. There is nothing in the *Autobiography* that resembles them: the only indecorum besides the mild anecdote told in connection with Andrew Carnegie describes how a dear little girl embarrassed her elders with some innocent *double entendres*. It may have brought repentant tears to the eyes of the banqueting millionaires who are several times described in this book, but in 1940 it is not only maudlin but tiresome and I have left it out. And exactly that principle has determined my other omissions. I have left out what seems to me irrelevant or uninteresting.

Mark Twain's notion was that he could produce a fascinating book by the method of free association —by talking about whatever came into his mind, no matter what he had been talking about a moment ago. The two volumes previously published show that the method frequently let him down. If the reader will follow through these two volumes any single incident, for example Mark's serial indignation at the President's secretary who ejected a woman from the White House (other parts of which have been woven into this text), he will understand the method I have substituted. After determining which portions of the unpublished typescript I wanted to print, I first deleted from them interpolations, headlines and newspaper stories, and such other interruptions as I considered disfiguring, and then brought them together in a kind of order. It is a loose order but it is the tightest one that can be given the *Autobiography*; and occasionally I have chosen to let the original order stand, at some cost in incoherence. But related things have been given an explicit relationship in this book which they lack in the typescript.

In brief, I have given the book a more coherent plan than Mark Twain's and I have left out what seemed to me uninteresting. That statement holds for everything except three passages in which I have reverted to Mr. Paine's method. The typescript contains a number of further dictations on Mark Twain's experiences with publishers, which I have omitted not only because the passages printed here are quite long enough but also because what he said was fantastic and injurious. Practically all of the *Autobiography* is colored by the events of the 1890's, especially by the failure of Mark Twain's publishing firm and of the Paige typesetting machine. Throughout his life Mark nourished violent animosities against those who he thought had taken advantage of him, and after the disasters of the 90's this trait became obsessive. He began to believe that all his publishers had swindled him. The reader should be cautioned not to take the passages published here as history; they are crowded with inaccuracies, distortions, and exaggerations. I have not had access to the books of the American Publishing Company, but I am confident that, though the firm did indeed make a good thing of its property in Mark's books, it protected its own interest in him, treated him with complete probity, and gave him as good terms as any writer could have got from any publisher—very likely, if I know Mark Twain, better terms. There can be no doubt that the affairs of Webster & Company were badly mismanaged. If the firm had been managed with ordinary publishing sagacity it need not have failed, and many letters in the Mark Twain

Papers and innumerable notebook entries show that Mark is remembering, herein, a grievance that was much more realistic than the one he had built up against Elisha Bliss. But Mark shared in the commercial stupidity and inflation that wrecked the firm quite as much as the inept management he hired, and none of his managers appears to have treated him dishonestly. I publish these passages because they are interesting and because they help to reveal Mark Twain. But I have left out other passages because the exaggeration gets so far into phantasy that it becomes a trivial rage. I have left them out as units, and the texts I publish are not emended.

I have also left out one whole dictation that belongs at the end of the passage relating to Bret Harte. The passage as it stands here is complete in itself, and not only interesting but privileged as a part of the history of American literature. The omitted passage, quoting the usual newspaper headlines, rakes up a distressing episode which was intended to add to the portrait of Harte, but it is irrelevant.

Finally, I have worked over the text of one passage, leaving as much of it as I could but trying to reduce its vindictiveness. Here and there the typescript of the *Autobiography* contains a marginal notation in Mr. Paine's hand that the context was not intended to be published for a certain number of years. The Mark Twain Estate agrees with me that sufficient time has now passed to fulfill Mark Twain's final intention. (Some of the passages so marked were published in the *North American Review* during Mark's lifetime and others in Mr. Paine's edition.) In the dictations about the Thomas Bailey Aldrich Memorial Museum, however, a prohibition is made in the text itself. Mark Twain formally directs his heirs and executors not to publish this passage until seventy-five years after its date—not, he says, because it is not true but because he wants to speak freely without injuring or offending anyone.

Wanting to publish his account of the dedication but believing that certain other passages, which were not only biased but vindictive, would cause pain to living persons, I put the question to the Estate. The Estate's decision seems to me sensible: it would regard the prohibition as no longer operative, provided that I could so edit the passage as to remove the offense. I have therefore, in this single instance, abandoned my editorial position and omitted relevant parts of the text. The reader is denied several pages of personalities that are full of flavor, but he also gains the amusing account of the dedication which neither the Estate nor I would otherwise be willing to publish.

A number of portions of the typescript that seem to me interesting enough to be included in this book are not included in it because Mr. Paine used or reproduced the greater part of them in his *Mark Twain: a Biography.*

The last section of the book is composed of fragments lifted from contexts that did not seem to me interesting enough to be run in their entirety. They contain moods, anecdotes, opinions, or sometimes merely phrases that delighted me and so would conceivably delight others, and I was unwilling to leave them unpublished even though they could not be fitted into the scheme adopted for the book.

Some portions of the book were published in the *North American Review* in 1906-1907, and in *Harper's Magazine* in 1922. If anyone compares those texts with the ones used here, he will observe a number of discrepancies. The portions published in *Harper's* were not troublesome, for Mr. Paine edited them after Mark's death and I have restored the text of the typescript after deciding, where I could, which of the two copies was last corrected by the author. Those in the *North American Review*, however, were proofread by Mark himself. Most of the changes in the typescript are later than the *Review's* text and I have usually preferred them, but in several places there is reason to suppose that they are earlier and I have had to follow my own judgment. How far I may have erred must be determined by scholars when the Papers have passed into the possession of a university.

I have supplied almost all the half titles and subtitles. Every dictation in the typescript is prefaced by a cumbersome summary like those which are retained in the two earlier volumes. I have thought it best to omit them. Except where otherwise noted, the footnotes are also mine. I have inserted as few as possible, in the belief that the people who will read this book will be sufficiently acquainted with Mark Twain's career and the events he talks about to follow him without editorial assistance. I have pointed out a few flagrant mistakes of fact and chronology. Any informed person will recognize many less important errors and many misinterpretations. I have not corrected them because they are a part of the man and the mood. In other contexts it will be desirable to correct a number of statements made by Mark Twain and a number of other statements that have been made about him, in relation to the material printed here, but that will be an exercise in scholarship without interest to the general public.

The portions of the typescript that remain unpublished are also, in my opinion, without general interest. Scholars will eventually have a gorgeous time working them over, sifting them, and trying to make out how true or false they may be and what relation they may have to the biography and criticism of Mark Twain (the Papers I have gone over could furnish forth several dozen Ph.D. dissertations), and collectors will regret that the whole typescript has not been published. I can only say that my desire —which is supported by my instructions from the Estate and the publishers—has been to produce a book for the public, not for the special interests of scholars and collectors. I have left out nothing that seemed to me important, and I assume responsibility for the omissions as well as for what is printed.

II

This book is presented not as autobiography but as a kind of table talk, as Mark Twain discoursing about men he knew, events that interested him, and occasionally himself. One of the most autobiographical of writers, he is least autobiographical when he seriously tries to be and does not carry his attempt to reveal himself very far or very deep.

The formal autobiography offers criticism a number of paradoxes. It extends to more than four hundred thousand words, and there are besides a number of half-developed sketches for it and many notes that were never used. The impulse to write it came early and recurred often; it was an important impulse but he did not understand it and it is not easily clarified. What he said about it varied with his mood. From the *Letters* one may recover the enthusiasm which Mark sometimes described to Howells: now for the first time in history a man was going to tell the whole truth about himself and was also going to reveal himself in relation to his times, so that in the end he would have a book which would live for a thousand years and then begin all over again and live for another millennium or two. He sometimes thought in that way about it. Also he sometimes regarded it as a mere defense against boredom; he was happier when writing than when not writing, and why not write this? And also he sometimes thought of it as no more than a device by which he might outwit the copyright law, which he hated as an economic exploitation of writers. Several times he declares that his sole reason for writing it is to provide material which may be distributed among his published books as their copyrights expire, so that the copyrights may be renewed and his children may enjoy the fruits of his labor as securely as if they were the children of inventors, bankers, or real estate brokers.

All these explanations correspond to traits of Mark Twain's and yet none of them has much bearing on what he wrote. Unquestionably he thought he

would like to reveal the natural man stripped of pretense and defense, but he never came within shouting
distance of self-revelation. Unquestionably parts of
the autobiography were written because once he had
got started inertia kept him going. Unquestionably
he had a Republican party sense of property in his
books and sometimes raged torridly against the system that would protect Standard Oil and a mechanic's
savings account but seemed to be expropriating literary genius. But he would have written his autobiography, and would have written it as it is, if his
royalties had been confiscated by Act of Congress in
advance.

In his other books the autobiographical impulse
takes two forms. *The Innocents Abroad, Roughing
It, A Tramp Abroad, Life on the Mississippi,* and
Following the Equator are loosely strung together
narratives in the first person, basically true, basically
factual, discursive and episodic but centered on himself, frankly personal but not in the least introspective. In them he developed a species of personal
commentary that is unique in our literature, and it
gave him his earliest reputation. In kind, the autobiography is the same thing, and it is interesting that
the earliest notes made for it appear in the notebook
from which *A Tramp Abroad* grew. But it is per-
sonalized—and also it is shaped and colored by the
deeper impulse, the one which gets free expression
only in his fiction. If his fiction is not introspective
it has a subjective quality not present in his other
work.

He wrote hundreds of pages about Hartford,
Vienna, London, Palestine, South Africa, and other

portions of the map, but he made no fiction out of them or out of Virginia City, San Francisco, the experiences of his piloting, his soldiering, or the vicissitudes of a publisher, a speculator, and a globe-trotter. When he wrote fiction, he was impelled to write about the society in which his boyhood had been spent, and to write it out of the phantasies, the ecstasy, and the apprehension which he remembered from his boyhood. *Tom Sawyer, Huckleberry Finn, Pudd'nhead Wilson, The Man That Corrupted Hadleyburg, The Mysterious Stranger,* and the bulk of his shorter pieces give us Hannibal with little alteration. Fifteenth-century France under Joan of Arc is Hannibal again, and so is England under Edward VI, though in these two books, and still more in *A Connecticut Yankee,* a kind of projection has occurred. It is not a transformation, however, and the roads by which he traveled to the farther past are clearly marked. When he wrote fiction, which is to say when the bases of his personality were finding instinctive expression, the human race was the race he had known in Hannibal. Life was confined within the circumstances of his boyhood. There is a profound difference between Tom Sawyer and Huck Finn, but one or the other of them is holding the pen in the best, the deepest, and the truest of Mark's work.

Hannibal was the master condition of his fiction, and fiction was the instinctual part of his work. His artistic creativeness, his phantasy-making, was rooted in his boyhood. Why this should be so is a question not germane to this Introduction; one, furthermore, which could be answered only speculatively and only in analytical psychology. But we can recognize two elements in that repeated invocation of Hannibal. One of them has been widely remarked: that his memory of boyhood was lyrical, a memory of free- dom, irresponsibility, and security, islanded in a countryside and a society as pleasant as any in the American past. That is true, but there is also another element in that invocation which has been less dis- cussed. When he invoked Hannibal he found there not only the idyll of boyhood but anxiety, violence, supernatural horror, and an uncrystallized but en- veloping dread. Much of his fiction, most of his mas- terpiece, flows from that phantasy-bound anxiety.

I think that the impulse to write his autobiog- raphy was in part an impulse to examine and under- stand that dread. And I think that the impulse was arrested short of genuine self-revelation because the dread was so central in him that he could approach it only symbolically, by way of fiction. This belief is supported by the circumstances in which he actually began to write the *Autobiography*.

As I have said, the urge to write it goes back many years, the first real notes appear in a notebook of 1878, and in fact he wrote at least one fragment ("The Tennessee Land," Vol. I) as early as 1870. The first account of his association with General Grant was written in 1885 and "Jane Lampton Clemens" a few years later; "The Machine Episode" is dated 1890; a number of fragmentary, uncollected sketches also belong to that period. But all these are episodic and so are the jottings in his notebooks. It is in a notebook of 1897 that the first systematic intention to write his autobiography appears, and it was in the following year, 1898, that he wrote "Playing Bear," "Macfarlane," "Old Lecture Days," and "Ralph Keeler" of the published volumes, several autobiographical pieces published separately, other pieces that were later incorporated in the typescript, and still others that were not. (Some of the dates I give here correct those given by Paine.) That is, he turned purposefully to autobiography in the late 1890's. Although he did not work continuously at the job until 1906, when the dictations began which produced more than half of the typescript (and that fact too is significant)—he did work recurrently at it from 1898 on. And he worked at it with a purpose which the events of the 90's had freed and focused— and made dominant.

This period of Mark Twain's life has not been adequately described. A series of disasters brought about a reorientation of his personality and gave his talent a different shape. His publishing firm failed; his fortune and his wife's were dissipated in the failure of the Paige typesetting machine; his health broke and, a bankrupt at the age of sixty, he had to make a heartbreaking effort to pay off his debts; his oldest daughter died; his youngest daughter developed epilepsy; his wife declined into permanent invalidism. His world toppled in ruins round him, all the bases of his belief were called into question, and his talent was so impaired that for a long time it seemed to have been destroyed. When at last it was integrated again there is no longer to be seen the Mark Twain who had had a coherent development up to *A Connecticut Yankee.* There is a new Mark Twain, the author of *What Is Man?* and *The Mysterious Stranger.*

It is a long story and cannot be told here. (I out-
lined it in a little more detail in *Harper's* for January, 1940, and enlarged the summary in a William
Vaughn Moody lecture at the University of Chicago
in March, 1940, "Mark Twain and the Symbols of
Despair.") The essence of it is this:

Wholly an artist, he was under an imperative obligation, a psychological necessity, to deal with the
catastrophes that had shattered him. For a period
of years he wrote obsessively—and was repeatedly
frustrated—in an effort to understand what had happened to him, how far he was the author of his fate,
what his responsibility was, and what relation might
exist between personal tragedy and the moral foundations of the universe. It was a protracted agony.
Manuscript after manuscript came to nothing. He
returned to many of them, to some of them many
times, tried to work them out, reached a solid inhibi-
tion, and went on to try the same thing in some new
form. The abandoned efforts make an astonishing, a
heartbreaking bulk, perhaps fifteen thousand pages.
Through that bewildered groping one is eventually
able to trace the development of three things: a
sequence of homilies on man's weakness and God's
hostility, some of which were eventually formed into
What Is Man?, a sequence of stories which shift
through many artistic and psychological adaptations
till they produce *The Mysterious Stranger*—and the
Autobiography.

All three begin at the same time, all three orig-
inate in the same need, all three are essentially the
same thing. They are an interpretation of personal
tragedy, a confession of guilt, a plea for understand-

ing and pardon, a defiance of fate, and a judgment
passed on mankind and its place in the universe.
They were made necessary by the events of the 90's
—and are an effort to explain them. They were produced by the climactic experiences of Mark's life and
they represent, not a complete change certainly, for
their elements were always in him though held in the
healthy equilibrium of his artistic success and personal happiness, but a new orientation of his personality and a new if minor expression of his genius.

It is true, therefore, that the *Autobiography*, begun
under stress of disaster, tried instinctively to be what
he sometimes thought it was: the naked revelation of
a man in the light of eternity. The intent was there—
but the capability was not. He could not make the
revelation directly. He could make it only by indirec-
tion, by forging it into the symbols of fiction. The
Autobiography has exactly the same relation to *The
Mysterious Stranger* that *Life on the Mississippi*
has to *The Adventures of Huckleberry Finn*. It discourses with charm and the greatest satisfaction
about Samuel Clemens, what he has done, the places
he has seen, the people he has known, but it does
not get inside him. It undertakes to tell us what he
was, without palliation and to the uttermost depth.
But it never comes near that confession—which is
made, instead, in *The Mysterious Stranger*. That
deeply symbolical story is Mark's final word on what
he found inside himself and his final expression of
the years in Hannibal that had shaped him once and
for all. Once he had made that peace with himself,
he could—and did—freely complete the *Autobiography*, which he had begun with the same intent.

But this is merely to make a commonplace observation, one which is familiar to everyone who reads his books though it is sometimes forgotten by those who write about them: that fundamentally he was a novelist.

III

I should not care, however, to commit the irrationality I have charged against others, that of discussing Mark Twain's books as what they are not rather than as what they are. Providence owed us no obligation to make him the kind of autobiographer who could anatomize his soul. If his autobiography is not a document of the inner life, it is nevertheless rich with reminiscence. At its best it has the enchantment which his friends found in his conversation, and even when it is least interesting intrinsically it has the fine vitality of his prose. We could not spare from the collected works the fragrance of Hannibal in Volume I, nor the Hartford of Volume II, nor the fantasia composed about Orion Clemens, nor the pitiful tenderness in the portrait of Susy. We could not spare the nuggets and flashes of light that are plentifully distributed through both volumes.

Similarly, it is good to have the sketches of his publishers and literary friends brought together in this volume, decorated with his prejudices and enhanced by the precision of his prose. It is good to have his memories of how his books were written. Most of all, I am glad to spread on the record the feelings and opinions of a man who had grown old as the nineteenth century in America ran out and who found himself not too assured about his country and his countrymen in the first decade of the twentieth century. What is added to the portrait of Mark Twain by this book is the citizen of the first Roosevelt Era looking toward our own time with a strong foreboding. I have said elsewhere that when *The Adventures of Huckleberry Finn* is examined from a point of view much recommended to criticism since I wrote, that of social implications, it may be seen as the American democratic hope colliding with a realization of the limits implicit in American democracy. In what Mark has to say about the government and the plutocracy at the moment when the American empire is achieved he typifies his generation's confused surprise at finding contradictions in the American axioms. The man of good will, the Mugwump, not only perceives that there is something wrong but wonders, against his belief, whether something may not have been wrong from the beginning.

His own life had surpassed Tom Sawyer's daydreams. The one-gallus backwoods boy had achieved the greatest literary reputation in the English-speaking world, and with it such corollaries as wealth, acceptance as a fellow by the great ones of the earth, and authority freely acknowledged as a spokesman of his time. All this by virtue of his own talent, enterprise, and labor—which was exactly what the axioms had promised. He had moved from canal boy to President, from the tinker's cart to the chairmanship of the Colt Patent Firearms Manufacturing Company, and the Republic lived because it kept open the avenue by which talent, intelligence, energy, and integrity might travel just as far as their potential

made possible. Mark seemed to himself a proof
of what has been called the American dream. "Who
began it? [the ovation when he landed in England
to receive the Oxford degree] The very people of
all people in the world whom I would have chosen:
a hundred men of my own class—grimy sons of labor,
the real builders of empires and civilization, the
stevedores!" He was a grimy son of labor who had
been made a doctor of letters by the greatest university in the world. And who had come to associate
with those other grimy laborers, John D. Rockefeller,
the richest man in the world, Andrew Carnegie, the
greatest philanthropist, and Theodore Roosevelt,
the President of the United States.

Yet there was a dim sense that he did not belong
to that company and did not want to, and a livelier
sense that something must be wrong with the whole
process. The nineteenth century was the greatest age
of mankind—had he not repeatedly shown as much
in his books?—and it had ended in such a welter of
war and organized cruelty as he could not find elsewhere in history. The Boer War, the suppression of
the Boxer uprising, King Leopold's butchery in the
Congo, the Republic's suppression of the Filipinos—
such things were in the harvest and must have been
in the planting, which he had shared. And the Empire
had destroyed the virtues of the Republic. There had
not been before Jay Gould (there had not been, that
is, in Hannibal) the worship of wealth which he saw
everywhere about him, the elevation of wealth beyond all other values. The plutocrats had seized the
government and were using it to corrupt the people.
They were using That Man in the White House to

destroy our liberties and corner the common wealth. They had bought patriotism, they had bought integrity, they had bought liberty for cash on the barrelhead. They had corrupted private standards and public decency. They had taken over the Republic—and they were going to finish it pretty soon.

Yet this betrayal could not be the work of any friend of Mark's. It could not be charged, for instance, to Standard Oil. Who but a Standard Oil millionaire had stepped in when his disasters came, organized his affairs, and enabled him to achieve solvency again? (And when it was achieved, had doubled his capital in a few months by putting it into Federal Steel.) And look at the achievement of Standard Oil: its gigantic organization, its freedom from labor troubles, the progress it had brought to the poor and the backward. Moreover, Standard Oil was a product of the American axioms: it was the result of enterprise, energy, intelligence, and (since Henry Rogers was a part of it) rigorous and undeviating integrity. It was a fulfillment of the same dream that Mark fulfilled. To be sure, that small skinful of vanity and pretense, Andrew Carnegie, was a good deal of a fool—as young Rockefeller was surely no shining flame of genius. But, in his proper province, see what Carnegie had achieved. By the free exercise of his talents in the Republic which permitted talent to go just as far as it could, Carnegie had raised himself from nothing at all, had developed a great industry, had given employment to thousands, and had made possible the spread of education among Mark's own class, the stevedores. Obviously such an achievement absolved Carnegie of any guilt in the decay and betrayal of the Republic. That must be charged to others, a vaguer and partly anonymous class, to Roosevelt who bought old soldiers on behalf of the Republican party, Guggenheim and Clark alleged to have bought legislatures, other plutocrats who bought foreign titles, and Jay Gould who bought everyone and everything that was for sale.

Mark Twain had no awareness of the forces which men like Rogers and Carnegie expressed or the kind of power they were using. He saw Roosevelt's timidity and exhibitionism, he saw Carnegie's absurdity, he saw the enfranchised arrogance of the plutocracy, but he did not even speculate about the current that ran beneath the froth. In complete innocence of heart he could let himself be used at the propaganda luncheon described in this book (I have verified his account of it from other sources), and he came away from it with no further thought than that the Rockefeller Institute was doing a noble work.[1] He could not argue against the Rockefeller Institute—nor against Standard Oil or any other achievement that appeared to have been worked out from the same axioms he saw exemplified by his own life. His life proved that a man might go just as far as his talent and energy would take him. A man could make himself wanted; he could work at his job, better his condition, raise himself higher, and go on. It was not possible to deny that, either on the evidence or in the assumption. And yet there was the overmastering sense, rather in his nerve ends than in his mind, that some term of the equation had been false, that

[1] Once the research on meningitis was mentioned, Mark was captured. For Susy had died of meningitis.

America, in attaining its heritage, had lost it. If he did not understand the forces, he perceived their products.

Artists are the least analytical of men and he was the least analytical of artists. He had no gift for disentangling social, economic, and historical energies; what he knew about was the motives and especially the weaknesses and cruelties of mankind, of men as men. So when he added up the integers he got the same sum he had been getting all his life from other propositions.

The process of debauchery and decay, he concluded, could not be arrested. He said that the end was monarchy; he meant what our generation calls dictatorship. In two apocalyptic treatises on history which he began at this time but did not finish, he works out the curve more fully than he does here. Every civilization carries the seeds of its own destruction, and the same cycle shows in them all. The Republic is born, flourishes, decays into plutocracy, and is captured by the shoemaker whom the mercenaries and millionaires make into a king. It will be born again later on, to the same cycle. The people could will otherwise but they do not; they form their procession behind the shoemaker. And that proves something. The people invent their oppressors, and the oppressors serve the function for which they are invented . . . It comes back to the old question, What Is Man? Man is a noisome bacillus whom Our Heavenly Father created because he was disappointed in the monkey. Mark Twain will vote for the monarchy. He is not only marching in the procession, he is carrying a banner.

At the moment when Mark Twain was describing his shoemaker, a Brahmin dilettante who was as unlike him as possible was putting this *Götterdämmerung* into spurious mathematical formulas. Pretty widely over America the afterglow of the nineteenth century was experiencing the same doubt, and Henry Adams hoping for "a world that sensitive and timid natures could regard without a shudder" was no clearer than Mark Twain about his own distress. We must not demand too much accuracy or comprehension from either of them, or from anyone else who, looking back to 1865 and forward to 1940, felt in 1906 the same consternation. Here it is enough to remember that Mark Twain, who had expressed so much else that was typical of his generation, made this last expression also.

BERNARD DeVoto

Cambridge, Massachusetts
April 15, 1940

Every man is in his own person the whole human race, with not a detail lacking. I am the whole human race without a detail lacking; I have studied the human race with diligence and strong interest all these years in my own person; in myself I find in big or little proportion every quality and every defect that is findable in the mass of the race. I knew I should not find in any philosophy a single thought which had not passed through my own head, nor a single thought which had not passed through the heads of millions and millions of men before I was born; I knew I should not find a single original thought in any philosophy, and I knew I could not furnish one to the world myself, if I had five centuries to invent it in. Nietzsche published his book, and was at once pronounced crazy by the world—by a world which included tens of thousands of bright, sane men who believed exactly as Nietzsche believed but concealed the fact and scoffed at Nietzsche. What a coward every man is! and how surely he will find it out if he will just let other people alone and sit down and examine himself. The human race is a race of cowards; and I am not only marching in that procession but carrying a banner.

(September 4, 1907)

THEODORE ROOSEVELT

1. The Monarchy. (July 16, 1908)

Thirty-five years ago in a letter to my wife ostensibly, but really to Mr. Howells, I amused myself—and endeavored to amuse him—with forecasting the monarchy and imagining what the country would be like when the monarchy should replace the republic.[1] That letter interests me now. Not because of anything it says—for there are no serious sentences in it—but because it refreshes my memory and enables me to recall the substance of a letter which preceded it and which treated the coming monarchy seriously.

I was not expecting the monarchy to come in my own time, nor in my children's time, nor at any period which one might forecast with anything approaching definiteness. It might come soon, it might come late; it might come in a century, it might be delayed two centuries, even three. But it would come.

Because of a special and particular reason? Yes. Two special reasons and one condition.

1. It is the nature of man to want a definite something to love, honor, reverently look up to, and obey: God and King, for example.

2. Little republics have lasted long, protected by

---

[1] See Appendix M of Paine's *Mark Twain, a Biography*. Written in 1874, the letter was dated 1935.

their poverty and insignificance, but great ones have not.

3. The Condition: vast power and wealth, which breed commercial and political corruption and incite public favorites to dangerous ambitions.

The idea was, republics are impermanent; in time they perish and in most cases stay under the sod, but the overthrown monarchy gets back into the saddle again by and by. The idea was—in other and familiar words—history repeats itself: whatever has been the rule in history may be depended upon to remain the rule. Not because, in the case under present consideration, men would deliberately desire the destruction of their republic and plan it out, but because *circumstances* which they create without suspecting what they are doing will by and by *compel* that destruction—to their grief and dismay. My notion was that in some near or some distant day circumstances would so shape themselves, unnoticed by the people, as to make it possible for some ambitious idol of the nation to upset the republic and build his throne out of its ruins; and that then history would stand ready to back him.

But all this was thirty-five years ago. It seems curious now that I should have been dreaming dreams about a *future* monarchy and never suspecting that the monarchy was already present and the republic a thing of the past. Yet that was the case. The republic in name remained but the republic in fact was gone.

For fifty years our country has been a constitutional monarchy, with the Republican party sitting on the throne. Mr. Cleveland's couple of brief interruptions do not count; they were accidents and temporary, they made no permanent inroad upon Republican supremacy. Ours is not only a monarchy but a hereditary monarchy—in the one political family. It passes from heir to heir as regularly and as surely and as unpreventably as does any throne in Europe. Our monarch is more powerful, more arbitrary, more autocratic than any in Europe, its White House commands are not under restraint of law or custom or the Constitution, it can ride down the Congress as the Czar cannot ride down the Duma. It can concentrate and augment power at the Capital by despoiling the States of their reserved rights, and by the voice of a Secretary of State it has indicated its purpose to do this. It can pack the Supreme Court with judges friendly to its ambitions, and it has threatened—by the voice of a Secretary of State—to do this. In many and admirably conceived ways it has so formidably intrenched itself and so tightened its grip upon the throne that I think it is there for good. By a system of extraordinary tariffs it has created a number of giant corporations in the interest of a few rich men, and by most ingenious and persuasive reasoning has convinced the multitudinous and grateful unrich that the tariffs were instituted in *their* interest! Next, the monarchy proclaims itself the enemy of its child the monopoly, and lets on that it wants to destroy that child. But it is wary and judicious, and never says anything about attacking the monopolies at their life source—the tariffs. It thoughtfully puts off that assault till "after election." A thousand years after is quite plainly what it means, but the people do not know that. Our monarchy takes no backward step; it moves always forward, always toward its ultimate and now assured goal, the *real* thing.

I was not expecting to live to see it reach it, but a recent step—the newest advance step and the startlingest—has encouraged me. It is this: formerly our monarchy went through the form of electing its Shadow by the voice of the people, but now the Shadow has gone and *appointed* the succession Shadow!

I judge that that strips off about the last rag that was left upon our dissolving wax-figure republic. It was the last one in the case of the Roman Republic.

. . . . .

2. The Panic. (November 1, 1907)

This has been a strange panic. It has not strongly resembled any other panic in the history of the country. The panic to which we have long been accustomed is a tempest, a cyclone, a hurricane, which sweeps away values and lays industries waste much as the cyclone fells forests and leaves towns a tumultuous confusion of wreckage; but this new panic is of a new sort; it is a still panic, a noiseless panic, a smothered panic; it makes no noise, there are no hysterics, no frenzies; it is not like a storm, it is like a blight, a paralysis; it is as if the business activities of our eighty millions of people had suddenly come to a standstill, leaving everybody idle, frightened, wondering. The conditions make one think of a mighty machine which has slipped its belt and is still running by previous and perishing impulse but accomplishing nothing. There has not been a single important failure in the financial world. There are

no crashes, no thunderbursts, no earthquakes; there
is nothing but a creepy and awful stillness and an
atmosphere charged with apprehension.

The phrase "laying off" has become common, almost wearisomely so. We hear of this and that and
the other vast concern laying off a thousand men,
two thousand men, three thousand men—and this
makes us familiar with the conditions obtaining
among the multitude of millionaire industries of
the country; but there is a far wider and more disastrous laying off that does not find its way into the
newspapers; this is the laying off that is going on
under the surface, all over the land—the discharging
of one employee out of every three in all the humble
little shops and industries from one end of America
to the other—a laying off which is not to be counted
by thousands, as in the case of the giant industries,
but by hundreds of thousands, with an aggregate
reaching into millions and making the laying off by
the great companies a trifle and insignificant by
comparison. The four-servant families are getting
along with three now; the three-servant families are
getting along with two; the two-servant families are
getting along with one; the one-servant families are
getting along without any. The day governess with
six pupils has lost three of them; the day governess
with three pupils has lost all of them; counter clerks,
male and female, have been discharged in shoals;
there is not a single trade in the country that has
not reduced its force and imperiled the bread and
butter of one family or a thousand. A blight has
fallen everywhere and Mr. Roosevelt is the author
of it.

Last week a prodigious and universal crash was impending and but for one thing would have happened: the millionaire "bandits" whom the President is so fond of abusing in order to get the applause of the gallery, stepped in and stayed the desolation. Mr. Roosevelt promptly claimed the credit of it, and there is much evidence that this inebriated nation thinks he is entitled to it. The great financiers saved every important bank and trust company in New York but one—the Knickerbocker Trust Company. That one had no friends and was obliged to suspend, with obligations amounting to forty-two millions—mainly deposits. No one will lose by the temporary suspension but twenty-two thousand depositors are more or less inconvenienced by it. Its Board of Blunderers have been shilly-shallying for a week and trying to invent ways to save its stockholders from an assessment. Of course I had to be a depositor in the only concern that got into trouble—it was just my luck. I had fifty-one thousand dollars there. I feel hurt, I feel abused; I feel a deep sympathy for that man who ——

I think I have spoken of that Young Christian long ago in an earlier chapter of this *Autobiography* —I don't remember; however, this was the incident. I was to talk to a lot of Young Men's Christian Associations in the Majestic Theater on a Sunday afternoon. My secretary and I entered the place by the stage door and sat down in a box and looked out over a desert expanse of empty benches—wondering. My secretary presently went to the main entrance in the other street, to see what the matter was; just as she started the Young Christians came pouring in like a tidal wave; she plowed through the wave and by the time she reached the main door the place was full and the police, mounted and on foot, were struggling with a multitude of remaining Young Christians and keeping them back. The doors were being closed against the people. There was one last man, of course—there always is. He almost got his body into the closing door but was pushed back by a big officer. He realized that his chance was gone. He was mute for a moment while his feelings were rising in him, then he said: "I have been a member of the Young Men's Christian Association in good standing for seven years and never got any reward for it, and here it is again—just my God damned luck!" I do not feel as profane as that—still I sense the situation, and I sympathize with that man.

· · · · ·

3. The Hunting of the Cow. (October 18, 1907)

Two colossal historical incidents took place yesterday, incidents which must go echoing down the corridors of time for ages, incidents which can never be forgotten while histories shall continue to be written. Yesterday, for the first time, business was opened to commerce by the Marconi Company and wireless messages sent entirely across the Atlantic, straight from shore to shore; and on that same day the President of the United States for the fourteenth time came within three miles of flushing a bear. As usual he was far away, nobody knew where, when the bear burst upon the multitude of dogs and hunters and equerries and chamberlains in waiting,

and sutlers and cooks and scullions, and Rough
Riders and infantry and artillery, and had his customary swim to the other side of a pond and disappeared in the woods. While half the multitude
watched the place where he vanished, the other half
galloped off, with horns blowing, to scour the State
of Louisiana in search of the great hunter. Why
don't they stop hunting the bear altogether and
hunt the President? He is the only one of the pair
that can't be found when he is wanted.

By and by the President was found and laid upon
the track and he and the dogs followed it several
miles through the woods, then gave it up, because
Rev. Dr. Long, the "nature fakir," came along
and explained that it was a cow track. This is a
sorrowful ending to a mighty enterprise. His Excellency leaves for Washington today, to interest
himself further in his scheme of provoking a war
with Japan with his battleships. Many wise people
contend that his idea, on the contrary, is to compel
peace with Japan but I think he wants a war. He
was in a skirmish once at San Juan Hill, and he got
so much moonshine glory out of it that he has never
been able to stop talking about it since. I remember
that at a small luncheon party of men at Brander
Matthews's house once, he dragged San Juan Hill
in three or four times, in spite of all attempts of
the judicious to abolish the subject and introduce
an interesting one in its place. I think the President
is clearly insane in several ways, and insanest upon
war and its supreme glories. I think he longs for a
big war wherein he can spectacularly perform as
chief general and chief admiral, and go down in

history as the only monarch of modern times that has served both offices at the same time.

Yesterday Marconi's stations on the two sides of the Atlantic exchanged messages aggregating five thousand words, at the rate of forty or fifty words per minute. It is a world event. I met Mr. Marconi in London seven years ago in company with Sir Hiram Maxim; he was confident at that time that he would some day be able to send wireless telegrams across the ocean without relays, but not many other persons shared this confidence with him. I am glad to have seen him and talked with him, and glad that I have seen and talked with Professor Morse and Graham Bell and Edison and others among the men who have added the top story to the majestic edifice of the world's modern material civilization. No fuss was made over the great event of yesterday, either in England or America; the time for that will come later, as was the case with Morse's telegraph.

I remember the wave of jubilation and astonishment that swept the planet in the summer of 1858 when the first electric message was sent across the Atlantic under the sea, by cable. It did not seem believable; it seemed altogether unbelievable, yet we had to believe it and go through the several stages of getting reconciled to it and adjusted to it; then, as usual in these vast matters, it presently became a commonplace. That was the year of the great comet—the most illustrious wanderer of the skies that has ever appeared in the heavens within the memory of men now living. It was a wonderful spray of white light, a light so powerful that I think it was able to cast shadows—however, necessarily it *could*, there is no occasion to seek for evidence of that; there is sufficient evidence of it in the fact that one could read a newspaper by that light at any time in the night. I was a cub pilot in those days, and had the glory and the splendor of that great companionship for my solace and delight on my lonely watch in the pilothouse during many and many a night. More than once I read a newspaper by the light that streamed from that stupendous explorer of the glittering archipelagoes of space.

By and by Marconi, like Morse, will have his triumph. It was not my fortune to be present when Morse had his but I remember the stir it made. Morse, clothed in stars and ribbons and crosses contributed in his honor by the chief scientific societies and sceptered rulers of the world, sat old and bowed with age upon the stage of the Academy of Music, in the presence of several thousand persons, and worked the key himself and exchanged messages over land and under sea with monarchs and municipalities scattered far and wide around the rotundity of the globe. I missed that colossal event but I hope to be present when it is repeated, with Marconi at the key.

·   ·   ·   ·   ·

(October 21, 1907)

Alas, the President has got that cow after all! If it was a cow. Some say it was a bear—a real bear. These were eyewitnesses, but they were all White House domestics; they are all under wages to the great hunter, and when a witness is in that condition it makes his testimony doubtful. The fact that the President himself thinks it was a bear does not diminish the doubt but enlarges it. He was once a reasonably modest man, but his judgment has been out of focus so long now that he imagines that everything he does, little or big, is colossal.

I am sure he honestly thinks it was a bear, but the circumstantial evidence that it was a cow is overwhelming. It acted just as a cow would act; in every detail from the beginning to the end it acted precisely as a cow would act when in trouble; it even left a cow track behind, which is what a cow would do when in distress, or indeed at any other time if it knew a President of the United States was after it—hoping to move his pity, you see; thinking maybe he would spare her life on account of her sex, her helpless situation, and her notorious harmlessness. In her flight she acted just as a cow would have done when in a frenzy of fright, with a President of the United States and a squadron of bellowing dogs chasing after her; when her strength was exhausted, and she could drag herself no further, she did as any other despairing cow would have done—she stopped in an open spot, fifty feet wide, and humbly faced the President of the United States with the tears running down her cheeks, and said to him with the mute eloquence of surrender: "Have pity, sir, and spare me. I am alone, you are many; I have no weapon but my helplessness, you are a walking arsenal; I am in awful peril, you are as safe as you would be in a Sunday school; have pity, sir—there is no heroism in killing an exhausted cow."

Here are the scareheads that introduce the wonderful dime-novel performance:

ROOSEVELT TELLS OF HUNTING TRIP

Ate All the Game, Except a Wildcat, and That Had a Narrow Escape.

Swam Despite Alligators.

Charged Into the Canebrake After Bear and Hugged the Guides After the Kill.

There it is—he hugged the guides after the kill. It is the President all over; he is still only fourteen years old after living half a century; he takes a boy's delight in showing off; he is always hugging something or somebody—when there is a crowd around to see the hugging and envy the hugged. A grown person would have milked the cow and let her go; but no, nothing would do this lad but he must kill her and be a hero. The account says: "The bear slain by the President was killed Thursday, and the killing was witnessed by one of the McKenzies and by Alex Ennolds."

These names will go down in history forever, in the company of an exploit which will take a good deal of the shine out of the twelve labors of Hercules. Testimony of the witnesses: "They say that the President's bearing was extremely sportsmanlike."

Very likely. Everybody knows what mere sportsmanlike bearing is, unqualified by an adverb, but none of us knows quite what it is when it is extremely sportsmanlike, because we have never encountered that inflamed form of the thing before. The probabilities are that the sportsmanlike bearing was not any more extremely sportsmanlike than was that of Hercules; it is quite likely that the adverb is merely emotional and has the hope of a raise of wages back of it. The chase of the frightened creature lasted three hours and reads like a hectic chapter in a dime novel—and this time it is a chapter of pathetically humble heroics.

In the outcome the credit is all with the cow, none of it is with the President. When the poor hunted thing could go no further it turned, in fine and picturesque defiance, and gallantly faced its enemies and its assassin. From a safe distance Hercules sent a bullet to the sources of its life; then, dying, it made fight—so there *was* a hero present after all. Another bullet closed the tragedy, and Hercules was so carried away with admiration of himself that he hugged his domestics and bought a compliment from one of them for twenty dollars. But this resumé of mine is pale; let us send it down to history with the colors all in it:

The bear slain by the President was killed Thursday, and the killing was witnessed by one of the McKenzies and by Alex Ennolds. They say that the President's bearing was extremely sportsmanlike. The animal had been chased by the dogs for three hours, the President following all the time. When at last they came within hearing distance the President dismounted, threw off his coat and dashed into the canebrake, going to within twenty paces of the beast. The dogs were coming up rapidly, with the President's favorite, Rowdy, in the lead.

The bear had stopped to bid defiance to the canines when the President sent a fatal bullet from his rifle through the animal's vitals. With the little life left in it the bear turned on the dogs. The President then lodged a second bullet between the bear's shoulders, breaking the creature's neck. Other members of the party soon came up, and the President was so rejoiced over his success that he embraced each of his companions. Ennolds said: "Mr. President, you are no tenderfoot."

Mr. Roosevelt responded by giving Ennold a $20 note.

There was little hunting yesterday, because the dogs encountered a drove of wild hogs, more ferocious than bears. One of the best dogs was killed by a boar.

There were daily swims in the lake by members of the party, including the President.

"The water was fine," he said, "and I did not have the fear of alligators that some seem to have."

Whatever Hercules does is to him remarkable; when other people are neglectful and fail to notice a detail, here and there, proper for admiration and comment, he supplies the omission himself. Mr. Ennolds lost a chance; if he had been judiciously on watch he could have done the alligator compliment himself, and got another twenty for it.

.   .   .   .   .

4. The President as Advertiser. (September 7, 1907)

Three days ago the *World* newspaper convicted Mr. Roosevelt beyond redemption of having bought his election to the Presidency with money. That he committed this stupendous crime has long been suspected—ever since election day, in fact—but the proofs have never been furnished until now. Judge

Parker, the opposition candidate, made the charge at the time in courteous parliamentary terms, but Mr. Roosevelt fiercely denied it—thus adding falsehood to his burden of misconduct. However, that was not much of an addition—for him; he is accustomed to it and has a talent for it, although he detests false speaking in other people and cannot abide it. At one time and another during the past three years he has frankly charged a dozen of the cleanest men in the country with being unveracious, and in every instance has seemed almost really and sincerely shocked at it.

Mr. Roosevelt is easily the most astonishing event in American history—if we except the discovery of the country by Columbus. The details of Mr. Roosevelt's purchase of the Presidency by bribery of voters are all exposed now, even to the names of the men who furnished the money and the amounts which each contributed. The men are great corporation chiefs and three of them are Standard Oil monopolists. It is now known that when the canvass was over a week before election day and all legitimate uses for election money at an end, Mr. Roosevelt got frightened and sent for Mr. Harriman to come to Washington and arrange measures to save the State of New York for the Republican party. The meeting took place and Harriman was urged to raise two hundred thousand dollars for the cause. He raised two hundred and sixty thousand and it was spent upon the election in the last week of the campaign— necessarily for the purchase of votes, since the time had gone by for using money in any other way. In a printed statement Judge Parker now says:

Obviously in the closing hours of the campaign but one practical use could be made of it, and that was to swell the fund already accumulated to secure beyond peradventure the large floating vote, builded up by years of effort to corrupt the electorate by means of moneys contributed by those who were willing to buy favors from those willing to sell them.

Of the money subscribed, two hundred thousand dollars were spent in the City of New York and Mr. Harriman claims that it changed the votes of fifty thousand floaters, thereby making a change in Mr. Roosevelt's favor of a hundred thousand votes.

For years the rich corporations have furnished vast sums of money to keep the Republican party in power, and have done this upon the understanding that their monopolies were to be shielded and protected in return. During all these years this protection has been faithfully furnished in accordance with the agreement, but this time treachery intervened. Mr. Roosevelt saw that it would be popular to attack the great corporations, and he did not hesitate to retire from his contract and do it. Mr. Harriman and those others had bought him and paid for him, but that was nothing to a man who stands always ready to sell his honor for such a price as he can get for it in the market—for even a large advertisement, for that matter.

Mr. Roosevelt is now rejoicing over the act of a federal judge, of Chicago, who is a man after his own heart. This judge has fined the Standard Oil Company twenty-nine million, two hundred and forty thousand dollars, upon a quibble, and the President is delighted for it is a large and showy advertisement. It is quite unlikely that a higher court will affirm the

decision on appeal, but the President will care little
for that; he has had his advertisement.

He has sent Secretary Taft around the world on
an electioneering trip—another advertisement.

He is sending the United States Navy to San Francisco by way of the Strait of Magellan—all for
show, all for advertisement—although he is aware
that if it gets disabled on its adventurous trip it cannot be repaired in the Pacific, for lack of docks; but
the excursion will make a great noise and this will
satisfy Mr. Roosevelt.

Mr. Roosevelt has done what he could to destroy
the industries of the country, and they all stand now
in a half-wrecked condition and waiting in an ague
to see what he will do next. One more shake up and
they will go, perhaps. He will certainly provide that
shake up, if he can get a sufficient advertisement out
of it. That San Francisco earthquake which shook
the city down and made such a noise in the world
was but a poor thing, and local; it confined itself to
a narrow strip of the Pacific strand and was a
poor little back-settlement thing compared with Mr.
Roosevelt; he is the real earthquake and the most
colossal one in history; when he quakes he convulses
the entire land, from the Atlantic to the Pacific and
from Canada to the Gulf; not even a village escapes.

In six months he has reduced the value of every
species of property in the United States—in some
cases ten per cent, in others twenty per cent, in still
others fifty per cent. Six months ago the country was
worth a hundred and fourteen billions; it is not
worth more than ninety billions now. The public
confidence is gone; it is possible that the public credit

may follow. Mr. Roosevelt is the most formidable disaster that has befallen the country since the Civil War—but the vast mass of the nation loves him, is frantically fond of him, even idolizes him. This is the simple truth. It sounds like a libel upon the intelligence of the human race but it isn't; there isn't any way to libel the intelligence of the human race.

To descend to small matters: the President is about to start out on another advertising tour; two or three weeks hence he is going to review the Mississippi River—that poor old abandoned waterway which was my field of usefulness when I was a pilot in the days of its high prosperity, nearly fifty years ago. He will start at Cairo and go down the river on a steamboat and make a noise all the way. He is ready to lend himself to any wildcat scheme that any one can invent for the bilking of the Treasury, provided he can get an advertisement out of it. This time he goes as cat's-paw for that ancient and insatiable gang, the Mississippi Improvement conspirators, who for thirty years have been annually sucking the blood of the Treasury and spending it in fantastic attempts to ameliorate the condition of that useless river— apparently that, really to feed the Republican vote out there. These efforts have never improved the river, for the reason that no effort of man can do that. The Mississippi will always have its own way; no engineering skill can persuade it to do otherwise; it has always torn down the petty basketwork of the engineers and poured its giant floods whithersoever it chose, and it will continue to do this. The President's trip is in the interest of another wasted appropriation, and the project will succeed—succeed and furnish an advertisement.

.   .   .   .   .

5. *Naturalist and Nature-Fakir. (May 29, 1907)*

President Roosevelt has been having a scrap with the Rev. Dr. Long, who is a naturalist equipped with a pleasant and entertaining pen. Mr. Long is not a heavyweight like John Burroughs and has never intimated, as John has seemed to intimate, that he knows more about an animal than the animal knows about itself. Mr. Long's books are very popular, particularly among young people. He tells many amusing and interesting things about the wild creatures of the forest, and he does not speak from hearsay but from observation. He tells what *he* has seen the animal do, not what it is reported to have done. If he misinterprets the actions of the animals and infers from them intellectual qualities of a higher order than they perhaps possess, is that a crime? I think not—although the President of the United States thinks it is. I think it is far from being a crime. Ninety-six per cent of our newspapers and ninety-eight per cent of our eighty million citizens believe that the President is possessed of high intellectual qualities. Is that a crime? I do not think so. I think it is merely stupidity, and stupidity is not a crime. The other day the President allowed the affairs of the universe to stand unmolested during thirty minutes, while he got himself interviewed for the *Outlook* and launched a devastating assault upon poor obscure little Mr. Long, and made a noise over him the like of which has not been heard on the planet since the hostile fleets opened upon each other with two thousand shells a minute in the Japan Sea.

What had Mr. Long been doing? He had merely been telling how he had found a deer whose breast had just been fatally torn by a wolf, and how he had also seen a wild bird mend its broken leg by smart devices invented by itself and successfully consummated without anybody else's help. No doubt these were extraordinary incidents, but what of that? Does their unusualness make them incredible? Indeed it does not. Wild creatures often do extraordinary things. Look at Mr. Roosevelt's own performances. Did he not fling the faithful Bowen out of office and whitewash and deodorize the mephitic Loomis? Didn't he promulgate the illegal Order 78?[2] Hasn't he tunneled so many subways under the Constitution that the transportation facilities through that document are only rivaled, not surpassed, by those now enjoyed by the City of New York? Didn't he send a bouquet and a broken heart to lay upon the corpse of Mr. Quay? Hasn't he tacitly claimed some dozens of times that he is the only person in America who knows how to speak the truth—quite ignoring me and other professionals? Hasn't he kept up such a continual thundering from our Olympus about football and baseball and mollycoddles and all sorts of little nursery matters that we have come to stand in fear that the first time an exigency of real importance shall arise, our thunders will not be able to attract the world's notice or exert any valuable influence upon ourselves. And so on and so on——the

[2] The once notorious Executive Order by which Roosevelt had considerably enlarged the pension list in an election year.

list of unpresidential things, things hitherto deemed
impossible, wholly impossible, measurelessly impossible for a president of the United States to do, is
much too long for invoicing here.

When a president can do these extraordinary
things, why can't he allow a poor little unoffending
bird to work a marvelous surgical operation without
finding fault with it? That surgical operation is impossible at first glance, but it is not any more impossible than is Order 78. It is not easy to believe
that either of them happened; but we all know that
Order 78 happened, therefore we are justified in believing in the bird's surgery. Order 78 should make
it easy for us to believe in anything that can be
charged against a bird. I should think that if a person were offered his choice as between risking his
character upon the bird story or upon the authorship
of Order 78, he ought not to have any difficulty
about which of the two to choose. I should think that
a judicious person would rather father all the lies
that have ever been told about the animal world than
have it found out that he invented Order 78.

Perhaps it is a marvelous thing for a bird to mend
its broken leg; but is it half as marvelous, as extraordinary, as incredible, as that the autocrat over
a nation of eighty millions should come down from
his summit in the clouds to destroy a wee little naturalist who was engaged in the harmless business of
amusing a nursery? Is it as extraordinary as the
spectacle of a president of the United States attacking a private citizen without offering anything de-
scribable as evidence that he is qualified for the office
of critic—and then refusing to listen to the man's

defense, and following this uncourteous attack by backing out of the dispute upon the plea that it would not be consonant with the dignity of his great office to further notice such a person?

The President is badly worsted in the scrap, and I think he is wise in backing out of it. There was no respectable way out, and I think it was plainly best for him to accept and confess defeat in silence. And he would be safe in any course he might pursue, whatever that course might be, for the newspapers would praise it and admire it and the nation would applaud. It is long since the head of any nation has been so blindly and unreasoningly worshiped as is President Roosevelt by this nation today. If he should die now, he would be mourned as no ruler has been mourned save Nero.

.   .   .   .   .

(May 30, 1907)

I think it is not wise for an emperor, or a king, or a president, to come down into the boxing ring, so to speak, and lower the dignity of his office by meddling in the small affairs of private citizens. I think it is not even discreet in a private citizen to come out in public and make a large noise, and by criticism and faultfinding try to cough down and injure another citizen whose trade he knows nothing valuable about. It seems to me that natural history is a pretty poor thing to squabble about anyway, because it is not an exact science. What we know about it is built out of the careful or careless observations of students of animal nature, and no man can be accurate enough in his observations to safely pose as the last and unassailable authority in the matter—not even Aristotle, not even Pliny, not even Sir John Mandeville, not even Jonah, not even Theodore Roosevelt.

All these professionals ought to stand ready to accept each other's facts, closing one eye furtively now and then, perhaps, but keeping strictly quiet and saying nothing. The professional who disputes another professional's facts damages the business and imperils his own statistics, there being no statistics connected with the business that are absolute and unassailable. The only wise and safe course is for all the naturalists to stand by each other and accept and endorse every discovery, or seeming discovery, that any one of them makes. Mr. Roosevelt is immeasurably indiscreet. He accepts as an established fact that the ravens fed Elijah; it is then bad policy in him to question the surgical ability of Mr. Long's bird. I accept the raven's work, and admire it. I know the raven; I know him well; I know he has no disposition to share his food, inferior and overdue as it is, with prophets or presidents or any one else— yet I feel that it would not be right nor judicious in me to question the validity of the hospitalities of those ravens while trying to market natural-history marvels of my own which are of a similar magnitude.

I know of a turkey hen that tried during several weeks to hatch out a porcelain egg, then the gobbler took the job and sat on that egg two entire summers and at last hatched it. He hatched out of it a doll's tea set of fourteen pieces, and all perfect except that the teapot had no spout, on account of the material running out. I know this to be true, of my own personal knowledge, and I do as Mr. Roosevelt and

Mr. Burroughs and Jonah and Aristotle, and all the other naturalists do—that is to say, I merely make assertions and back them up with just my say-so, offering no other evidence of any kind. I personally know that that unusual thing happened; I knew the turkey; I furnished the egg and I have got the crockery. It establishes, once and for all, the validity of Mr. Long's statement about his bird—because it is twice as remarkable as that bird's performance and yet it happened. If I must speak plainly, I think it is rank folly for the President, or John Burroughs, or any other professional, to try to bear any other naturalist's stock in the public market. It is all watered— I even regard some of my own discoveries in that light—and so it is but common prudence for those of us who got in on the ground floor to refrain from boring holes in it.

.   .   .   .   .

6. *The True Character of Mr. Roosevelt.* (*July 14, 1908*)

The principal editorial comment in *Collier's Weekly* for July 11th contains seven or eight sentences—short ones, therefore it is a brief paragraph. It is a wonderful accumulation of rubbish to be packed into so small a space. It is a burst of servile and insane admiration and adulation of President Roosevelt. It purports to be a reflection of the sentiment of the nation; that is to say, the Republican bulk of the nation. It ought to grieve me to concede that it does reflect the sentiment of the Republican bulk of the nation, but it doesn't. To my mind, the bulk of any nation's opinion about its president, or its king, or its emperor, or its politics, or its religion, is without value and not worth weighing or considering or examining. There is nothing mental in it; it is all feeling, and procured at secondhand without any assistance from the proprietor's reasoning powers.

On the other hand, it would grieve me deeply to be obliged to believe that any very large number of sane and thinking and intelligent Republicans privately admire Mr. Roosevelt and do not despise him. Publicly, all sane and intelligent Republicans worship Mr. Roosevelt and would not dare to do otherwise where any considerable company of listeners was present; and this is quite natural, since sane and intelligent human beings are like all other human beings, and carefully and cautiously and diligently conceal their private real opinions from the world and give out fictitious ones in their stead for general consumption.

Norman Hapgood wrote that paragraph. He is an able young man; well read, well educated, and as honest and honorable as any man whom I am as intimately acquainted with as I am with him. But do I believe that this diseased paragraph came out of his private heart and reflects his real feeling toward this disgraced outgoing president? No, I am not able to believe that. If I had him here in private a while I should expect him to find it very difficult to put his finger on half a dozen considerable benefits conferred upon this country since he ceased to be president, four years ago, and became Czar. Hapgood's paragraph begins thus:

Mr. Roosevelt will leave office secure in the hearts of his countrymen. The dexterity and sincerity with which he avoided a renomination for himself, and secured it for a believer in his policies, have solidified the affection and the confidence of mankind.

That sentence is itself about as dexterous as was the presidential dexterity which it admires. The sentence mixes together a possibly creditable act and a distinctly discreditable one, and the mixing is so cleverly done as to divert attention from the discreditable one and make one or two important words seem to apply to it as well as to the other member of the sentence, when in fact no such application of those words is justifiable. That wily sentence should be bitten in two and each half of it chewed by itself: "The dexterity and sincerity with which he avoided a renomination for himself ———"

That half of the sentence is true. No, that is putting it too strong; it isn't quite true. If we leave the "dexterity" out and put in "reluctance," then it is true. Mr. Roosevelt did avoid a renomination of himself, after trying for two years to find some decent way to get out of his bombastic pledges and renunciations of the great office for all future time. The public press kept after him like a swarm of bees, and they pestered and pestered him for two years before they were able to sting a definite and final renunciation out of him. And so we will leave the "dexterity" out of that half of the sentence and put "reluctance" in its place, as being some four hundred thousand miles nearer the truth—but "dexterity" comes good, and exceedingly good, in the last half of that sentence: "The dexterity with which he secured the nomination for a believer in his policies ——"

Yes, he dexterously secured Mr. Taft's nomination. But dexterity doesn't cover the whole ground; it needs the help of some more words, in order that the whole truth may be arrived at. The dexterity itself needs these qualifying words; mere dexterity carries with it a suggestion of compliment, but no compliment is due in this case. The President's dexterity in the matter of Mr. Taft's nomination was a dishonest and dishonorable dexterity—the same kind used by him when he jumped that horse doctor, Leonard Wood, over the heads of fifty regular army brigadiers, real soldiers, and made that Rooseveltian flunky a major-general by help of the famous "interval," a trick which was merely and simply a lie and a swindle; and also—so to speak—a criminal assault upon the Senate. The President's act was not superior in respectability to the raping of a blind idiot—a blind and very reluctant idiot, a pleading idiot, a beseeching idiot; in fact that was just about what the Senate was—a blind and rapable idiot, and upon her the President "accomplished his hellish purpose," as the Western papers used to say, fifty years ago, in these cases.

Examined by the facts of Mr. Roosevelt's presidential career, the rest of Mr. Hapgood's paragraph becomes matter for laughter:

Turned aside by none of the flattering and plausible arguments which were daily showered upon him, he gave up power, kept his word, and set a high example. Scarcely was Mr. Taft nominated when the President gave another example of his quality by springing enthusiastically to the aid of Henry Spreckels, and their friends in San Francisco, at a time when the current had set strongly in the opposite direction. A few days more, and, in his praise of Cleveland, Mr. Roosevelt once again struck with hearty truthfulness those notes which celebrate earnestness and the truth. He has been a good Police Commissioner, a good Governor, a good President, and a good man. Twenty years of active life may still be his. Meanwhile he has already done splendid service for a thankful nation.

In what way has Mr. Roosevelt given up power? He hasn't given it up; he has merely gone through the form of transferring it to his serf, Mr. Taft, who runs to him daily with the docility of a spaniel to get his permission to do things. Taft even carries his speech of acceptance to his master to be edited and made the utterance of the master, not the voice of the serf. In what way has the President set a high example? Is it a high example for a president of the United States to keep his word? Is keeping one's word such a very extraordinary thing, when the person achieving the feat is the first citizen of a civilized nation? It could be a compliment to say of a burglar that he has kept his word and has thereby set a high example for the other burglars, but it is probably the poorest compliment that has ever been fired at a president of the United States up to this time.

And yet there is some little reason why Hapgood should consider it a compliment, and praiseworthy, in this President's case, for this President has never been servilely addicted to keeping his word. A man's acts are also his word. Look at Mr. Roosevelt. He is always vaporing about purity and righteousness and fairness and justice, just the same as if he really respected those things and regarded himself as their pet champion, whereas there is little or nothing in his history to show that he even knows the meaning of those words. Mr. Roosevelt's character and conduct have undergone many changes since he rose upon the political horizon and became notorious, but the changes are not to his credit, since they have been persistently not for the better but for the worse.

Years ago he was the champion and vigorous fighter for civil service reform, and in this character he won the strong and outspoken praises of a public sick unto death of the spoils system. This was before he was President. The other day this stately foe of the blending of public office with politics sent three hundred federal officeholders to represent his interests at the Republican Convention in Chicago and help nominate his shadow. Mr. Roosevelt is always talking about his policies but he is discreetly silent about his principles. If he has any principles they look so like policies that they cannot be told from that commodity, and they have that commodity's chiefest earmark—the quality of impermanency, a disposition to fade out and disappear at convenience.

In the matter of justice and fairness he evidently has no fixed idea; he talks fairness and justice noisily but he is quite ready to sacrifice these things to expediency at any time, and apparently without a pang. He admires the dime-novel hero and has always made him his model but he has always failed to "make good," as the slang phrase has it; he has always been ready to do the fine and spectacular hero act, and he has always been equally ready to wish he had let it alone when he found that it pleased only half of the people and not the other half.

Six or seven years ago he had a chance to do some dime-novel heroics and he eagerly accepted the opportunity to make a big sensation and set the whole American world applauding—applauding his nerve, his courage, his daring. He invited a negro to lunch with him at the White House, and the negro did it. That was Booker T. Washington, a man worth a hundred Roosevelts, a man whose shoe-latchets Mr. Roosevelt is not worthy to untie. A negro feeding at the White House table! The storm that burst on us from one end of the country to the other must have enthused the circus soul of the little imitation cowboy to the utmost limit for a few hours, for the whole eighty millions were helping to make that noise, but when the inspirer of it found that it wasn't all praise but that the Southern half of it was furious censure, it was not in his nature to remain happy.

I am speaking as if I knew. I think I do know; I think I know he was an unhappy man over that incident. For this reason: there was a freshet of honorary degrees at Yale, and the President was there to get part of the ducking and I was there on the same errand, and there were sixty more gowned and hooded for baptism. The President asked me if I thought he was right in inviting Booker Washington to lunch at the White House. I judged by his tone that he was worried and troubled and sorry about that showy adventure, and wanted a little word of comfort and approval. I said it was a private citizen's privilege to invite whom he pleased to his table, but that perhaps a president's liberties were more limited; that if a president's duty required it there was no alternative but that in a case where it was not required by duty it might be best to let it alone, since the act would give offense to so many people when no profit to the country was to be gained by offending them.

I didn't tell him all I thought about it—we never do that; we keep half of what we think hidden away on our inside and only deliver ourselves of that remnant of it which is proper for general consumption. Privately, I thought it a president's duty to refrain from offending the nation merely to advertise himself and make a noise, but I didn't say that. But I believed that he would not leave that mistake of his alone; I believed he would watch for a chance to rectify it and get himself back into Southern favor. His opportunity came, by and by, and he seized it with avidity, and instantly made himself as splendidly popular in the South as Alexander VI is in hell. It was the Brownsville incident that gave him his chance. Some unimaginable ass in the War Department—surely not Taft—and it couldn't be Taft anyway, because Taft was always away from home around the globe somewhere electioneering for Roosevelt at the nation's expense—ordered the 25th Colored Infantry to take post at Brownsville, on the Mexican border. The Brownsville people heard of this proposition and they implored the War Department not to fling this firebrand into their midst; saying that the sight of a nigger soldier could not

be endured by Texans and disaster must certainly
follow if the colored soldiers came there.

Whoever was doing the particular assing in the
War Office at that time paid no attention to these
appeals. The negro soldiers went into barracks there,
and by and by the prophesied hatred and bad blood
manifested itself between the two colors, and presently there was some shooting done at midnight,
manifestly with government arms and by negro soldiers. To please the Brownsville folk the government
did several strange and shabby things: it sent a commission of officers of the regular army down there to
take testimony and they took it; took such of it as
would go toward convicting some of the negro soldiers and stopped there—they were not interested in
any testimony that could go to the favor of those
men. By the testimony of Captain McDonald, Texan
Ranger, a man whose character for veracity is well
established, the government and its agents acted in
a shabby and dishonest and dishonorable way from
the beginning to the end. Mr. Roosevelt was anxious
to convict some of those soldiers and thus get back
into Southern favor, but as he was not able to do it
he did the next best thing; he convicted the entire
command himself, without evidence and without excuse, and dismissed them from the army, adding those
malignant and cowardly words, "without honor."

How long would it take me to set down a list of
the acts and utterances of the President which are at
variance with Norman Hapgood's estimate of Mr.
Roosevelt as crystallized in his closing sentence? It
would take me a good while; too long for this day

and this weather, and so I will leave that interminable list unregistered until another time.

.   .   .   .   .

7. *The American Gentleman. (April 3, 1906)*[3]

I am not jesting, but am in deep earnest, when I give it as my opinion that our President is *the* representative American gentleman—of today. I think he is as distinctly and definitely the representative American gentleman of today as was Washington the representative American gentleman of his day. Roosevelt is the whole argument for and against, in his own person. He represents what the American gentleman ought not to be, and does it as clearly, intelligibly, and exhaustively as he represents what the American gentleman *is.* We are by long odds the most ill-mannered nation, civilized or savage, that exists on the planet today, and our President stands for us like a colossal monument visible from all ends of the earth. He is fearfully hard and coarse where another gentleman would exhibit kindliness and delicacy. Lately, when that creature of his, that misplaced doctor, that Governor of Cuba, that sleight-of-hand major-general, Leonard Wood, penned up six hundred helpless savages in a hole and butchered every one of them, allowing not even a woman or a child to escape, President Roosevelt—representative American gentleman, first American gentleman— put the heart and soul of our whole nation of gentlemen into the scream of delight which he cabled to

[3] This is restored from a day's dictation which Paine omitted from Volume II of the published *Autobiography.* As the date shows, it would have begun on p. 310 of Volume II.

Wood congratulating him on this "brilliant feat of arms," and praising him for thus "upholding the honor of the American flag."

Roosevelt is far and away the worst President we have ever had, and also the most admired and the most satisfactory. The nation's admiration of him and pride in him and worship of him is far wider, far warmer, and far more general than it has ever before lavished upon a president, even including McKinley, Jackson, and Grant.

.   .   .   .   .

8. Domitian. (September 12, 1908)

I shall vote for the continuance of the monarchy. That is to say, I shall vote for Mr. Taft. If the monarchy could be permanently abolished and the republic restored to us by electing Mr. Bryan, I would vote the Democratic ticket; but it could not happen. The monarchy is here to stay. Nothing can ever unseat it. From now on, the new policy will be continued and perpetuated: the outgoing president will appoint his successor, and the Party will go through the form of ratifying the appointment. Things will go on well enough under this arrangement so long as a Titus succeeds a Vespasian, and we shall best not trouble about a Domitian until we get him. All in good time he will arrive. The Lord will provide—as heretofore. My humble vote is for Titus Taft, inherited insane policies and all, and may it elect him! I do not believe he will appoint a Domitian to succeed him; I only know that if he shall disappoint us and appoint Domitian, Domitian will be elected. But I am not personally concerned in the matter; I shall not be here to grieve about it.

ANDREW CARNEGIE

(August 11, 1906)

The first thing I notice in this morning's paper is a note which I wrote to Andrew Carnegie some years ago.

MARK TWAIN ASKS FOR HYMNBOOK

My dear Mr. Carnegie,—I see by the papers that you are very prosperous. I want to get a hymnbook. It costs six shillings. I will bless you, God will bless you, and it will do a great deal of good.

> Yours truly,
> Mark Twain.

P.S.—Don't send me the hymnbook; send me the six shillings.

Many a stranger would think that the hymnbook was only a blind; that at bottom I didn't really want the hymnbook but only wanted to get my hands on the money. Such a suspicion would do me wrong. I only wanted the hymnbook. I was most anxious to get it but I wanted to select it myself. If I had succeeded in getting the money I would have bought a hymn-book with it and not any other thing. Although I have no evidence but my own as to this I believe it to be trustworthy and sufficient. I am speaking from my grave, and it is not likely that I would break through the sod with an untruth in my mouth.

(December 2, 1907)

Yesterday I had a message for Andrew Carnegie who has just been celebrating his seventieth birthday with the help of friends, and I went uptown to deliver it, first notifying him by telephone that I should arrive at midafternoon or thereabouts. I arrived at his palace a little after three o'clock and delivered my message; then we adjourned to a room which he called his "cozy corner" to have a general chat while I should wait for Mr. Bryce, the British ambassador, who had gone to fill an appointment but had left word that I must wait, as he would soon return. I was glad to comply, for I have known Mr. Bryce a good many years, mainly at his own hospitable table in London, and have always not only respected and esteemed him but have also revered him. I waited an hour and then had to give it up, but the hour was not ill spent, for Andrew Carnegie, long as I have known him, has never yet been an uninteresting study, and he was up to standard yesterday.

If I were going to describe him in a phrase I think I should call him the Human Being Unconcealed. He is just like the rest of the human race but with this difference, that the rest of the race try to conceal what they are and succeed, whereas Andrew tries to conceal what he is but doesn't succeed. Yesterday he was at his best; he went on exposing himself all the time, yet he seemed to be unaware of it. I cannot go so far as to say he *was* unaware of it— seemed is the safer word to use, perhaps. He never has any but one theme, himself. Not that he deals in autobiography; not that he tells you about his brave struggles for a livelihood as a friendless poor boy in a strange land; not that he tells you how he advanced his fortunes steadily and successfully against obstructions that would have defeated almost any other human being similarly placed; not that he tells you how he finally reached the summit of his ambition and became lord over twenty-two thousand men and possessor of one of the three giant fortunes of his day; no, as regards these achievements he is as modest a man as you could meet anywhere, and seldom makes even a fleeting reference to them; yet it is as I say, he is himself his one darling subject, the only subject he for the moment—the social moment—seems stupendously interested in. I think he would surely talk himself to death upon it if you would stay and listen.

Then in what way does he make himself his subject? In this way. He talks forever and ever and ever and untiringly of the attentions which have been shown him. Sometimes they have been large attentions, most frequently they are very small ones; but no matter, no attention comes amiss to him and he likes to revel in them. His friends are coming to observe with consternation that while he adds new attentions to his list every now and then, he never drops an old and shopworn one out of the catalogue to make room for one of these fresh ones. He keeps the whole list, keeps it complete; and you must take it all, along with the new additions, if there is time and you survive. It is the deadliest affliction I know of. He is the Ancient Mariner over again; it is not possible to divert him from his subject; in your weariness and despair you try to do it whenever you think you see a chance, but it always fails; he will use your remark for his occasion and make of it a pretext to get straight back upon his subject again.

A year or two ago Gilder, of *The Century*, and I called at Mr. Carnegie's upon some matter connected with Gen. Carl Schurz, who was very ill at the time. We arranged for a visit to the Schurz family with Mr. Carnegie, who was Schurz's nearest neighbor; then our business was over and we wanted to get away but we couldn't manage it. In the study Mr. Carnegie flew from photograph to photograph, from autograph to autograph, from presentation book to presentation book, and so on, buzzing over each like a happy hummingbird, for each represented a compliment to Mr. Carnegie. Some of these compliments were worth having and remembering but some of them were not; some of them were tokens of honest admiration of the man for the liberal way in which he had devoted millions of dollars to "Carnegie Libraries," while others were merely sorrowfully transparent tokens of reverence for his moneybags; but they were all a delight to him and he loved to talk about them and explain them and enlarge upon them.

One was a poem written by a workingman in Scotland. It was a good piece of literary work, and sang Andrew's glories quite musically. It was in the Scotch dialect, and Andrew read it to us, and read it well—so well that no one born out of Scotland could understand it. Then he told us about King Edward's visit to him at Skibo Castle in Scotland. We had heard him read the poem before and tell about the King's visit; we were doomed to hear him read that

poem many times and also tell about that visit many
times, afterward. When his study seemed to be exhausted we were hoping to get away, but it was not
to be. He headed us off at this and that and the
other room, and made us enter each and every room
under the pretext that there was something important
in there for us to consider—but it was always the
same old thing: a gold box containing the freedom
of the city of London, or Edinburgh, or Jerusalem,
or Jericho; or a great photograph with the pictures
of all the iron masters whom he had reared and
trained and made millionaires of—a picture which
they had presented him, along with a banquet; or it
was shelves which we must inspect loaded to the
guards with applications from everywhere in the
world for a Carnegie library; or it was this or that
or the other God-knows-what in the form of some
damned attention that had been conferred upon him;
and one exasperating feature of it was that it never
seemed to occur to him for a moment that these attentions were mainly tributes to his money and not to
himself.

He has bought fame and paid cash for it; he has
deliberately projected and planned out this fame for
himself; he has arranged that his name shall be
famous in the mouths of men for centuries to come.
He has planned shrewdly, safely, securely, and will
have his desire. Any town or village or hamlet on
the globe can have a public library upon these following unvarying terms: when the applicant shall
have raised one-half of the necessary money, Carnegie will furnish the other half, and the library
building must permanently bear his name.

During the past six or eight years he has been spending six or seven million dollars a year on this scheme. He is still continuing it; there is already a multitude of Carnegie libraries scattered abroad over the planet and he is always making additions to the list. When he dies, I think it will be found that he has set apart a gigantic fund whose annual interest is to be devoted forever to the begetting of Carnegie libraries. I think that three or four centuries from now Carnegie libraries will be considerably thicker in the world than churches. It is a long-headed idea and will deceive many people into thinking Carnegie a long-headed man in other and larger ways. I am sure he is a long-headed man in many and many a wise small way—the way of the trimmer, the way of the smart calculator, the way that enables a man to correctly calculate the tides and come in with the flow and go out with the ebb, keeping a permanent place on the top of the wave of advantage while other men as intelligent as he, but more addicted to principle and less to policy, get stranded on the reefs and bars.

It is possible but not likely that Carnegie thinks the world regards his library scheme as a large and unselfish benevolence; whereas the world thinks nothing of the kind. The world thanks Mr. Carnegie for his libraries and is glad to see him spend his millions in that useful way, but it is not deceived as to the motive. It isn't because the world is intelligent, for the world isn't; it is only the world's prejudice against Mr. Carnegie that protects it from being deceived as to the Carnegie motive. The world was deceived as to President Roosevelt's motive when he issued that lawless Order 78, but that was because the world was saturated with adoration of our small idol. Even half-intelligent persons, outside of the holy Republican communion, knew that Order 78 was merely a vote-bribing raid on the Treasury. It would be by no means fair to say that Mr. Carnegie never gives away money with any other object in view than the purchase of fame. He does not give money to any large extent with a non-advertising purpose in view, still there are instances on record, instances where the notice required is but momentary and quickly forgettable and forgotten.

To return to the visit of yesterday to Mr. Carnegie in his palace. One of his first remarks was characteristic—characteristic in this way: that it brought forward a new attention which he had been receiving; characteristic also in this way: that he dragged it in by the ears, without beating around the bush for a pretext to introduce it.

He said, "I have been down to Washington to see the President."

Then he added, with that sort of studied and practiced casualness which some people assume when they are proposing to state a fact which they are proud of but do not wish to seem proud of, "He sent for me."

I knew he was going to say that. If you let Carnegie tell it, he never seeks the great—the great always seek him. He went on, and told me about the interview. The President had desired his advice regarding the calamitous conditions existing today, commercially, in America and Mr. Carnegie furnished that advice. It was characteristic of Mr. Carnegie that he did not enter into the details of the advice which he furnished and didn't try to glorify himself as an adviser. It is curious. He knew, and I knew, and he knew that I knew, that he was thoroughly competent to advise the President and that the advice furnished would be of the highest value and importance; yet he had no glorification to waste upon that; he has never a word of brag about his real achievements, his great achievements; they do not seem to interest him in the least degree; he is only interested—and intensely interested—in the flatteries lavished upon him in the disguise of compliments and in other little vanities which other men would value but conceal. I must repeat he is an astonishing man in his genuine modesty as regards the large things he has done, and in his juvenile delight in trivialities that feed his vanity.

Mr. Carnegie is not any better acquainted with himself than if he had met himself for the first time day before yesterday. He thinks he is a rude, bluff, independent spirit, who writes his mind and thinks his mind with an almost extravagant Fourth of July independence; whereas he is really the counterpart of the rest of the human race in that he does not boldly speak his mind except when there isn't any danger in it. He thinks he is a scorner of kings and emperors and dukes, whereas he is like the rest of the human race: a slight attention from one of these can make him drunk for a week and keep his happy tongue wagging for seven years.

I was there an hour or thereabouts, and was about to go when Mr. Carnegie just happened to remember by pure accident, apparently, something which had escaped his mind—this something which had escaped his mind being, in fact, a something which had not been out of his mind for a moment in the hour and which he was perishing to tell me about.

He jumped up and said, "Oh, wait a moment. I knew there was something I wanted to say. I want to tell you about my meeting with the Emperor."

The German Kaiser, he meant. His remark brought a picture to my mind at once, a picture of Carnegie and the Kaiser; a picture of a battleship and a Brooklyn ferryboat, so to speak; a picture of a stately big man and a wee little forkèd child of God that Goliath's wife would have pinned a shirt-waist onto a clothesline with—could have done it if she wanted to, anyway. I could see the Kaiser's bold big face, independent big face, as I remember it, and I could see that other face turned up toward it—that foxy, white-whiskered, cunning little face, happy, blessed, lit up with a sacred fire, and squeaking, without words: "Am I in Heaven or is it only a dream?"

I must dwell for a moment upon Carnegie's stat-ure—if one may call it by that large name—for the sake of the future centuries. The future centuries will be glad to hear about this feature from one who has actually looked upon it, for the matter of stature will always be a matter of interest to the future ages when they are reading about Caesar and Alexander and Napoleon and Carnegie. In truth Mr. Carnegie is no smaller than was Napoleon; he is no smaller than were several other men supremely re-nowned in history but for some reason or other he looks smaller than he really is. He looks incredibly small, almost unthinkably small. I do not know how to account for this; I do not know what the reason of it is, and so I have to leave it unexplained; but always when I see Carnegie I am reminded of a Hartford incident of the long, long ago—a thing which had occurred in a law court about a dozen years before I went there, in 1871, to take up my residence. There was a little wee bit of a lawyer there by the name of Clarke, who was famous for two things: his diminutiveness and his persecuting sharpness in cross-questioning witnesses. It was said that always when he got through with a witness there was nothing left of that witness, nothing but a limp and defeated and withered rag. Except once. Just that one time the witness did not wither. The witness was a vast Irishwoman and she was testifying in her own case. The charge was rape. She said she awoke in the morning and found the accused lying beside her, and she discovered that she had been outraged. The lawyer said, after elaborately measuring her great figure impressively with his eye, "Now, Madam, what an impossible miracle you are hoping to persuade this jury to believe! If one may take so preposterous a thing as that seriously, you might even charge it upon me. Come now, suppose you should wake up and find me lying beside you? What would you think?"

She measured him critically and at her leisure, with a calm, judicious eye, and said, "I'd think I'd had a miscarriage!"

As I was saying, Carnegie jumped up and said he wanted to tell me about his meeting with the Emperor; then he went on, something like this:

"We went aboard the *Hohenzollern*, Tower and I, in a perfectly informal way as far as I was concerned, for emperors and commoners are all one to me and so I didn't care to have any announcement made that I was coming. Well, there on the deck stood the Emperor, talking, with the usual imperial crowd of gilded and resplendent naval and civil dignitaries standing a little apart and reverently listening. I stood to one side quietly observing and thinking my own thoughts, the Emperor not conscious that I was there. Presently the Ambassador said, 'There is an American here, your majesty, whom you have more than once expressed a desire to see.'

" 'Who is that, your excellency?'

" 'Andrew Carnegie.'

"With a start which might be translated into a 'God bless my soul,' the Emperor said, 'Ha! a man I have so wanted to see. Bring him to me. Bring him to me,' and he advanced halfway himself and shook me cordially by the hand and said, laughing, 'Ah, Mr. Carnegie, I know you for a confirmed and incurable Independent, who thinks no more of kings and emperors than of other people, but I like it in you; I like a man that does his own thinking and speaks out what he thinks, whether the world approve or not; it's the right spirit, the brave spirit, and there's little enough of it on this planet.'

"I said, 'I am glad your majesty is willing to take me for what I am. It would not become me to disclaim or disown, or even to modify, what your majesty has said of me, since it is only the truth. I could not be otherwise than independent if I wanted

to, for the spirit of independence is a part of my
nature and a person's nature is born, not made. But
I have reverences, your majesty, just the same. What
I revere, respect, esteem, and do homage to is a
man!—a man, a whole man, a fearless man, a manly
and masculine and right-feeling and right-acting
man; let him be born in garret or palace, it is the
same to me—if he is a man he has my homage; your
majesty is a man, a whole man, a manly man, and
it is for this that I revere you, *not* for your mighty
place in the world.' "

And so on, and so on. It was a battle of compliments, appreciations, and almost indecently enthusiastic delight on both sides. One or two of the speeches
which Mr. Carnegie made to the Emperor were of
the soaring, high-voiced, ornate, and thunderously
oratorical sort, and in re-delivering them now he
acted them out with fire, energy, and effective ges-
ticulation. It was a fine and stirring thing to see.

We are all alike—on the inside. Also we are exteriorly all alike, if you leave out Carnegie. Scoffing
democrats as we are, we do dearly love to be noticed
by a duke, and when we are noticed by a monarch
we have softening of the brain for the rest of our
lives. We try our best to keep from referring to
these precious collisions, and in time some of us succeed in keeping our dukes and monarchs to ourselves;
it costs us something to do this but in time we accomplish it. In my own case, I have so carefully and
persistently trained myself in this kind of self-denial
that today I can look on calm and unmoved when a
returned American is casually and gratefully playing
the earls he has met; I can look on, silent and un-

excited, and never offer to call his hand, although I
have three kings and a pair of emperors up my
sleeve.

It takes a long time to reach this summit of self-
sacrifice, and Carnegie has not reached it and never
will. He loves to talk about his encounters with
sovereigns and aristocracies; loves to talk of these
splendid artificialities in a lightly scoffing and com-
passionate vein and try not to let on that those encounters are the most precious bric-a-brac in the
treasury of his memory; but he is just a human
being, and he can't even wholly deceive himself, let
alone the house cat. With all his gentle scoffings,
Carnegie's delight in his contacts with the great
amounts to a mania; it must be as much as four years
since King Edward visited him at Skibo Castle, yet
it is an even bet that not a day has passed since then
that he has not told somebody all about it, and enlarged with pride upon the fact that the visit was so
small a matter to him that he was able to forget
that it was impending, and so the King had to wait a
moment until Mr. Carnegie was sent for.

Mr. Carnegie cannot leave the King's visit alone;
he has told me about it at least four times, in detail.
When he applied that torture the second, third, and
fourth times, he certainly knew that it was the second,
third, and fourth time, for he has an excellent
memory. I am not able to believe that he ever allows
an opportunity to tell it to go by without getting out
of that opportunity all it is worth. He has likable
qualities and I like him, but I don't believe I can
stand the King Edward visit again.

In his talk about his recent visit—by request—to

the President, Mr. Carnegie very, very gently criti-
cized a couple of Mr. Roosevelt's latest insanities:
one of these is his departure from his last year's
requirement of a new battleship per year and his substituted policy of last week, requiring four new battleships right away at a cost of sixty-nine million
dollars. Carnegie suggested to him, in a guarded
and diplomatic way, that this amazing warlike outburst was not altogether in harmony with Mr.
Roosevelt's laboriously acquired position in the world
as the Dove of Peace and as the recipient of the
Nobel Prize of forty thousand dollars as the chiefest
dove of peace on the planet. Mr. Carnegie also suggested, in cautious, diplomatic language, that the
warships be postponed and the sixty-nine millions be
employed in improving the waterways of the country.

I said that the suggestion to drop the battleships
was good advice but that the President would not be
influenced by it, because dropping the battleships
would interfere with his policy—policy, not policies,
since the President has only one policy and that is to
do insanely spectacular things and get himself talked
about.

Mr. Carnegie toyed cautiously with that suggestion of insanity; he did not commit himself and I
didn't expect him to do it. He had no call to trade
dangerous political confessions with me—and besides, he didn't need to tell me what I already knew;
to wit, that there isn't an intelligent human being in
America that doesn't privately believe that the President is substantially and to all effects and purposes
insane, and ought to be in an asylum.

I added, without fishing for a response, and not

expecting one, "Mr. Roosevelt is the Tom Sawyer
of the political world of the twentieth century; always showing off; always hunting for a chance to
show off; in his frenzied imagination the Great Republic is a vast Barnum circus with him for a clown
and the whole world for audience; he would go to
Halifax for half a chance to show off, and he would
go to hell for a whole one."

Mr. Carnegie chuckled half approvingly but didn't
say anything, and I wasn't expecting him to say
anything.

As I have said, Mr. Carnegie mentioned two incidents of his Washington visit: one of them was the
one I have been talking about—the four battleships;
the other was the "In God We Trust." Away back
yonder in the days of the Civil War, a strong effort
was made to introduce the name of God into the
Constitution; it failed but a compromise was arrived
at which partially satisfied the friends of the Deity.
God was left out of the Constitution but was furnished a front seat on the coins of the country. After
that on one side of the coin we had an Injun, or a
Goddess of Liberty, or something of that kind, and
on the other side we engraved the legend, "In God
We Trust." Now then, after that legend had remained there forty years or so, unchallenged and
doing no harm to anybody, the President suddenly
"threw a fit" the other day, as the popular expression goes, and ordered that remark to be removed
from our coinage.

Mr. Carnegie granted that the matter was not of
consequence, that a coin had just exactly the same
value without the legend as with it, and he said he

had no fault to find with Mr. Roosevelt's action but only with his expressed reasons for the act. The President had ordered the suppression of that motto because a coin carried the name of God into improper places, and this was a profanation of the Holy Name. Carnegie said the name of God is used to being carried into improper places everywhere and all the time, and that he thought the President's reasoning rather weak and poor.

I thought the same, and said, "But that is just like the President. If you will notice, he is very much in the habit of furnishing a poor reason for his acts while there is an excellent reason staring him in the face, which he overlooks. There was a good reason for removing that motto; there was, indeed, an unassailably good reason—in the fact that the motto stated a lie. If this nation has ever trusted in God, that time has gone by; for nearly half a century almost its entire trust has been in the Republican party and the dollar—mainly the dollar. I recognize that I am only making an assertion and furnishing no proof; I am sorry, but this is a habit of mine; sorry also that I am not alone in it; everybody seems to have this disease.

"Take an instance: the removal of the motto fetched out a clamor from the pulpit; little groups and small conventions of clergymen gathered themselves together all over the country, and one of these little groups, consisting of twenty-two ministers, put up a prodigious assertion unbacked by any quoted statistics and passed it unanimously in the form of a resolution: the assertion, to wit, that this is a Christian country. Why, Carnegie, so is hell. Those clergymen know that, inasmuch as 'Strait is the way and narrow is the gate, and few—*few*—are they that enter in thereat' has had the natural effect of making hell the only really prominent Christian community in any of the worlds; but we don't brag of this and certainly it is not proper to brag and boast that America is a Christian country when we all know that certainly five-sixths of our population could not enter in at the narrow gate."

.   .   .   .   .

(December 10, 1907)

I have been leading a quiet and wholesome life now during two entire banqueteering, speechmaking seasons. These seasons begin in September and last until the end of April; it is half a year. Banquets run late, and by the end of the season the habitual banqueteer is haggard and worn facially, and drowsy in his mind and weak on his legs. Three seasons ago I was still keeping up the banqueteering habit—a habit which had its beginning in 1869 or '70 and had been continued season by season, thereafter, over that long stretch of thirty-five or thirty-six years.

I renounced that habit on the 29th of April, three seasons ago. I had been banqueteering and making speeches two or three times in every week for six months; I had tried to get out of this soul-wearing slavery every year for a long time but had failed of my desire through the adoption of a mistaken system, the system of tapering off used by hard drinkers. I said I would limit myself to three banquets in the season. This was naturally a mistake, for when a

weak person has said yes once he hasn't grit enough
to say no the rest of the time—but I adopted a
better policy on that 29th of April just referred to.
I took what may be called the teetotaler's pledge
and said I would not attend speechmaking banquets
any more. That pledge has saved me and has given
me a quiet and peaceful life; I think I have not
broken it more than three times since I made it.

I broke it last night and am not at all likely to
break it again for a twelvemonth. I had good reasons
for breaking it last night—I wanted to see some
more of Andrew Carnegie, who is always a subject
of intense interest for me. I like him; I am ashamed
of him; and it is a delight to me to be where he is
if he has new material on which to work his vanities
where they will show him off as with a limelight.

The banquet last night was given him by the Associated Societies of Engineers, a wonderful organization with a membership of fifteen thousand engineers of all sorts and kinds, an organization whose
industries cover every department of that extraordinary trade; that trade which by the help of the
inventor has created the marvel of the ages, this
modern material civilization of ours. Two hundred
and fifty members were present and not an unintel-
lectual face visible anywhere—a most remarkable
body of men to look at. The oldest member present,
Mr. Fritz, aged eighty-six, hale and hearty, was the
revolutionizer of the steel industries of the United
States, a small affair when he took hold of it with
Mr. Holley but now vast almost beyond the power
of figures to compute. Edison was there, looking
young and plump; and there were others of high

distinction present. The dinner was in honor of Mr. Carnegie, who had given to the Associated Societies their great building and the land it stands upon in 39th Street, a present which cost his pocketbook twelve hundred thousand dollars.

I wonder what the banquet will be a century from now. If it has not greatly improved by that time it ought to be abolished. It is a dreadful ordeal and in my long experience it has shown not a shade of improvement; I believe it is even worse now than it was a generation ago. The guests gather at half past seven in the evening and stand and chat half an hour and weary themselves with the standing and chatting; then they march out in procession in double file, with the chairman and the chief guest in the lead, and the crashing and deafening clamor of the music breaks out; the guests seat themselves and begin to talk to each other softly, sanely, then a little louder, and a little louder, and still a little louder, each group trying to make itself heard above the general din, and before long everybody is shrieking and shouting; knives and forks and plates are clattering, and a man might as well be in pandemonium as far as personal comfort is concerned. This used to continue an hour and a half; then at half past nine the speaking began, and continued for an hour; then the insurrection ceased and the survivors went home.

Years ago, in order to save my life, I adopted the system of feeding at home, then starting to the banquet in time to reach it when the banquet was over and the speaking ready to begin—say at half past nine; then leaving the place upon one pretext or another as soon as I had emptied my speech upon the assembled sufferers. But nowadays the menu is so intolerably long that the speaking is not likely to begin until fully ten o'clock, so I asked them not to come for me before ten and to allow me as early a place as they could in the list of speakers, so that I could get back home at a reasonable hour. But they came for me at nine, which cheered me and charmed me, because I supposed it meant that the banquet was about over. It was a mistake. I arrived at a quarter past nine, and the feeding was not over until a quarter to eleven. Then the intellectual labors of the evening began; the speeches of the chairman and Mr. Carnegie and Mr. Fritz occupied, altogether, thirty-five minutes; then I spoke ten minutes and got away at half past eleven, leaving behind me half a dozen speakers still to be heard from. It is likely that the last one did not finish before one o'clock.

I hope I shall not see another banquet in this life until Mr. Carnegie is chief guest again. He made a good speech—sound, sensible, to the point, not a minute too long; and it had humor in it and also quite distinct traces of modesty—but that was because it was a prepared speech and memorized; he had the typewritten manuscript on the table before him but I did not see him refer to it; he trusted to his memory and it was not strictly faithful to him; it failed him a couple of times when he tried to quote poetical passages from Kipling. They were forceful and would have been very effective if he had reeled them off easily and comfortably, but as he was obliged to stop in the middle of them and stand and wait and think, their effectiveness oozed out and was lost—but there was no other defect in his speech and it was received with high and vociferous approval. When he sat down, Mr. Fritz was called up and read a quiet speech of considerable length from manuscript and sat down.

Apparently it was my turn now but there was an interruption—a framed certificate of honorary membership was brought forward to be presented to Mr. Carnegie by Mr. Fritz. The chairman held the big frame up where all the house could see it and explained what it was, and everybody cheered; then Mr. Carnegie rose and from his low altitude beamed up at the tall and stately Fritz and reached up and took him by the hand and said, "I will not call him Mister, it is too distant; he is not Mister to us, he is Uncle John," whereat everybody shouted approval, and one man shouted "Unser Fritz," and the house took that up and reshouted it—Mr. Fritz has German blood in his veins—and altogether the incident was very pleasing and stirring.

The little episode was highly dramatic and if Mr. Carnegie had sat down then he would have scored the triumph of the evening; but no, he was Carnegie and that could not happen. He was Carnegie, and being Carnegie of course he was bursting to tell about his recent contact with the Emperor of Germany. He played the same casualness that he had played upon me in his palace the other day and in just about the same words—certainly in the same spirit. He pretended that he had been on the point of sitting down but had suddenly remembered something—which was an acted lie; without any doubt he had come there intending to tell about himself and the Emperor and he hadn't forgotten about it at all; it was fresh and boiling and steaming in his mind all the time; he was only waiting for a chance.

He said, ever so casually, "Oh, I forgot to tell you about my recent reception by the Emperor of Germany."

I don't see how a man of such principled and practiced veracity as Carnegie can lie in that easy and comfortable way and look just as if it came natural to him to do it. He went on at great length and told about the meeting with the Emperor in almost exactly the same words in which he had detailed it to me in his palace. I know that one sentence, at least, was in precisely the same words which I had heard him utter on that occasion; to wit, "His majesty said, 'Ah, well, Mr. Carnegie, I know you. I have read all your books, and I know you hate kings.' I said, 'Ah yes, your majesty, I am certainly a democrat of the democrats. I do hate kings; but, your majesty, I admire and revere the man behind the king, when he is a man, and that is what your majesty is.' "

I could see that Mr. Carnegie was tired and worn with the daily and hourly repetition of his encounter with the Emperor, and that his stupendous pride and joy in that imperial attention was shortening his life with pure ecstasy—but dear me, how full of it he was! How delighted he was to expose himself to those people while imagining that he was deceiving them all the time! He filled his talk with his brave scorn of royalties, and those people cheered those handsome and intrepid remarks to the echo, and in their kindness of heart they never once betrayed their

perception of the fact that his only reason for remembering to tell them about that contact was that
he might brag about it and intoxicate himself with
it, and send them home filled with the immortal glory
of having seen with their own eyes a man who had
talked face to face with an emperor.

He was interrupted by the heartiest applause all
the way through, and by and by he made a hit that
almost fetched the house to its feet—and perhaps a
hundred did rise and wave their napkins at him,
while every man present made all the noise he could.
Carnegie ought to have sat down then but it wouldn't
have been Carnegie if he had done that; when he is
happy he can't stop, he has to go on and wind up
with an anticlimax—and that is what he did.

Well, then we had some music, and at last the
chairman called me up.

I said I had been chief guest myself several times
and knew by experience what this one was suffering.
He had said himself that he was embarrassed by the
chairman's splendid compliments. I said that that
was always what happened to the chief guest and
that it was a pity that he should be so treated; there
ought always to be some friend present humane
enough to act as devil's advocate in the preliminaries
of a beatification and do the guest the kindness of
calling some little attention to the uncomplimentable
side of his career and character, since no man, not
even Mr. Carnegie, has led a life that is wholly free
from crime.

I said, "Look at him where he sits, his face softly,
sweetly, benignantly scintillating with the signs and
symbols of a fictitious innocence. Is he free from

crime? Look at his pestiferous simplified spelling! It has disordered the minds of this whole nation and brought upon this people sorrow and disaster in a hundred forms; it has broken up families; it has ruined households; it produced the San Francisco earthquake; it has brought the vast industries of this country to a standstill and spread a blight of commercial stagnation and undeserved poverty, hunger, nakedness and suffering from Florida to Alaska and from the Great Lakes to the Gulf—and not even the solar system has escaped; the sun is blanketed as never before with sunspots—sunspots which will bring upon us cyclones, hurricanes, electrical storms of all descriptions throughout the coming year; and the astronomers lay all this to Mr. Carnegie's pernicious simplified spelling. He has attacked orthography at the wrong end; he has attacked the symptoms, not the disease itself.

"The real disease is in the alphabet; there is not a vowel in it that has a definite and permanent and inalterable value, and sometimes a consonant is placed where it has no value at all. The *h* in *honor, honesty, gherkin,* and in a multitude of other words, has no value, and it ought to be flung out; in *wheat* and *which* and *what,* and so on, it is misplaced: it should be the first letter of the word, not the second, for the sound of the *h* precedes the sound of the *w*; we don't say *w-heat,* we say *h-weat*; it isn't *w-hich,* it is *h-wich*—and so on. The consonants that begin *mnemonics* and *pneumonia,* and three of the consonants in *phthisis,* are wasted—and so on.

"Adequate reform would give each consonant a sole and definite office to perform, and restrict it to

that. Adequate reform would give each vowel and
its modifications a sole and definite office to perform,
and restrict it to that. Then you wouldn't have to be
taught spelling, you would only need to be taught
the alphabet—then every word that fell upon your
ear would instantly and automatically spell itself.

"After three hours' labor in mastering that re-
formed alphabet you could promptly and correctly
spell every word in the Unabridged Dictionary with
your eyes shut; whereas by reason of the immeasur-
able silliness of our present alphabet there isn't a
man in this house that doesn't have to leave fifteen
hundred words out of his correspondence every day
because he doesn't know how to spell them—yet he
spent many weary weeks, and many, many dreary
months of his life trying to learn how to spell; it's as
idiotic as trying to do a St. Vitus dance with wooden
legs. Is there anybody here that knows how to spell
pterodactyl? No, not one. Except perhaps the prisoner at the bar. God only knows how he would simplify it. When he got done with it you wouldn't
know whether it was a bird or a reptile, and the
chances are that he would give it tusks and a trunk
and make it lay eggs.

"A system of accents assigning to each vowel its
special and sole and definite shade of sound would
enable us to spell rationally and with precision all
kinds of words, let them come from what language
they might; and that would be *real* simplifying,
thorough simplifying, competent simplifying—*not*
inadequate and halfway simplifying by removing the
hair, cauterizing the warts, lancing the tumors,
medicating the cancers—leaving the old thing sub-

stantially what it was before, only bald-headed and unsightly.

"If I ask you what *b-o-w* spells you can't answer till you know which bow I am referring to; the same with *r-o-w*; the same with *sore*, and *bore*, and *tear*, and *lead*, and *read*—and all the rest of that asinine family of bastard words born out of wedlock and don't know their own origin and nobody else does; and if I ask you to pronounce *s-o-w*, instead of promptly telling me, as you would if we had a sane and healthy and competent alphabet instead of a hospital of compound comminuted cripples and eunuchs in the place of it, you have to waste time asking me which sow I mean, the one that is poetic, and recalls to you the furrowed field and the farmer scattering seed, or the one that recalls the lady hog and the future ham.

"It's a rotten alphabet! O Carnegie, O prisoner at the bar, reform, reform! There's never been a noble, upright, right-feeling prophet in this world, from David and Goliath down to Sodom and Gomorrah who wouldn't censure you for what you've done! And yet you have meant well; you have not been purposely criminal, and your simplified spelling is not destitute of virtue and value. It has a certain degree of merit—but I must be just, I must be sternly just, and I say to you this: your simplified spelling is well enough, but like chastity—(*artful pause of a moment or two, here, to let the word sink in and give the audience a chance to guess out where the resemblance lies*)—it can be carried too far!"

THE PLUTOCRACY

1. The Drift toward Centralized Power. (December 13, 1906)[1]

As regards the coming American monarchy. It was before the Secretary of State had been heard from that the chairman of the banquet said: "In this time of unrest it is of great satisfaction that such a man as you, Mr. Root, is chief adviser of the President."

Mr. Root then got up and in the most quiet and orderly manner touched off the successor to the San Francisco earthquake. As a result, the several State governments were well shaken up and considerably weakened. Mr. Root was prophesying. He was prophesying, and it seems to me that no shrewder and surer forecasting has been done in this country for a good many years.

He did not say in so many words that we are proceeding in a steady march toward eventual and unavoidable replacement of the republic by monarchy, but I suppose he was aware that that is the case. He notes the several steps, the customary steps, which

---

[1] The *Autobiography* has no entry under this date. All but the first three paragraphs of this section were written about a year earlier, under the title "Comment on Mr. Root's Utterances." Mark Twain apparently decided to insert the passage in the *Autobiography* when he published portions in the *North American Review*, where, with the introductory two paragraphs and the date as given, it appears in the issue of January 4, 1907.

in all the ages have led to the consolidation of loose
and scattered governmental forces into formidable
centralizations of authority but he stops there and
doesn't add up the sum. He is not unaware that heretofore the sum has been ultimate monarchy, and
that the same figures can fairly be depended upon to
furnish the same sum whenever and wherever they
can be produced, so long as human nature shall remain as it is; but it was not needful that he do the
adding since anyone can do it, neither would it have
been gracious in him to do it.

In observing the changed conditions which in the
course of time have made certain and sure the
eventual seizure by the Washington government of
a number of State duties and prerogatives which
have been betrayed and neglected by the several
States, he does not attribute those changes and the
vast results which are to flow from them to any
thought-out policy of any party or of any body of
dreamers or schemers, but properly and rightly
attributes them to that stupendous power—Circumstance—which moves by laws of its own, regardless
of parties and policies, and whose decrees are final
and must be obeyed by all—and will be. The railway
is a Circumstance, the steamship is a Circumstance,
the telegraph is a Circumstance. They were mere
happenings; and to the whole world, the wise and
the foolish alike, they were entirely trivial, wholly
inconsequential; indeed silly, comical, grotesque. No
man, and no party, and no thought-out policy said,
"Behold, we will build railways and steamships and
telegraphs, and presently you will see the condition
and way of life of every man and woman and child

in the nation totally changed; unimaginable changes of law and custom will follow, in spite of anything that anybody can do to prevent it."

The changed conditions have come and Circumstance knows what is following and will follow. So does Mr. Root. His language is not unclear, it is crystal.

"Our whole life has swung away from the old State centres and is crystallizing about national centres . . . the old barriers which kept the States as separate communities are completely lost from sight.

". . . that (State) power of regulation and control is gradually passing into the hands of the national government.

"Sometimes by an assertion of the inter-State commerce power, sometimes by an assertion of the taxing power, the national government is taking up the performance of duties which under the changed conditions the separate States are no longer capable of adequately performing.

"We are urging forward in a development of business and social life which tends more and more to the obliteration of State lines and the decrease of State power as compared with national power.

"It is useless for the advocates of State rights to inveigh against . . . the extension of national authority in the fields of necessary control where the States themselves fail in the performance of their duty."

He is not announcing a policy, he is not forecasting what a party of planners will bring about, he is merely telling what the people will require and compel. And he could have added—which would be perfectly true—that the people will not be moved to it by speculation and cogitation and planning but by *Circumstance*—that power which arbitrarily compels all their actions and over which they have not the slightest control.

"*The end is not yet.*"

It is a true word. We are on the march, but at present we are only just getting started.

If the States continue to fail to do their duty as required by the people—". . . *Constructions of the Constitution will be found* to vest the power where it will be exercised—in the national government."

I do not know whether that has a sinister meaning or not and so I will not enlarge upon it lest I should chance to be in the wrong. It sounds like ship money come again but it may not be so intended.

Human nature being what it is, I suppose we must expect to drift into monarchy by and by. It is a saddening thought but we cannot change our nature —we are all alike, we human beings; and in our blood and bone, and ineradicably, we carry the seeds out of which monarchies and aristocracies are grown: worship of gauds, titles, distinctions, power. We have to worship these things and their posses- sors, we are all born so and we cannot help it. We have to be despised by somebody whom we regard as above us or we are not happy; we have to have somebody to worship and envy or we cannot be content. In America we manifest this in all the ancient and customary ways. In public we scoff at titles and hereditary privilege but privately we hanker after them, and when we get a chance we buy them for cash and a daughter. Sometimes we get a good man and worth the price but we are ready to take him anyway, whether he be ripe or rotten, whether he be clean and decent or merely a basket of noble and sacred and long-descended offal. And when we get him the whole nation publicly chaffs and scoffs—and privately envies, and also is proud of the honor which has been conferred upon us. We run over our list of titled purchases every now and then in the newspapers and discuss them and caress them, and are thankful and happy.

Like all the other nations, we worship money and the possessors of it—they being our aristocracy, and we have to have one. We like to read about rich people in the papers; the papers know it, and they do their best to keep this appetite liberally fed. They even leave out a football game or a bull fight now and then to get room for all the particulars of how—according to the display heading— "Rich Woman Fell Down Cellar—Not Hurt." The falling down the cellar is of no interest to us when the woman is not rich, but no rich woman can fall down a cellar and we not yearn to know all about it and wish it was us.

In a monarchy the people willingly and rejoicingly revere and take pride in their nobilities, and are not humiliated by the reflection that this humble and hearty homage gets no return but contempt. Contempt does not shame them, they are used to it and they recognize that it is their proper due. We are all made like that. In Europe we easily and quickly learn to take that attitude toward the sovereigns and the aristocracies; moreover, it has been observed that when we get the attitude we go on and exaggerate it, presently becoming more servile than the natives and vainer of it. The next step is to rail and scoff at republics and democracies. All of which is natural, for we have not ceased to be human beings by becoming Americans, and the human race was always intended to be governed by kingship, not by popular vote.

I suppose we must expect that unavoidable and irresistible Circumstances will gradually take away the powers of the States and concentrate them in the central government, and that the republic will then repeat the history of all time and become a monarchy; but I believe that if we obstruct these encroachments and steadily resist them the monarchy can be postponed for a good while yet.

.   .   .   .   .

2. *Purchasing Civic Virtue. (January 15, 1907)*

The human race was always interesting, and we know by its past that it will always continue so. Monotonously. It is always the same; it never changes. Its circumstances change from time to time, for better or worse, but the race's *character* is permanent, and never changes. In the course of the ages it has built up several great and worshipful civilizations and has seen unlooked-for circumstances slily emerge bearing deadly gifts which looked like benefits and were welcomed, whereupon the decay and destruction of each of these stately civilizations has followed.

It is not worth while to try to keep history from repeating itself, for man's character will always

make the preventing of the repetitions impossible.
Whenever man makes a large stride in material
prosperity and progress he is sure to think that *he*
has progressed, whereas he has not advanced an
inch; nothing has progressed but his circumstances.
He stands where he stood before. He knows more
than his forebears knew but his intellect is no better
than theirs and never will be. He is richer than his
forebears but his character is no improvement upon
theirs. Riches and education are not a permanent
possession; they will pass away, as in the case of
Rome and Greece and Egypt and Babylon; and a
moral and mental midnight will follow—with a dull
long sleep and a slow reawakening. From time to
time he makes what looks like a change in his character but it is not a real change; and it is only
transitory anyway. He cannot even invent a religion
and keep it intact; circumstances are stronger than
he and all his works. Circumstances and conditions
are always changing, and they always compel him
to modify his religions to harmonize with the new
situation.

For twenty-five or thirty years I have squandered
a deal of my time—too much of it perhaps—in trying to guess what is going to be the process which
will turn our republic into a monarchy and how far
off that event might be. Every man is a master and
also a servant, a vassal. There is always someone
who looks up to him and admires and envies him;
there is always someone to whom he looks up and
whom he admires and envies. This is his nature;
this is his character; and it is unchangeable, inde-
structible; therefore republics and democracies are

not for such as he; they cannot satisfy the requirements of his nature. The inspirations of his character will always breed circumstances and conditions which must in time furnish him a king and an aristocracy to look up to and worship. In a democracy he will try—and honestly—to keep the crown away, but Circumstance is a powerful master and will eventually defeat him.

Republics have lived long but monarchy lives forever. By our teaching we learn that vast material prosperity always brings in its train conditions which debase the morals and enervate the manhood of a nation—then the country's liberties come into the market and are bought, sold, squandered, thrown away, and a popular idol is carried to the throne upon the shields or shoulders of the worshiping people and planted there in permanency. We are always being taught—no, formerly we were always being taught—to look at Rome and beware. The teacher pointed to Rome's stern virtue, incorruptibility, love of liberty, and all-sacrificing patriotism —this when she was young and poor; then he pointed to her later days when her sunbursts of material prosperity and spreading dominion came and were exultingly welcomed by the people, they not suspecting that these were not fortunate glories, happy benefits, but were a disease and freighted with death.

The teacher reminded us that Rome's liberties were not auctioned off in a day, but were bought slowly, gradually, furtively, little by little; first with a little corn and oil for the exceedingly poor and wretched, later with corn and oil for voters who were not quite so poor, later still with corn and oil for pretty much every man that had a vote to sell—exactly our own history over again. At first we granted deserved pensions, righteously and with a clean and honorable motive, to the disabled soldiers of the Civil War. The clean motive began and ended there. We have made many and amazing additions to the pension list but with a motive which dishonors the uniform and the Congresses which have voted the additions—the sole purpose back of the additions being the purchase of votes. It is corn and oil over again, and promises to do its full share in the eventual subversion of the republic and the substitution of monarchy in its place. The monarchy would come anyhow, without this, but this has a peculiar interest for us in that it prodigiously hastens the day. We have the two Roman conditions: stupendous wealth with its inevitable corruptions and moral blight, and the corn and oil pensions—that is to say, vote bribes, which have taken away the pride of thousands of tempted men and turned them into willing alms receivers and unashamed.

It is curious—curious that physical courage should be so common in the world, and moral courage so rare. A year or two ago a veteran of the Civil War asked me if I did not sometimes have a longing to attend the annual great Convention of the Grand Army of the Republic and make a speech. I was obliged to confess that I wouldn't have the necessary moral courage for the venture, for I would want to reproach the old soldiers for not rising up in indignant protest against our government's vote-purchasing additions to the pension list, which is making of the remnant of their brave lives one long blush. I might try to say the words but would lack the guts and would fail. It would be one tottering moral coward trying to rebuke a houseful of like breed—men nearly as timid as himself but not any more so.

Well, there it is—I am a moral coward like the rest; and yet it is amazing to me that out of the hundreds of thousands of physically dauntless men who faced death without a quiver of the nerves on a hundred bloody fields, not one solitary individual of them all has had courage enough to rise up and bravely curse the Congresses which have degraded him to the level of the bounty-jumper and the bastards of the same. Everybody laughs at the grotesque additions to the pension fund; everybody laughs at the grotesque-est of them all, the most shameless of them all, the most transparent of them all, the only frankly lawless one of them all—the immortal Executive Order 78. Everybody laughs— privately; everybody scoffs—privately; everybody is indignant—privately; everybody is ashamed to look a real soldier in the face—but none of them exposes his feelings publicly. This is perfectly natural, and wholly inevitable, for it is the nature of man to hate to say the disagreeable thing. It is his character, his nature; it has always been so; his character cannot change; while he continues to exist it will never change by a shade.

.   .   .   .   .

3. Senator Clark of Montana. (January 28, 1907)

In the middle of the afternoon day before yesterday, a particular friend of mine whom I will call

Jones for this day and train only, telephoned and said he would like to call for me at half past seven and take me to a dinner at the Union League Club. He said he would send me home as early as I pleased, he being aware that I am declining all invitations this year—and for the rest of my life—that make it necessary for me to go out at night, at least to places where speeches are made and the sessions last until past ten o'clock. But Jones is a very particular friend of mine and therefore it cost me no discomfort to transgress my rule and accept his invitation; no, I am in error—it did cost me a pang, a decided pang, for although he said that the dinner was a private one with only ten persons invited, he mentioned Senator Clark of Montana as one of the ten. I am a person of elevated tone and of morals that can bear scrutiny, and am much above associating with animals of Mr. Clark's breed.

I am sorry to be vain—at least I am sorry to expose the fact that I am vain—but I do confess it and expose it; I cannot help being vain of myself for giving such a large proof of my friendship for Jones as is involved in my accepting an invitation to break bread with such a person as Clark of Montana. It is not because he is a United States Senator —it is at least not wholly because he occupies that doubtful position—for there are many Senators whom I hold in a certain respect and would not think of declining to meet socially, if I believed it was the will of God. We have lately sent a United States Senator to the penitentiary, but I am quite well aware that of those who have escaped this promotion there are several who are in some regards guiltless of crime—not guiltless of all crimes, for that cannot be said of any United States Senator, I think, but guiltless of some kinds of crime. They all rob the Treasury by voting for iniquitous pension bills in order to keep on good terms with the Grand Army of the Republic, and with the Grand Army of the Republic Jr., and with the Grand Army of the Republic Jr., Jr., and with other great-grandchildren of the war—and these bills distinctly represent crime and violated senatorial oaths.

However, while I am willing to waive moral rank and associate with the moderately criminal among the Senators—even including Platt and Chauncey Depew—I have to draw the line at Clark of Montana. He is said to have bought legislatures and judges as other men buy food and raiment. By his example he has so excused and so sweetened corruption that in Montana it no longer has an offensive smell. His history is known to everybody; he is as rotten a human being as can be found anywhere under the flag; he is a shame to the American nation, and no one has helped to send him to the Senate who did not know that his proper place was the penitentiary, with a chain and ball on his legs. To my mind he is the most disgusting creature that the republic has produced since Tweed's time.

I went to the dinner, which was served in a small private room of the club with the usual piano and fiddlers present to make conversation difficult and comfort impossible. I found that the Montana citizen was not merely a guest but that the dinner was given in his honor. While the feeding was going on two of my elbow neighbors supplied me with information concerning the reasons for this tribute of respect to Mr. Clark. Mr. Clark had lately lent to the Union League Club, which is the most powerful political club in America and perhaps the richest, a million dollars' worth of European pictures for exhibition. It was quite plain that my informant regarded this as an act of almost superhuman generosity. One of my informants said, under his breath and with awe and admiration, that if you should put together all of Mr. Clark's several generosities to the club, including this gaudy one, the cost to Mr. Clark first and last would doubtless amount to a hundred thousand dollars. I saw that I was expected to exclaim, applaud, and adore, but I was not tempted to do it, because I had been informed five minutes earlier that Clark's income, as stated under the worshiping informant's breath, was thirty million dollars a year.

Human beings have no sense of proportion. A benefaction of a hundred thousand dollars subtracted from an income of thirty million dollars is not a matter to go into hysterics of admiration and adulation about. If I should contribute ten thousand dollars to a cause, it would be one-ninth of my past year's income, and I could feel it; as matter for admiration and wonder and astonishment and gratitude, it would far and away outrank a contribution of twenty-five million dollars from the Montana jailbird, who would still have a hundred thousand dollars a week left over from his year's income to subsist upon.

It reminded me of the only instance of benevolence exploded upon the world by the late Jay Gould that I had ever heard of. When that first and most

infamous corrupter of American commercial morals
was wallowing in uncountable stolen millions, he contributed five thousand dollars for the relief of the
stricken population of Memphis, Tennessee, at a
time when an epidemic of yellow fever was raging
in that city. Mr. Gould's contribution cost him no
sacrifice; it was only the income of the hour which
he daily spent in prayer—for he was a most godly
man—yet the storm of worshiping gratitude which
welcomed it all over the United States in the newspaper, the pulpit, and in the private circle might
have persuaded a stranger that for a millionaire
American to give five thousand dollars to the dead
and dying poor—when he could have bought a cir-
cuit judge with it—was the noblest thing in American history, and the holiest.

In time, the President of the Art Committee of
the club rose and began with that aged and long-ago
discredited remark that there were not to be any
speeches on this occasion but only friendly and
chatty conversation; then he went on, in the ancient
and long-ago discredited fashion, and made a speech
himself—a speech which was well calculated to make
any sober hearer ashamed of the human race. If a
stranger had come in at that time he might have
supposed that this was a divine service and that the
Divinity was present. He would have gathered that
Mr. Clark was about the noblest human being the
great republic had yet produced and the most mag-
nanimous, the most self-sacrificing, the most limit-
lessly and squanderingly prodigal benefactor of
good causes living in any land today. And it never
occurred to this worshiper of money, and money's

possessor, that in effect Mr. Clark had merely dropped a dime into the League's hat. Mr. Clark couldn't miss his benefaction any more than he could miss ten cents.

When this wearisome orator had finished his devotions, the President of the Union League got up and continued the service in the same vein, vomiting adulations upon that jailbird which, estimated by any right standard of values, were the coarsest sarcasms, although the speaker was not aware of that. Both of these orators had been applauded all along but the present one ultimately came out with a remark which I judged would fetch a cold silence, a very chilly chill; he revealed the fact that the expenses of the club's loan exhibition of the Senator's pictures had exceeded the income from the tickets of admission; then he paused—as speakers always do when they are going to spring a grand effect—and said that at that crucial time Senator Clark stepped forward of his own motion and put his hand in his pocket and handed out fifteen hundred dollars wherewith to pay half of the insurance on the pictures, and thus the club's pocket was saved whole. I wish I may never die if the worshipers present at this religious service did not break out in grateful applause at that astonishing statement; and I wish I may never permanently die, if the jailbird didn't smile all over his face and look as radiantly happy as he will look some day when Satan gives him a Sunday vacation in the cold storage vault.

Finally, while I was still alive, the President of the club finished his dreary and fatiguing marketing of juvenile commonplaces, and introduced Clark, and sat down. Clark rose to the tune of "The Star-Spangled Banner"—no, it was "God Save the King," frantically sawed and thumped by the fiddlers and the piano, and this was followed by "For he's a jolly good fellow," sung by the whole strength of the happy worshipers. A miracle followed. I have always maintained that no man could make a speech with nothing but a compliment for a text but I know now that a reptile can. Senator Clark twaddled and twaddled and twaddled along for a full half-hour with no text but those praises which had been lavished upon his trifling generosities; and he not only accepted at par all these silly phrases but added to them a pile—praising his own so-called generosities and magnanimities with such intensity and color that he took the pigment all out of those other men's compliments and made them look pallid and shadowy. With forty years' experience of human assfulness and vanity at banquets, I have never seen anything of the sort that could remotely approach the assfulness and complacency of this coarse and vulgar and incomparably ignorant peasant's glorification of himself.

I shall always be grateful to Jones for giving me the opportunity to be present at these sacred orgies. I had believed that in my time I had seen at banquets all the different kinds of speechmaking animals there are and also all the different kinds of people that go to make our population, but it was a mistake. This was the first time I had ever seen men get down in the gutter and frankly worship dollars and their possessors. Of course I was familiar with such things through our newspapers, but I had never before heard men worship the dollar with their mouths or seen them on their knees in the act.

.　　.　　.　　.　　.

4. The Teaching of Jay Gould. (February 16, 1906)

Jay Gould was the mightiest disaster which has ever befallen this country. The people had *desired* money before his day, but *he* taught them to fall down and worship it. They had respected men of means before his day, but along with this respect was joined the respect due to the character and industry which had accumulated it. But Jay Gould taught the entire nation to make a god of the money and the man, no matter how the money might have been acquired. In my youth there was nothing resembling a worship of money or of its possessor, in our region. And in our region no well-to-do man was ever charged with having acquired his money by shady methods.

The gospel left behind by Jay Gould is doing giant work in our days. Its message is "Get money. Get it quickly. Get it in abundance. Get it in prodigious abundance. Get it dishonestly if you can, honestly if you must."

This gospel does seem to be almost universal. Its great apostles, today, are the McCurdies, McCalls, Hydes, Alexanders, and the rest of that robber gang who have lately been driven out of their violated positions of trust in the colossal insurance companies of New York. President McCall was reported to be dying day before yesterday. The others have been several times reported, in the past two or three

months, as engaged in dying. It has been imagined
that the cause of these death strokes was sorrow and
shame for the robberies committed upon the two or
three million policy holders and their families, and
the widow and the orphan—but every now and then
one is astonished to find that it is not the outraged
conscience of these men that is at work; they are
merely sick and sore because they have been exposed.

Yesterday—as I see by the morning paper—John
A. McCall quite forgot about his obsequies and sat
up and became impressive, and worked his morals for
the benefit of the nation. He knew quite well that
anything which a prodigiously rich man may say—
whether in health or moribund—will be spread by
the newspapers from one end of this continent to the
other and be eagerly read by every creature who is
able to read. McCall sits up and preaches to his son
—ostensibly to his son—really to the nation. The
man seems to be sincere, and I think he *is* sincere.
I believe his moral sense is atrophied. I believe he
really regards himself as a high and holy man. And
I believe he thinks he is so regarded by the people
of the United States. He has been worshiped because
of his wealth, and particularly because of his shady
methods of acquiring it for twenty years. And I
think he has become so accustomed to this adulation,
and so beguiled and deceived by it that he does
really think himself a fine and great and noble being,
and a proper model for the emulation of the rising
generation of young men. He snivels owlishly along
and is evidently as happy and as well satisfied with
himself as if there wasn't a stain upon his name, nor

a crime in his record. Listen—here is his little sermon:

February 16, 1906.
WORK, WORK, SAYS McCALL

Tells of His Last Cigar in a Talk with His Son.
Special to The New York Times.

LAKEWOOD, Feb. 15.—John A. McCall felt so much better today that he had a long talk with his son, John C. McCall, and told many incidents of his career.

"John," he said to his son, "I have done many things in my life for which I am sorry, but I've never done anything of which I feel ashamed.

"My counsel to young men who would succeed is that they should take the world as they find it, and then work—work!"

Mr. McCall thought the guiding force of mankind was will power, and in illustration he said:

"Some time ago, John, your mother and I were sitting together, chatting. I was smoking a cigar. I liked a cigar, and enjoyed a good, quiet smoke. She objected to it.

" 'John,' said she, 'why don't you throw that cigar away?'
"I did so.
" 'John,' she added, 'I hope you'll never smoke again.'

"The cigar I threw away was my last. I determined to quit then and there, and did so. That was exactly thirty-five years ago."

Mr. McCall told his son many stories of his business life and seemed in a happier frame of mind than usual. This condition was attributed partly to the fact that he received hundreds of telegrams today congratulating him on his statement of yesterday reiterating his friendship for Andrew Hamilton.

"Father received a basketful of dispatches from friends in the North, South, East, and West commending him for his statement about his friend Judge Hamilton," said young Mr. McCall tonight. "The telegrams came from persons who wished him good health and recovery. It has made him very happy."

Mr. McCall had a sinking spell at 3 o'clock this morning, but it was slight, and he recovered before it was deemed necessary to send for a physician.

Milk and bouillons are now his sole form of nourishment. He eats no solids and is rapidly losing weight.

Drs. Vanderpoel and Charles L. Lindley held a conference at the McCall house at 5 o'clock this evening, and later told Mrs. McCall and Mrs. Darwin P. Kingsley, his daughter, that Mr. McCall's condition was good, and that there was no immediate danger.

John C. McCall gave out this statement tonight: "Mr. McCall has had a very favorable day and is somewhat better."

Following it comes the kind of bulletin which is given out from day to day when a king or other prodigious personage has had a favorable day and is somewhat better—a fact which will interest and cheer and comfort the rest of the human race, nobody can explain why.

The sons and daughters of Jay Gould move today in what is regarded as the best society—the aristocratic society—of New York. One of his daughters married a titled Frenchman ten or twelve years ago, a noisy and silly ruffian, gambler, and gentleman, and agreed to pay his debts, which amounted to a million or so. But she only agreed to pay the existing debts, not the future ones. The future ones have become present ones now and are colossal. Today she is suing for a separation from her shabby purchase,

and the world's sympathy and compassion are with
her, where it belongs.

.   .   .   .   .

5. The Teaching Applied. (January 30, 1907)

The political and commercial morals of the
United States are not merely food for laughter, they
are an entire banquet. The human being is a curious
and interesting invention. It takes a Cromwell and
some thousands of preaching and praying soldiers
and parsons ten years to raise the standards of English official and commercial morals to a respectworthy altitude, but it takes only one Charles II a
couple of years to pull them down into the mud
again. Our standards were fairly high a generation
ago, and they had been brought to that grade by
some generations of wholesome labor on the part of
the nation's multitudinous teachers; but Jay Gould,
all by himself, was able to undermine the structure
in half a dozen years; and in thirty years his little
band of successors—the Senator Clarks and their
kind—have been able to sodden it with decay from
roof to cellar and render it shaky beyond repair,
apparently.

Before Jay Gould's time there was a fine phrase,
a quite elegant phrase, that was on everybody's lips,
and everybody enjoyed repeating it, day and night,
and everywhere, and enjoyed the thrill of it: "The
press is the palladium of our liberties." It was a
serious saying and it was a true saying, but it is long
ago dead and has been tucked safely away in the
limbo of oblivion. No one would venture it now except as a sarcasm.

Mr. Guggenheim has lately been chosen United States Senator reputedly by a bought legislature in Colorado—which is almost the customary way, now, of electing United States Senators. Mr. Guggenheim is said to have purchased his legislature and paid for it. By his public utterances it is plain that the general political rottenness has entered into him and saturated him, and he is not aware that he has been guilty of even an indelicacy, let alone a gross crime. In many instances the palladium of our liberties has nothing but compliment for him, and justification. The Denver *Post*, which is recognized as the principal and most trustworthy reflector of the public opinion of his State, says:

It is true that Mr. Guggenheim spent a large sum of money, but he only followed the precedents set in many other States. There is nothing essentially wrong in what he has done. Mr. Guggenheim will make the best Senator Colorado has ever had. His election will result in bringing to Colorado what the State needs, capitalists and population of the desirable quality. Mr. Guggenheim will get for Colorado many improvements which Tom Patterson failed to obtain from Washington. He is just the man for the place. There is no use trying to reform the world. They have been trying that for two thousand years and haven't succeeded. Mr. Guggenheim is the choice of the people and they ought to have him, even if he spent a million dollars. The issue of the election was Tom Patterson and Simon Guggenheim, and the people chose Guggenheim. The Denver *Post* bows to the will of the people.

Mr. Guggenheim, in buying what an obsolete phrase called senatorial "honors," did not buy the

entire legislature but practiced the customary econ-
omy and bought only enough of it to elect him. This
has been resented by some of the unbought; they
offered a motion to inquire into the methods by
which his election was achieved, but the bought
majority not only voted the motion down but actually *sponged it from the records*. It looks like
sensitiveness but it probably isn't; it is human nature
that even the most conscienceless thieves do not like
to be pilloried in the Rogues' Gallery.

.   .   .   .   .

6. *Mr. Rockefeller's Bible Class. (March 20, 1906)*

One of the standing delights of the American
nation in these days is John D. Rockefeller, Junior's,
Bible Class adventures in theology. Every Sunday
young Rockefeller explains the Bible to his class.
The next day the newspapers and the Associated
Press distribute his explanations all over the continent and everybody laughs. The entire nation
laughs, yet in its innocent dullness never suspects
that it is laughing at itself. But that is what it is
doing.

Young Rockefeller, who is perhaps thirty-five
years old, is a plain, simple, earnest, sincere, honest,
well-meaning, commonplace person, destitute of
originality or any suggestion of it. And if he were
traveling upon his mental merit instead of upon his
father's money, his explanations of the Bible would
fall silent and not be heard of by the public. But his
father ranks as the richest man in the world, and
this makes his son's theological gymnastics inter-

esting and important. The world believes that the
elder Rockefeller is worth a billion dollars. He pays
taxes on two million and a half. He is an earnest,
uneducated Christian and for years and years has
been Admiral of a Sunday school in Cleveland, Ohio.
For years and years he has discoursed about himself
to his Sunday school and explained how he got his
dollars; and during all these years his Sunday school
has listened in rapture and has divided its worship
between him and his Creator—unequally. His Sunday-school talks are telegraphed about the country
and are as eagerly read by the nation as are his son's.

As I have said, the nation laughs at young Rockefeller's analyzations of the Scriptures. Yet the nation
must know that these analyzations are exactly like
those which it hears every Sunday from its pulpits,
and which its forbears have been listening to for centuries without a change of an idea—in case an idea
has ever occurred in one of these discourses. Young
John's methods are the ordinary pulpit methods. His
deductions of golden fancy from sordid fact are
exactly the same which the pulpit has traded in for
centuries. Every argument he uses was already worn
threadbare by the theologians of all the ages before
it came in its rags to him. All his reasonings are
like the reasonings of all the pulpit's stale borrowings from the dull pulpits of the centuries.

Young John has never studied a doctrine for himself; he has never examined a doctrine for any purpose but to make it fit the notions which he got at
secondhand from his teachers. His talks are quite
as original and quite as valuable as any that proceed
from any other theologian's lips, from the Pope of

Rome down to himself. The nation laughs at young John's profound and clumsy examinations of Joseph's character and conduct, yet the nation has always heard Joseph's character and conduct examined in the same clumsy and stupid way by its pulpits, and the nation should reflect that when they laugh at young John they are laughing at themselves. They should reflect that young John is using no new whitewash upon Joseph. He is using the same old brush and the same old whitewash that have made Joseph grotesque in all the centuries.

I have known and liked young John for many years and I have long felt that his right place was in the pulpit. I am sure that the fox fire of his mind would make a proper glow there—but I suppose he must do as destiny has decreed and succeed his father as master of the colossal Standard Oil Corporation. One of his most delightful theological deliverances was his exposition, three years ago, of the meaning—the real meaning, the bottom meaning—of Christ's admonition to the young man who was overburdened with wealth yet wanted to save himself if a convenient way could be found: "Sell all thou hast and give to the poor." Young John reasoned it out to this effect:

"Whatever thing stands between you and salvation, remove that obstruction at any cost. If it is money, give it away, to the poor; if it is property, sell the whole of it and give the proceeds to the poor; if it is military ambition, retire from the service; if it is an absorbing infatuation for any person or thing or pursuit, fling it far from you and proceed with a single mind to achieve your salvation."

The inference was plain. Young John's father's millions and his own were a mere incident in their lives and not in any way an obstruction in their pursuit of salvation. Therefore Christ's admonition could have no application to them. One of the newspapers sent interviewers to six or seven New York clergymen to get their views upon this matter, with this result: that all of them except one agreed with young Rockefeller. I do not know what we should do without the pulpit. We could better spare the sun —the moon, anyway.

Three years ago I went with young John to his Bible Class and talked to it—not theologically, that would not have been in good taste, and I prefer good taste to righteousness. Now whoever—on the outside—goes there and talks to that Bible Class is by that act entitled to honorary membership in it. Therefore I am an honorary member. Some days ago a Bible Class official sent me word that there would be a quinquennial meeting of these honoraries in their church day after tomorrow evening, and it was desired that I should come there and help do the talking. If I could not come, would I send a letter which could be read to those people?

I was already overburdened with engagements, so I sent my regrets and the following letter:

March 14, 1906.

Mr. Edward M. Foote, Chairman.

Dear Friend and Fellow-Member:

Indeed I should like to attend the reunion of the fellowship of honorary members of Mr. Rockefeller's Bible Class (of whom I am one, by grace of

service rendered) but I must be discreet and not
venture. This is on account of Joseph. He might
come up as an issue and then I could get into trouble,
for Mr. Rockefeller and I do not agree as to Joseph.
Eight years ago I quite painstakingly and exhaustively explained Joseph by the light of the 47th chapter of Genesis, in a *North American Review* article
which has since been transferred to volume XXII of
my Collected Works; then I turned my attention to
other subjects, under the impression that I had settled Joseph for good and all and left nothing further
for anybody to say about him. Judge, then, of my
surprise and sorrow, when by the newspapers I lately
saw that Mr. Rockefeller had taken hold of Joseph
—quite manifestly unaware that I had already settled Joseph—and was trying to settle him again.

In every sentence uttered by Mr. Rockefeller there
was evidence that he was not acquainted with Joseph.
Therefore it was plain to me that he had never read
my article. He has certainly not read it, because his
published estimate of Joseph differs from mine. This
could not be, if he had read the article. He thinks
Joseph was Mary's little lamb; this is an error. He
was—but you look at the article, then you will see
what he was.

For ages Joseph has been a most delicate and
difficult problem. That is, for everybody but me.
It is because I examine him on the facts as they
stand recorded, the other theologians don't. Over-
borne by a sense of duty, they paint the facts. They
paint some of them clear out. Paint them out and
paint some better ones in, which they get out of their
own imaginations. They make up a Joseph-statement

on the plan of the statement which a shaky bank gets
up for the beguilement of the bank inspector. They
spirit away light-throwing liabilities and insert fanci-
ful assets in their places. Am I saying the thing that
isn't true? Sunday before last the very learned and
able Dr. Silverman was thus reported in the *Times*:

But the farmers, the agriculturists, and the shepherds, who
depended for their living on the product of the land, suffered most during a famine. To prevent utter starvation
Joseph had the people from the country removed to the
cities, from one end of the borders of Egypt even to the
other end thereof (Genesis xlvii, 21), and there he supported
them. As long as they had money he gave them food for
money, but when this was exhausted he took their cattle,
their horses, their herds and asses, and even their land, when
necessary, as a pledge for food. The government then fed the
cattle, horses, &c., which otherwise would have died.

Later the land (the ownership?) was returned to the
former owners; they were given seed to sow the land; they
received as many of their cattle, horses, herds, &c., as they
needed, and in payment were only required to give the government one-fifth part of all their increase in animals or
produce.

The whole plan of Joseph was statesmanlike, as well as
humanitarian. It appealed at once to Pharaoh and his coun-
selors, and it is no wonder that Joseph was appointed Viceroy
of all Egypt. Joseph successfully combated all the human
sharks and speculators who had for years despoiled the poor
in the season of famine and reduced them to starvation and
beggary. He held the land and animals of the needy as
pledge, and then returned them their patrimony. (The
ownership?) He charged them only a fair market price for
the food they received. Without the wise institutions of
public storehouses which Joseph had erected the people

would have lost all their possessions, the whole country would have been reduced to misery, and thousands upon thousands would have died, as had been the case in previous seasons of famine.

This is Dr. Silverman's bank statement—all painted and gilded and ready for the inspector. This is the Bible's statement. The italics are mine:

And there was no bread in all the land; for the famine was very sore, so that the land of Egypt and all the land of Canaan fainted by reason of the famine.

And Joseph gathered up *all* of the money that was found in the land of Egypt, and in the land of Canaan, for the corn which they bought; and Joseph brought the money into Pharaoh's house.

And when money failed in the land of Egypt, and in the land of Canaan, *all* the Egyptians came unto Joseph and said, Give us bread: for why should we die in thy presence? for the money faileth.

And Joseph said, Give your cattle; and I will give you for your cattle, if money fail.

And they brought their cattle unto Joseph; and Joseph gave them bread in exchange for horses, and for the flocks, and for the cattle of the herds, and for the asses; and he fed them with bread *for all their cattle for that year.*

When that year was ended, they came unto him the second year, and said unto him, We will not hide it from my lord, how that our money is spent; my lord also hath our herds of cattle; there is *not aught left* in the sight of my lord, but *our bodies*, and *our lands*:

Wherefore shall we die before thine eyes, both we and our land? buy *us* and *our land* for bread, and we and our land will be servants unto Pharaoh: and give us seed that we may live, and not die, that the land be not desolate.

And Joseph *bought* all the land of Egypt for Pharaoh; for the Egyptians *sold* every man his field, because the famine prevailed over them: so *the land became Pharaoh's.*

And as for the people, he removed them to cities from one end of the borders of Egypt even to the other end thereof.

Only the land of the priests bought he not; for the priests had a portion assigned them of Pharaoh, and did eat their portion which Pharaoh gave them: wherefore they sold not their lands.

Then Joseph said unto the people, Behold I have *bought you* this day *and your land* for Pharaoh: lo, here is seed for you, and ye shall sow the land.

And it shall come to pass in the increase, that ye shall give the fifth part unto Pharaoh, and four parts shall be your own, for seed of the fields, and for your own food, and for them of your households, and for food for your little ones.

And they said, Thou hast saved our lives: let us find grace in the sight of my lord, and we shall be Pharaoh's servants.

And Joseph made it a law over the land of Egypt unto this day, that Pharaoh should have the fifth part; except the land of the priests only, which became not Pharaoh's.

I do not find anything there about a "pledge." It looks to me like a brand-new asset—for Joseph. And a most handsome and ameliorating one, too—if a body could find some kind of authority for it. But I can't find it; I do not find that Joseph made loans to those distressed peasants and secured the loans by mortgage on their lands and animals. I seem to find that he took the land itself, to the last acre; and the animals too, to the last hoof. And I do not get the impression that Joseph charged those starving unfortunates "only a fair market price for the food they received." No, I get the impression that he skinned them of every last penny they had, of every last acre they had, of every last animal they had; then bought the whole nation's *bodies* and *liberties* on a "fair market" valuation for bread and the chains of slavery. Is it conceivable that there can be a "fair market price," or any price whatever, estimable in gold, or diamonds, or bank notes, or government bonds, for a man's supremest possession— that one possession without which his life is totally worthless—his liberty? Joseph acted handsome by the clergy; it is the most I can say for him. Politic, too. They haven't forgotten it yet.

No, I thank you cordially and in all sincerity, but I am afraid to come, I must not venture to come, for I am sensitive, I am humane, I am tender in my feelings, and I could not bear it if young Mr. Rockefeller, whom I think a great deal of, should get up and go to whitewashing Joseph again. But you have my very best wishes.

Mark Twain,
Honorary Member of the Bible Class.

· · · · ·

7. *The Little Tale.* (*January 30, 1907*)

It was told me the other night by one of the guests present at the service of praise given by the Union League Club in adulation of Senator Clark, the fragrant. He said:

"The Rev. Elliot B. X., of the City of XX, is an eager and passionate collector of rare books; by grace of his wife's wealth, he is able to exploit his passion freely. Several years ago he was traveling through a sparsely settled farming country and he stopped at a farmhouse to rest, or feed, or something. It was a poor little humble place but the farmer and his wife and their two little children seemed contented and happy. Presently the clergyman's attention was attracted by a large book which in their play the little children were using as a stool. It seemed to be a family Bible. Mr. X. was troubled to see the Scriptures used in such a way; also, the ancient aspect of the book inflamed his book-collecting lust, and he took up the volume and examined it. An earthquake of sudden joy shook him from dome to cellar—the book was a Shakespeare, first edition, and in good repair!

"As soon as he was able to compose himself, he asked the farmer where he got the book. The farmer said it had been in the possession of his people in New England no one knew how many years or generations, and that when he removed to the West to find a new home he brought the book along merely because it was a book; one doesn't throw books away.

"Mr. X. asked him if he would sell it. The farmer said 'Yes,' that he would like to trade it for a book or two of some other character—books of a fresher interest than this one.

"Mr. X. said he would take it home, then, and ——"

Somebody broke into the conversation at this point and it was not resumed. I went home thinking about the unfinished tale and in bed I continued to think about it. It was an interesting situation and I was sorry the interruption had occurred; then, as I was not sleepy, I thought I would finish the tale myself. I knew it would be easy to do, because such tales always move along a certain well-defined course and they all fetch up at one and the same goal at the end.

I must go back for a moment, for I have forgotten a detail. The book had furnished the clergyman not merely one joyful earthquake, but two, for in it he found what was manifestly Shakespeare's autograph —a prodigious find, there being only two others known to be in existence on the planet! Along with Shakespeare's name was another name—Ward. Without doubt this name would be a help in tracing the book's pedigree and in establishing its authenticity.

As I have said, it would be easy to finish the tale, so I began to think it out. I thought it out to my satisfaction—as follows:

My Version

Upon his arrival at home, the clergyman examined the latest quotations of the rare-book market and found that perfect copies of first-edition Shakespeares had advanced five per cent since the autumn quotations of the previous year, therefore the farmer's copy was worth $7,300; also, he found that the standing offer of $55,000 for an authentic autograph of Shakespeare had been advanced to $60,-000. He returned humble and fervent thanks for the happy fortune which had thrown these treasures in his way, and he resolved to add them to his collection, and thus make that collection illustrious and establish its renown forever; so he sent his check for $67,300 to the farmer, whose astonishment and gratitude were beyond his ability to express in words.

I was very well satisfied with my version and not unproud of it; wherefore I was eager to get hold of the rest of the other version and see if I had fallen into any discrepancies. I hunted up the narrator and he furnished me what I wanted, as follows:

Conclusion of the First Version

The gigantic find proved to be genuine and worth many thousands of dollars in the market; indeed the value of the autograph was quite beyond estimate in dollars, there being American multi-millionaires who would be glad to pay three-fourths of a year's income for it. The generous clergyman did not forget the poor farmer, but sent him an encyclopedia and $800.

Caesar's ghost! I was disappointed, and said so. A discussion followed, in which several of us took part, I maintaining that the clergyman had not been generous to the farmer, but had taken advantage of his ignorance to rob him; the others insisted that the clergyman's knowledge was a valuable acquisition which had been earned by study and diligence, and that he was entitled to all the profit he could get out of it—that there was no call for him to give away that valuable knowledge to a person who had been interesting himself in potatoes, and corn, and hogs, when he might have been devoting his leisure hours

to acquiring the same knowledge which had turned
out to be so valuable to the clergyman.

I was not persuaded, but still insisted that the
transaction was not fair to the farmer, and that he
ought to have had half of the value of his book and
the autograph anyway. I believed I would have allowed him half, and I said so. I could not be sure of
this but I at least believed it. Privately I *knew* that
in my first burst of emotion, if I had been in the
clergyman's place, I would have given the farmer
the entire value; that when the burst of emotion had
had time to modify, I would have reduced the
farmer's share by ten per cent; that when the second
burst had had time to cool off a little the farmer's
share would suffer another shrinkage; and if there
should be still further extensions of time for cooling
off, I thought it more than likely that I should end
by sending the farmer the cyclopedia and stopping
there; for this would be the way of the human race,
and I am the human race compacted and crammed
into a single suit of clothes but quite able to represent its entire massed multitude in all its moods and
inspirations.

But there are exceptions; I am aware of that; I
do not represent those exceptions, but only the
massed generality of the race. The late Hammond
Trumbull of Hartford was an exception. He was a
very great scholar and a very fine human being. If
he had used his vast knowledge commercially, he
could have made himself rich out of it, but he didn't;
he never made a penny out of it at the expense of
some other person's ignorance; he was always ready
to help the poor possessor of any rare and precious

thing, out of his store of knowledge, and he did it gladly, and without charge. I remember an instance: twenty years after the war a lady wrote him from the South that among the flotsam and jetsam left unappropriated by the Union soldiers when they destroyed her father's house in the wartime, was a copy of the Eliot Indian Bible; that she had been told it was worth a hundred dollars; that she had also been told that Mr. Trumbull would know the book's value, and would be able to advise her in the matter; that she was poor, and the hundred dollars would be an important sum for her.

Trumbull replied that if the volume was perfect the British Museum would take it at its standing price, which was a thousand dollars. He asked the lady to send the book to him, which she did. It turned out to be a perfect copy, and he sent her the money, without rebate.

I recall an instance of the other sort: a poverty-stricken sister or other female relative of Audubon possessed a copy, in perfect condition, of Audubon's great book and she wished to sell it for she was very poor. Among collectors it had an established price, which was a thousand dollars, but she did not know that. She offered it to a professor in a university, who *did* know it, and he gave her a hundred dollars for it; and not only did he play this swindle upon her but had no more wit and no more heart than to boast about it afterwards.

.   .   .   .   .

8. *Illustration of a Fine Art.* (*May 21, 1908*)

Yesterday the magazine publishers met together at a luncheon at the Aldine Club. They have been

meeting there once a month for the last two or three
years, with a very wise end in view—this end being
to get acquainted with each other, become friendly,
and work together for their mutual advantage instead of each fighting for his own hand as in the days
gone by. About forty of these men were present.
These are the men who are responsible for the policy
of their publications. Their editors are merely
salaried servants and have no authority and in fact
but little influence, perhaps, in the matter of policy.
For years now it has been policy for the magazines
to make war, along with the newspapers, against the
great corporations and monopolies, and this war has
been carried on as such wars are always likely to be
conducted where the persons assailed have to take
what they get and can't talk back. It has been a
cheap and easy matter to be bold and daringly ferocious in attacking the corporations, for the reason
that they had no friends—at least no friends that
were brave enough to face the general storm in their
defense. It was always possible, of course, that the
corporations had a defense worth examination and
consideration if they could only get a hearing, but
for several years such a hearing has been quite
impossible.

The hostility to the corporations was brought to
its height by President Roosevelt's attitude toward
them. The corporations were the creation of the
atrocious tariffs imposed upon everything by the Republican party, and Mr. Roosevelt and his party
have known all the time that all the burdensome
monopolies could be squelched by the simple process
of reducing the robber tariffs to a figure which would
allow the rest of the nation to prosper, instead of

conferring the bulk of the prosperity upon a few dozen multi-millionaire producers—but neither the President nor the party has ever confessed that this was the case; they have persisted in attacking the symptoms and in letting the disease carefully alone. They have had their reasons for it: the vast election contributions of the money of stockholders have kept that party in power, and the President's ferocious attacks upon them of the last two or three years have been merely a sham and a pretense. He has inspired no real move against them in the courts, he has merely indulged in wordy bluster about what he was going to do.

Among mighty corporations the chief sinner selected for attack was the Standard Oil Company. For some years now that Company has been freely and volubly charged with every crime and every villainy known to commercial oppression and misconduct, and anybody who could think of any vindictive thing to say about that corporation could promptly get a hearing in the newspapers and the magazines; and so the American world was brought to believe that the Standard Oil people were conscienceless criminals, one and all. The Standard Oil employs sixty-five thousand persons. The Company has been in existence about forty-five years, yet in all that time it has never had a strike. For years now strikes have been persistently frequent in all the other industries of the country; the newspapers are always full of them; rioting and bloodshed are common because of the strikes. The fact that the Standard Oil Company has never had a strike might suggest to a sane person here and there that the Standard Oil chiefs cannot be altogether bad or they would oppress their sixty-five thousand employees from habit and instinct, if they are so constituted that it is instinctive with them to oppress everybody else. But neither their good standing with their wage earners nor any other testimony that exists in their favor can get even a passing hearing in any newspaper or magazine in the United States.

Of the forty-five magazine publishers that were present at that luncheon yesterday, there was probably not one whose magazine had not had the habit for the past few years of abusing the Rockefellers, Henry Rogers, and the other chiefs of the Standard Oil, and without doubt those publishers had acquired the habit of heartily hating the said chiefs and of experiencing emotions of horror at the mere mention of their names—and so they must have had some curious sensations when John D. Rockefeller, Sr., John D., Jr., and Henry Rogers walked in in single file, yesterday, and sat down at the head of the table, elbow to elbow with the President of their association. To me it was an interesting spectacle, and dramatic. Three-fourths of those magazine publishers had never seen those three persons in their lives before, except in a couple of million photographs and caricatures.

How did these notorious criminals come to venture their persons in this den of their deadly enemies? It happened in this way: Doubleday came here a few days ago and said he had been thinking it was time for somebody connected with the public prints to go and look at a Standard Oil magnate and see what kind of a devil he might seem to be, from an outside inspection; and time also for the said publisher to come into actual contact with the fiend and talk with him and try to get on the inside of him and see what he might look like in there. He had been moved to this strange and unchristian project by something he found in the Annual Report of Mr. Rockefeller's Institute for Medical Research—a Report which showed that the ten million dollars which Mr. Rockefeller had put into that Institute was bearing good fruit, such good fruit in fact that it would not be popular for the newspaper or magazine press to say much about it, and not good policy to notice it otherwise than in a three-line remark followed by a judicious permanent silence; a Report no paragraph of which could find its way into a newspaper where room was needed for an account of the latest rape.

One of the facts in that Report was this: one of the results of the Institute's patient, continuous, and unflagging research into that awful malady, meningitis, was the reduction of its death rate from seventy-five per cent of the persons attacked to twenty-five, with the hopeful prospect that that death rate would presently be still further reduced. There were other great things in that Report and Doubleday told me about them, but I will not set them down at this time.

Doubleday had been vaguely aware that Mr. Rockefeller had been known to make large contributions to charities and to good causes of one sort or another, privately, in addition to the $138,000,-000 he has publicly contributed to such things. He hunted out some of these cases and found that the facts were in accordance with the rumors; therefore it seemed to Doubleday that perhaps Mr. Rockefeller was not giving away his tens of millions at a time wholly to buy public charity for his Standard Oil offenses. Finally he concluded to go and get acquainted with Mr. Rockefeller and see how much of him was Standard Oil fiend and how much of him was average human being. He went to Rockefeller, got acquainted with him down in the country, played golf with him every day, talked with him hour by hour, got acquainted with his sister-in-law and talked with her about Rockefeller, and it ended in his conceiving a great respect and liking for the man, and also in his conceiving a considerable degree of shame for disrespecting the man this long time upon evidence which presented only one side of his case.

Now then, the idea of Doubleday's visit to me was this: he wanted to bring Rockefeller face to face with all the magazine publishers—and did I think it would be wise for him to do this? He wanted to do Rockefeller a good turn but possibly it might be a bad turn. The men who had lent their magazines to harsh criticisms of him might resent his appearance among them as an impertinence. He had asked Mr. Rockefeller if he would be willing to meet those men and Rockefeller said, "Certainly. Why not? I am willing to meet and talk with any body of men, friends or enemies."

Doubleday asked me what I thought of the project —ought he to go on with it? I said I thought it was a very good idea; that I knew Mr. Rockefeller fairly well and was sure he would favorably impress those hostiles. Doubleday said he would go on with the project but he wanted all the strength he could get; he would like to have Mr. Rogers there. What would I think of that? I said Mr. Rogers's face would destroy any harsh evidence that had ever been brought against him, he wouldn't need to say a word; those men would look at him and would recognize and realize that if he was a villain there wasn't anybody left in the country that wasn't.

Well, then, would I come to the luncheon? And would I get Mr. Rogers to come?

I said I didn't think he would decline; indeed I was quite sure he would accept, and that Doubleday could tell Mr. Rogers I would go if he would come and fetch me.

Mr. Rogers arrived at our house on time yesterday and drove me to the Aldine Club, and that pleasant little dramatic surprise occurred which I have already mentioned: Rockefeller, his son John, Mr. Rogers and I, filed in and sat with the chairman on the firing line. After a speech from the chairman and a speech from an officer of the organization, explaining the nature of the organization and its purpose, I followed with a speech. Then Mr. Rockefeller was asked by the chairman to make a few remarks. Mr. Rockefeller got up and talked sweetly, sanely, simply, humanly, and with astonishing effectiveness, being interrupted by bursts of applause at the end of almost every sentence; and when he sat down all those men were his friends and he had achieved one of the completest victories I have ever had any knowledge of. Then the meeting broke up, and by a common impulse the crowd moved forward and each individual of it gave the victor a hearty handshake, and along with it some hearty compliments upon his performance as an orator.

But I have forgotten one rather striking incident. This was the reading of a letter in which a physician described an impressively interesting surgical operation which was performed on a child last March. It was a physician's child; it was four months old; it had been stricken by a fearful malady which sometimes attacks grown persons and attacks children with some little frequency; it is an internal hemorrhage, whose details I am not able to describe, and is in almost all cases fatal. The attack was making rapid progress; the physicians in attendance knew of nothing that could be done; the child was evidently dying; the hour was midnight.

Someone suggested that one of Mr. Rockefeller's Institute researchers had been making experiments upon kittens which promised a hope—at least a slight hope—for this child.[2] One of the doctors drove to the house of that physician, reached there at one o'clock, routed him out of his bed, and they drove to the Institute and gathered a few instruments but could not get all that were needed, because the others were locked up and the holder of the key was not there; but that Institute physician had with him, fortunately, one instrument which was absolutely essential; it was a needle so fine and delicate as to be next to invisible, and its thread was wholly invisible except when held against a black background. They proceeded to the house of the patient. The child was

[2] By blood transfusion, the father to furnish the blood. To mingle old blood and infant blood had never been ventured before, nor considered worth the trial. (M.T.)

too young for the use of anesthetics and none were given.

The thing necessary to be done, if I remember the details rightly, was to sever a vein of the child and an artery of its father, sew the ends of these tubes together in an absolutely perfect way, making no mistakes in the joining of them, and renew the child's famished blood with the fresh blood of the strong and healthy father. The child was wasted and white and flabby, and it was so small a creature that it possessed no vein large enough for the operation except one hidden deep in the calf of its leg.

When they were ready for the operation they could not tell, and had no way of finding out, with absolute certainty, whether the child was still alive or not, but it seemed to be dead. But they proceeded with the operation. The new blood was flushed into the child, and everybody stood by watching to see if there would be any effect. For a time no effect was apparent; then a faint rosy tinge appeared on the tops of the child's ears; after a little this rosy tinge appeared upon the ends of the child's fingers. After a little while the same tinge began to rise in the death-white cheeks; then presently that rosy tinge burst out in a sudden flash all over the little creature, and it threw up its hands and broke into a cry— with its grateful mother there to hear that music! This was nearly three months ago. The child is well and flourishing now. It owes its life to the ten million dollars which Mr. Rockefeller put into that Institute.

The reading of the letter was listened to in a deep and impressive silence, and the interest and emotion which it excited were visible in the faces of every person present, and there were times when those men seemed hardly to breathe. When the end came there was a pause and a deep breath, and then followed a burst of grateful and uplifting applause which was another triumph for the criminal at the bar.

. . . . .

9. A B C Lesson[3]

Question. What enables the Standard Oil to pay 60 per cent on its capital?

Answer. The high tariff.

Q. What would reduce the price of oil one half, and at the same time reduce the Standard's profits to 10 per cent?

A. The removal of the duties.

Q. Who created the duties?

A. The majority of the nation—the Republican party.

Q. By whose will are the duties kept alive and the Standard's 60 per cent "protected"?

A. By the will of the majority of the nation—the Republican party.

Q. By whose will is oil kept at double price?

A. By the will of the majority of the nation—the Republican party.

Q. Who is it that has sworn to drive the Standard out of business.

A. Its creator and preserver, the Republican administration.

---

[3] This dialogue is not part of the *Autobiography*. I insert it to remind the reader that the believing mood of the last previous entry was not constant.

Q. Can it do it by fining it half a year's profits— or even a whole year's?

A. No.

Q. Why?

A. Because the Standard will put up the price, and collect the fine from the people. Fining the people is not going to hurt the Standard.

Q. The people are aroused. They will find a way to beat the Standard.

A. It is an error. There is only one way to beat the Standard. The people know they can beat the Standard any day they choose; but they also know that the Standard's best friend and powerful protector will not allow them to do it.

Q. You mean the administration and the party?

A. Yes.

Q. The one and only way is the removal of the tariff? Do you believe that that would really reduce the price of oil one half?

A. I know it would.

Q. Then why doesn't the administration stand up for the people and remove the tariff?

A. Ask me another funny one.

HANNIBAL DAYS

1. A Corn Pone Prayer. (August 15, 1906)

My school days began when I was four years and a half old. There were no public schools in Missouri in those early days, but there were two private schools—terms twenty-five cents per week per pupil and collect it if you can. Mrs. Horr taught the children in a small log house at the southern end of Main Street. Mr. Sam Cross taught the young people of larger growth in a frame schoolhouse on the hill. I was sent to Mrs. Horr's school and I remember my first day in that little log house with perfect clearness, after these sixty-five years and upwards— at least I remember an episode of that first day. I broke one of the rules and was warned not to do it again, and was told that the penalty for a second breach was a whipping. I presently broke the rule again and Mrs. Horr told me to go out and find a switch and fetch it. I was glad she appointed me, for I believed I could select a switch suitable to the occasion with more judiciousness than anybody else.

In the mud I found a cooper's shaving of the old-time pattern, oak, two inches broad, a quarter of an inch thick, and rising in a shallow curve at one end. There were nice new shavings of the same breed close by but I took this one, although it was rotten. I carried it to Mrs. Horr, presented it, and stood before her in an attitude of meekness and resignation which seemed to me calculated to win favor and sympathy, but it did not happen. She divided a long look of strong disapprobation equally between me and the shaving; then she called me by my entire name, Samuel Langhorne Clemens—probably the first time I had ever heard it all strung together in one procession—and said she was ashamed of me. I was to learn later that when a teacher calls a boy by his entire name it means trouble. She said she would try and appoint a boy with a better judgment than mine in the matter of switches, and it saddens me yet to remember how many faces lighted up with the hope of getting that appointment. Jim Dunlap got it, and when he returned with the switch of his choice I recognized that he was an expert.

Mrs. Horr was a New England lady of middle age with New England ways and principles, and she always opened school with prayer and a chapter from the New Testament; also she explained the chapter with a brief talk. In one of these talks she dwelt upon the text, "Ask and ye shall receive," and said that whosoever prayed for a thing with earnestness and strong desire need not doubt that his prayer would be answered.

I was so forcibly struck by this information and so gratified by the opportunities which it offered that this was probably the first time I had heard of it. I thought I would give it a trial. I believed in Mrs. Horr thoroughly and I had no doubts as to the result. I prayed for gingerbread. Margaret Kooneman, who was the baker's daughter, brought a slab of gingerbread to school every morning; she had always kept it out of sight before but when I finished my prayer and glanced up, there it was in easy reach and she was looking the other way. In all my life I believe I never enjoyed an answer to prayer more than I enjoyed that one; and I was a convert, too. I had no end of wants and they had always remained unsatisfied up to that time, but I meant to supply them and extend them now that I had found out how to do it.

But this dream was like almost all the other dreams we indulge in in life, there was nothing in it. I did as much praying during the next two or three days as any one in that town, I suppose, and I was very sincere and earnest about it too, but nothing came of it. I found that not even the most powerful prayer was competent to lift that gingerbread again, and I came to the conclusion that if a person remains faithful to his gingerbread and keeps his eye on it, he need not trouble himself about your prayers.

Something about my conduct and bearing troubled my mother, and she took me aside and questioned me concerning it with much solicitude. I was reluctant to reveal to her the change that had come over me, for it would grieve me to distress her kind heart, but at last I confessed, with many tears, that I had ceased to be a Christian. She was heartbroken, and asked me why.

I said it was because I had found out that I was a Christian for revenue only and I could not bear the thought of that, it was so ignoble.

She gathered me to her breast and comforted me.

I gathered from what she said that if I would continue in that condition I would never be lonesome.

.   .   .   .   .

2. *The Minstrel Show. (November 30, 1906)*

Where now is Billy Rice? He was a joy to me, and so were the other stars of the nigger show— Billy Birch, David Wambold, Backus, and a delightful dozen of their brethren who made life a pleasure to me forty years ago and later. Birch, Wambold, and Backus are gone years ago; and with them departed to return no more forever, I suppose, the real nigger show—the genuine nigger show, the extravagant nigger show—the show which to me had no peer and whose peer has not yet arrived, in my experience. We have the grand opera; and I have witnessed and greatly enjoyed the first act of everything which Wagner created, but the effect on me has always been so powerful that one act was quite sufficient; whenever I have witnessed two acts I have gone away physically exhausted; and whenever I have ventured an entire opera the result has been the next thing to suicide. But if I could have the nigger show back again in its pristine purity and perfection, I should have but little further use for opera. It seems to me that to the elevated mind and the sensitive spirit, the hand organ and the nigger show are a standard and a summit to whose rarefied altitude the other forms of musical art may not hope to reach.

I remember the first negro musical show I ever saw. It must have been in the early forties. It was a new institution. In our village of Hannibal we had not heard of it before, and it burst upon us as a glad and stunning surprise.

The show remained a week and gave a perform-ance every night. Church members did not attend these performances, but all the worldlings flocked to them and were enchanted. Church members did not attend shows out there in those days. The minstrels appeared with coal-black hands and faces and their clothing was a loud and extravagant burlesque of the clothing worn by the plantation slave of the time; not that the rags of the poor slave were bur-lesqued, for that would not have been possible; burlesque could have added nothing in the way of extravagance to the sorrowful accumulation of rags and patches which constituted his costume; it was the form and color of his dress that was burlesqued. Standing collars were in fashion in that day, and the minstrel appeared in a collar which engulfed and hid the half of his head and projected so far for-ward that he could hardly see sideways over its points. His coat was sometimes made of curtain calico with a swallowtail that hung nearly to his heels and had buttons as big as a blacking box. His shoes were rusty and clumsy and cumbersome, and five or six sizes too large for him. There were many variations upon this costume and they were all ex-travagant, and were by many believed to be funny.

The minstrel used a very broad negro dialect; he used it competently and with easy facility, and it was funny—delightfully and satisfyingly funny. How-ever, there was one member of the minstrel troupe of those early days who was not extravagantly dressed and did not use the negro dialect. He was clothed in the faultless evening costume of the white society gentleman and used a stilted, courtly, artificial, and painfully grammatical form of speech, which the innocent villagers took for the real thing as exhibited in high and citified society, and they vastly admired it and envied the man who could frame it on the spot without reflection and deliver it in this easy and fluent and artistic fashion. "Bones" sat at one end of the row of minstrels, "Banjo" sat at the other end, and the dainty gentleman just described sat in the middle. This middleman was the spokesman of the show. The neatness and elegance of his dress, the studied courtliness of his manners and speech, and the shapeliness of his undoctored features made him a contrast to the rest of the troupe and particularly to "Bones" and "Banjo." "Bones" and "Banjo" were the prime jokers and whatever funniness was to be gotten out of paint and exaggerated clothing they utilized to the limit. Their lips were thickened and lengthened with bright red paint to such a degree that their mouths resembled slices cut in a ripe watermelon.

The original ground plan of the minstrel show was maintained without change for a good many years. There was no curtain to the stage in the beginning; while the audience waited they had nothing to look at except the row of empty chairs back of the footlights; presently the minstrels filed in and were received with a wholehearted welcome; they took their seats, each with his musical instrument in his hand; then the aristocrat in the middle began with a remark like this:

"I hope, gentlemen, I have the pleasure of seeing

you in your accustomed excellent health, and that everything has proceeded prosperously with you since last we had the good fortune to meet."

"Bones" would reply for himself and go on and tell about something in the nature of peculiarly good fortune that had lately fallen to his share; but in the midst of it he would be interrupted by "Banjo," who would throw doubt upon his statement of the matter; then a delightful jangle of assertion and contradiction would break out between the two; the quarrel would gather emphasis, the voices would grow louder and louder and more and more energetic and vindictive, and the two would rise and approach each other, shaking fists and instruments and threatening bloodshed, the courtly middleman meantime imploring them to preserve the peace and observe the proprieties—but all in vain, of course. Sometimes the quarrel would last five minutes, the two contestants shouting deadly threats in each other's faces with their noses not six inches apart, the house shrieking with laughter all the while at this happy and accurate imitation of the usual and familiar negro quarrel, then finally the pair of malignants would gradually back away from each other, each making impressive threats as to what was going to happen the "next time" each should have the misfortune to cross the other's path; then they would sink into their chairs and growl back and forth at each other across the front of the line until the house had had time to recover from its convulsions and hysterics and quiet down.

The aristocrat in the middle of the row would now make a remark which was surreptitiously intended to remind one of the end men of an experience of his of a humorous nature and fetch it out of him—which it always did. It was usually an experience of a stale and moldy sort and as old as America. One of these things, which always delighted the audience of those days until the minstrels wore it threadbare, was "Bones's" account of the perils which he had once endured during a storm at sea. The storm lasted so long that in the course of time all the provisions were consumed. Then the middleman would inquire anxiously how the people managed to survive.

"Bones" would reply, "We lived on eggs."

"You lived on eggs! Where did you get eggs?"

"Every day, when the storm was so bad, the Captain laid *to*."

During the first five years that joke convulsed the house, but after that the population of the United States had heard it so many times that they respected it no longer and always received it in a deep and reproachful and indignant silence, along with others of its caliber which had achieved disfavor by long service.

The minstrel troupes had good voices and both their solos and their choruses were a delight to me as long as the negro show continued in existence. In the beginning the songs were rudely comic, such as "Buffalo Gals," "Camptown Races," "Old Dan Tucker," and so on; but a little later sentimental songs were introduced, such as "The Blue Juniata," "Sweet Ellen Bayne," "Nelly Bly," "A Life on the Ocean Wave," "The Larboard Watch," etc.

The minstrel show was born in the early forties

and it had a prosperous career for about thirty-five years; then it degenerated into a variety show and was nearly all variety show with a negro act or two thrown in incidentally. The real negro show has been stone dead for thirty years. To my mind it was a thoroughly delightful thing, and a most competent laughter-compeller and I am sorry it is gone.

As I have said, it was the worldlings that attended that first minstrel show in Hannibal. Ten or twelve years later the minstrel show was as common in America as the Fourth of July but my mother had never seen one. She was about sixty years old by this time and she came down to St. Louis with a dear and lovely lady of her own age, an old citizen of Hannibal, Aunt Betsey Smith. She wasn't anybody's aunt in particular, she was aunt to the whole town of Hannibal; this was because of her sweet and generous and benevolent nature and the winning simplicity of her character.

Like my mother, Aunt Betsey Smith had never seen a negro show. She and my mother were very much alive; their age counted for nothing; they were fond of excitement, fond of novelties, fond of anything going that was of a sort proper for members of the church to indulge in. They were always up early to see the circus procession enter the town and to grieve because their principles did not allow them to follow it into the tent; they were always ready for Fourth of July processions, Sunday-school processions, lectures, conventions, camp meetings, revivals in the church—in fact, for any and every kind of dissipation that could not be proven to have anything irreligious about it—and they never missed a funeral.

In St. Louis they were eager for novelties and they applied to me for help. They wanted something exciting and proper. I told them I knew of nothing in their line except a Convention which was to meet in the great hall of the Mercantile Library and listen to an exhibition and illustration of native African music by fourteen missionaries who had just returned from that dark continent. I said that if they actually and earnestly desired something instructive and elevating, I would recommend the Convention, but that if at bottom they really wanted something frivolous, I would look further. But no, they were charmed with the idea of the Convention and were eager to go. I was not telling them the strict truth and I knew it at the time, but it was no great matter; it is not worth while to strain one's self to tell the truth to people who habitually discount everything you tell them, whether it is true or isn't.

The alleged missionaries were the Christy minstrel troupe, in that day one of the most celebrated of such troupes and also one of the best. We went early and got seats in the front bench. By and by when all the seats on that spacious floor were occupied, there were sixteen hundred persons present. When the grotesque negroes came filing out on the stage in their extravagant costumes, the old ladies were almost speechless with astonishment. I explained to them that the missionaries always dressed like that in Africa.

But Aunt Betsey said, reproachfully, "But they're niggers."

I said, "That is no matter; they are Americans in a sense, for they are employed by the American Missionary Society."

Then both the ladies began to question the propriety of their countenancing the industries of a company of negroes, no matter what their trade might be, but I said that they could see by looking around that the best people in St. Louis were present and that certainly they would not be present if the show were not of a proper sort.

They were comforted and also quite shamelessly glad to be there. They were happy now and enchanted with the novelty of the situation; all that they had needed was a pretext of some kind or other to quiet their consciences, and their consciences were quiet now, quiet enough to be dead. They gazed on that long curved line of artistic mountebanks with devouring eyes. The middleman began. Presently he led up to that old joke which I was telling about a while ago. Everybody in the house except my novices had heard it a hundred times; a frozen and solemn and indignant silence settled down upon the sixteen hundred, and poor "Bones" sat there in that depressing atmosphere and went through with his joke. It was brand new to my venerable novices and when he got to the end and said, "We lived on eggs," and followed it by explaining that every day during the storm the Captain "laid to," they threw their heads back and went off into heart-whole cackles and convulsions of laughter that so astonished and delighted that great audience that it rose in a solid body to look, and see who it might be that had not heard that joke before. The laughter of my novices went on and on till their hilarity became contagious, and the whole sixteen hundred joined in and shook the place with the thunders of their joy.

Aunt Betsey and my mother achieved a brilliant success for the Christy minstrels that night, for all the jokes were as new to them as they were old to the rest of the house. They received them with screams of laughter and passed the hilarity on, and the audience left the place sore and weary with laughter and full of gratitude to the innocent pair that had furnished to their jaded souls that rare and precious pleasure.

·   ·   ·   ·   ·

3. The Mesmerist. (December 1, 1906)[1]

An exciting event in our village was the arrival of the mesmerizer. I think the year was 1850. As to that I am not sure but I know the month—it was May; that detail has survived the wear of fifty years. A pair of connected little incidents of that month have served to keep the memory of it green for me all this time; incidents of no consequence and not worth embalming, yet my memory has preserved them carefully and flung away things of real value to give them space and make them comfortable. The truth is, a person's memory has no more sense than his conscience, and no appreciation whatever of values and proportions. However, never mind those trifling incidents; my subject is the mesmerizer now.

[1] Published, somewhat abbreviated, in the *North American Review* for January 4, 1907. Though given in the dictations the date it bears here, it was written, not dictated, nearly four years before.

He advertised his show and promised marvels. Admission as usual: 25 cents, children and negroes half price. The village had heard of mesmerism in a general way but had not encountered it yet. Not many people attended the first night but next day they had so many wonders to tell that everybody's curiosity was fired, and after that for a fortnight the magician had prosperous times. I was fourteen or fifteen years old, the age at which a boy is willing to endure all things, suffer all things short of death by fire, if thereby he may be conspicuous and show off before the public; and so, when I saw the "sub-jects" perform their foolish antics on the platform and make the people laugh and shout and admire, I had a burning desire to be a subject myself.

Every night for three nights I sat in the row of candidates on the platform and held the magic disk in the palm of my hand and gazed at it and tried to get sleepy, but it was a failure; I remained wide awake and had to retire defeated, like the majority. Also, I had to sit there and be gnawed with envy of Hicks, our journeyman; I had to sit there and see him scamper and jump when Simmons the enchanter exclaimed, "See the snake! See the snake!" and hear him say, "My, how beautiful!" in response to the suggestion that he was observing a splendid sun-set, and so on—the whole insane business. I couldn't laugh, I couldn't applaud; it filled me with bitterness to have others do it and to have people make a hero of Hicks, and crowd around him when the show was over and ask him for more and more particulars of the wonders he had seen in his visions and manifest in many ways that they were proud to be acquainted with him. Hicks—the idea! I couldn't stand it; I was getting boiled to death in my own bile.

On the fourth night temptation came and I was not strong enough to resist. When I had gazed at the disk a while I pretended to be sleepy and began to nod. Straightway came the professor and made passes over my head and down my body and legs and arms, finishing each pass with a snap of his fingers in the air to discharge the surplus electricity; then he began to "draw" me with the disk, holding it in his fingers and telling me I could not take my eyes off it, try as I might; so I rose slowly, bent and gazing, and followed that disk all over the place, just as I had seen the others do. Then I was put through the other paces. Upon suggestion I fled from snakes, passed buckets at a fire, became excited over hot steamboat-races, made love to imaginary girls and kissed them, fished from the platform and landed mud cats that outweighed me—and so on, all the customary marvels. But not in the customary way. I was cautious at first and watchful, being afraid the professor would discover that I was an impostor and drive me from the platform in disgrace; but as soon as I realized that I was not in danger, I set myself the task of terminating Hicks's usefulness as a subject and of usurping his place.

It was a sufficiently easy task. Hicks was born honest, I without that incumbrance—so some people said. Hicks saw what he saw and reported accordingly, I saw more than was visible and added to it such details as could help. Hicks had no imagination, I had a double supply. He was born calm, I was born excited. No vision could start a rapture in him and he was constipated as to language, anyway, but if I saw a vision I emptied the dictionary onto it and lost the remnant of my mind into the bargain.

At the end of my first half-hour Hicks was a thing of the past, a fallen hero, a broken idol, and I knew it and was glad and said in my heart, "Success to crime!" Hicks could never have been mesmerized to the point where he could kiss an imaginary girl in public or a real one either, but I was competent. Whatever Hicks had failed in, I made it a point to succeed in, let the cost be what it might, physically or morally. He had shown several bad defects and I had made a note of them. For instance, if the magician asked, "What do you see?" and left him to invent a vision for himself, Hicks was dumb and blind, he couldn't see a thing nor say a word, whereas the magician soon found that when it came to seeing visions of a stunning and marketable sort I could get along better without his help than with it.

Then there was another thing: Hicks wasn't worth a tallow dip on mute mental suggestion. Whenever Simmons stood behind him and gazed at the back of his skull and tried to drive a mental suggestion into it, Hicks sat with vacant face and never suspected. If he had been noticing, he could have seen by the rapt faces of the audience that something was going on behind his back that required a response. Inasmuch as I was an impostor I dreaded to have this test put upon me, for I knew the professor would be "willing" me to do something and as I couldn't know what it was, I should be exposed and denounced. However, when my time came, I took my chance. I perceived by the tense and expectant faces of the people that Simmons was behind me willing me with all his might. I tried my best to imagine what he wanted but nothing suggested itself. I felt ashamed and miserable, then. I believed that the hour of my disgrace was come and that in another moment I should go out of that place disgraced. I ought to be ashamed to confess it but my next thought was, not how I could win the compassion of kindly hearts by going out humbly and in sorrow for my misdoings, but how I could go out most sensationally and spectacularly.

There was a rusty and empty old revolver lying on the table, among the "properties" employed in the performances. On May Day two or three weeks before there had been a celebration by the schools, and I had had a quarrel with a big boy who was the school bully, and I had not come out of it with credit. That boy was now seated in the middle of the house, halfway down the main aisle. I crept stealthily and impressively toward the table, with a dark and murderous scowl on my face, copied from a popular romance, seized the revolver suddenly, flourished it, shouted the bully's name, jumped off the platform, and made a rush for him and chased him out of the house before the paralyzed people could interfere to save him. There was a storm of applause and the magician, addressing the house, said, most impressively ——

"That you may know how really remarkable this is, and how wonderfully developed a subject we have in this boy, I assure you that without a single spoken word to guide him he has carried out what I mentally commanded him to do, to the minutest detail.

I could have stopped him at a moment in his venge-
ful career by a mere exertion of my will, therefore
the poor fellow who has escaped was at no time in
danger."

So I was not in disgrace. I returned to the platform a hero and happier than I have ever been in
this world since. As regards mental suggestion, my
fears of it were gone. I judged that in case I failed
to guess what the professor might be willing me to
do, I could count on putting up something that
would answer just as well. I was right, and exhibitions of unspoken suggestion became a favorite with
the public. Whenever I perceived that I was being
willed to do something I got up and did something—
anything that occurred to me—and the magician, not
being a fool, always ratified it. When people asked
me, "How *can* you tell what he is willing you to do?"
I said, "It's just as easy," and they always said
admiringly, "Well, it beats *me* how you can do it."

Hicks was weak in another detail. When the professor made passes over him and said "his whole
body is without sensation now—come forward and
test him, ladies and gentlemen," the ladies and gentlemen always complied eagerly and stuck pins into
Hicks, and if they went deep Hicks was sure to
wince, then that poor professor would have to explain that Hicks "wasn't sufficiently under the influence." But I didn't wince; I only suffered and shed
tears on the inside. The miseries that a conceited
boy will endure to keep up his "reputation!" And so
will a conceited man; I know it in my own person
and have seen it in a hundred thousand others. That
professor ought to have protected me and I often

hoped he would, when the tests were unusually severe, but he didn't. It may be that he was deceived as well as the others, though I did not believe it nor think it possible. Those were dear good people but they must have carried simplicity and credulity to the limit. They would stick a pin in my arm and bear on it until they drove it a third of its length in, and then be lost in wonder that by a mere exercise of will power the professor could turn my arm to iron and make it insensible to pain. Whereas it was not insensible at all; I was suffering agonies of pain.

After that fourth night, that proud night, that triumphant night, I was the only subject. Simmons invited no more candidates to the platform. I performed alone every night, the rest of the fortnight. Up to that time a dozen wise old heads, the intellectual aristocracy of the town, had held out as implacable unbelievers. I was as hurt by this as if I were engaged in some honest occupation. There is nothing surprising about this. Human beings feel dishonor the most, sometimes, when they most deserve it. That handful of overwise old gentlemen kept on shaking their heads all the first week, and saying they had seen no marvels there that could not have been produced by collusion; and they were pretty vain of their unbelief too, and liked to show it and air it and be superior to the ignorant and the gullible. Particularly old Dr. Peake, who was the ringleader of the irreconcilables, and very formidable; for he was an F.F.V., he was learned, white-haired and venerable, nobly and richly clad in the fashions of an earlier and a courtlier day, he was large and stately, and he not only seemed wise but was what he seemed in that regard. He had great influence and his opinion upon any matter was worth much more than that of any other person in the community. When I conquered him at last, I knew I was undisputed master of the field; and now after more than fifty years I acknowledge, with a few dry old tears, that I rejoiced without shame.

. . . . .

(December 2, 1906)

In 1847 we were living in a large white house on the corner of Hill and Main Streets—a house that still stands but isn't large now although it hasn't lost a plank; I saw it a year ago and noticed that shrinkage.[2] My father died in it in March of the year mentioned, but our family did not move out of it until some months afterward. Ours was not the only family in the house; there was another, Dr. Grant's. One day Dr. Grant and Dr. Reyburn argued a matter on the street with sword canes, and Grant was brought home multifariously punctured. Old Dr. Peake calked the leaks and came every day for a while, to look after him.

The Grants were Virginians, like Peake, and one day when Grant was getting well enough to be on his feet and sit around in the parlor and talk, the conversation fell upon Virginia and old times. I was present but the group were probably unconscious of me, I being only a lad and a negligible quantity. Two

[2] There is a discrepancy here. This passage is inserted in the typescript of the "Autobiography" as a dictation and under the date given above. Actually, it was written in 1903, before the dictations were begun. "A year ago" is, therefore, right: he visited Hannibal for the last time in 1902.

of the group—Dr. Peake and Mrs. Crawford, Mrs. Grant's mother—had been of the audience when the Richmond theater burned down thirty-six years before, and they talked over the frightful details of that memorable tragedy. These were eyewitnesses and with their eyes I saw it all with an intolerable vividness: I saw the black smoke rolling and tumbling toward the sky, I saw the flames burst through it and turn red, I heard the shrieks of the despairing, I glimpsed their faces at the windows caught fitfully through the veiling smoke, I saw them jump to their death or to mutilation worse than death. The picture is before me yet and can never fade.

In due course they talked of the colonial mansion of the Peakes with its stately columns and its spacious grounds, and by odds and ends I picked up a clearly defined idea of the place. I was strongly interested, for I had not before heard of such palatial things from the lips of people who had seen them with their own eyes. One detail, casually dropped, hit my imagination hard. In the wall by the great front door there was a round hole as big as a saucer—a British cannon ball had made it in the war of the Revolution. It was breathtaking; it made history real; history had never been real to me before.

Very well, three or four years later, as already mentioned, I was king bee and sole "subject" in the mesmeric show; it was the beginning of the second week; the performance was half over; just then the majestic Dr. Peake with his ruffled bosom and wristbands and his gold-headed cane entered, and a deferential citizen vacated his seat beside the Grants and made the great chief take it. This happened while I was trying to invent something fresh in the way of vision, in response to the professor's remark ——

"Concentrate your powers. Look—look attentively. There—don't you see something? Concentrate—concentrate! Now then—describe it."

Without suspecting it, Dr. Peake, by entering the place, had reminded me of the talk of three years before. He had also furnished me capital and was become my confederate, an accomplice in my frauds. I began on a vision, a vague and dim one (that was part of the game at the beginning of a vision, it isn't best to see it too clearly at first, it might look as if you had come loaded with it.) The vision developed by degrees and gathered swing, momentum, energy. It was the Richmond fire. Dr. Peake was cold at first and his fine face had a trace of polite scorn in it; but when he began to recognize that fire, that expression changed and his eyes began to light up. As soon as I saw that, I threw the valves wide open and turned on all the steam and gave those people a supper of fire and horrors that was calculated to last them one while! They couldn't gasp when I got through—they were petrified. Dr. Peake had risen and was standing —and breathing hard. He said, in a great voice:

"My doubts are ended. No collusion could produce that miracle. It was totally impossible for him to know those details, yet he has described them with the clarity of an eyewitness—and with what unassailable truthfulness God knows I know!"

I saved the colonial mansion for the last night and solidified and perpetuated Dr. Peake's conversion with the cannon-ball hole. He explained to the house that I could never have heard of that small detail, which differentiated this mansion from all other Virginian mansions and perfectly identified it, therefore the fact stood proven that I had *seen* it in my vision. Lawks!

It is curious. When the magician's engagement closed there was but one person in the village who did not believe in mesmerism, and I was the one. All the others were converted, but I was to remain an implacable and unpersuadable disbeliever in mesmerism and hypnotism for close upon fifty years. This was because I never would examine them, in after life. I couldn't. The subject revolted me. Perhaps it brought back to me a passage in my life which for pride's sake I wished to forget; though I thought, or persuaded myself I thought, I should never come across a "proof" which wasn't thin and cheap, and probably had a fraud like me behind it.

The truth is, I did not have to wait long to get tired of my triumphs. Not thirty days, I think. The glory which is built upon a lie soon becomes a most unpleasant incumbrance. No doubt for a while I enjoyed having my exploits told and retold and told again in my presence and wondered over and exclaimed about, but I quite distinctly remember that there presently came a time when the subject was wearisome and odious to me and I could not endure the disgusting discomfort of it. I remember how General Sherman used to rage and swear over "While we were marching through Georgia," which was played at him and sung at him everywhere he went.

How easy it is to make people believe a lie, and how hard it is to undo that work again! Thirty-five

years after those evil exploits of mine I visited my
old mother, whom I had not seen for ten years; and
being moved by what seemed to me a rather noble
and perhaps heroic impulse, I thought I would
humble myself and confess my ancient fault. It cost
me a great effort to make up my mind; I dreaded
the sorrow that would rise in her face, and the
shame that would look out of her eyes; but after
long and troubled reflection, the sacrifice seemed due
and right, and I gathered my resolution together and
made the confession.

To my astonishment there were no sentimentali-
ties, no dramatics, no George Washington effects;
she was not moved in the least degree; she simply
did not believe me and said so! I was not merely disappointed, I was nettled, to have my costly truthfulness flung out of the market in this placid and confident way when I was expecting to get a profit out
of it. I asserted and reasserted with rising heat my
statement that every single thing I had done on those
long-vanished nights was a lie and a swindle; and
when she shook her head tranquilly and said she knew
better, I put up my hand and *swore* to it—adding a
triumphant, "*Now* what do you say?"

It did not affect her at all; it did not budge her
the fraction of an inch from her position. If this
was hard for me to endure, it did not begin with
the blister she put upon the raw when she began to
put my sworn oath out of court with *arguments* to
prove that I was under a delusion and did not know
what I was talking about. She refused to believe that
I had invented my visions myself, she said it was
folly: that I was only a child at the time and could

not have done it. She cited the Richmond fire and the colonial mansion and said they were quite beyond my capacities. Then I saw my chance! I said she was right—I didn't invent those, I got them from Dr. Peake. Even this great shot did not damage. She said Dr. Peake's evidence was better than mine, and he had said in plain words that it was impossible for me to have heard about those things.

I realized with shame and with impotent vexation that I was defeated all along the line. I had but one card left, but it was a formidable one. I played it and stood from under. It seemed ignoble to demolish her fortress after she had defended it so valiantly, but the defeated know not mercy. I played that master card. It was the pin-sticking. I said solemnly ——

"I give you my honor, a pin was never stuck into me without causing me cruel pain."

She only said ——

"It is thirty-five years. I believe you do think that, now, but I was there and I know better. You never winced."

She was so calm! and I was so far from it, so nearly frantic.

"Oh, my goodness!" I said, "let me *show* you that I am speaking the truth. Here is my arm; drive a pin into it—drive it to the head—I shall not wince."

She only shook her gray head and said with simplicity and conviction ——

"You are a man, now, and could dissemble the hurt; but you were only a child then and could not have done it."

And so the lie which I played upon her in my

youth remained with her as an unchallengeable truth
to the day of her death. Carlyle said "a lie cannot
live." It shows that he did not know how to tell them.
If I had taken out a life policy on this one the pre-
miums would have bankrupted me ages ago.

.   .   .   .   .

(December 3, 1906)

One evening we dined with the C.'s (in Vienna, in
1897) and after dinner a number of friends of the
family dropped in to smoke and chat; among them
G., who had dined with the X.'s. He brought with
him an incident. It was to this effect. When dinner
was announced a guest was still lacking, the Baron
F., a cousin of Herr X. Ten minutes later he had
not yet arrived; then he was given up and the company went to the table. Between soup and fish the
Baron arrived and was ushered in, a large and
strongly built man about fifty years old, with iron-
gray hair and a harsh and hard face. With a per-
functory word of excuse for his tardiness he took his
seat and began to unfold his napkin; in the midst of
this function he stopped and began to stare across
the table at a Mr. B., a visiting Englishman of grave
mien and middle age. As he stared his countenance
darkened and assumed an expression of hatred of
the most bitter and uncompromising kind; the napkin fell from his hands and he got up abruptly and
stalked out of the room. X., astonished, left his
bewildered guests and followed, to see what the matter was. He found the Baron gloving himself for
departure. He was not exactly frothing at the mouth

but was near to doing it. In answer to X.'s anxious inquiries, he said ——

"No, give yourself no concern, it isn't anything that's happened here—it dates back, away back. I can't be mistaken; that's an Englishman and his name is B. Isn't it so?"

"Yes."

"Well, I've seen him only once before and it's twenty-seven years ago, but I know him, I would recognize him in Siberia, in Sahara, in hell! How fortunate that I couldn't reach him—I don't wish to be a murderer!"

"Why, what was the trouble? What did he do?"

"Do? Oh, oh, oh, it's too horrible to think of! Out of my way—don't detain me; do you want me to kill him?"

That was the incident and that was all that G. knew. Enough to heat our curiosity to the sizzling point and raise a world of excited wondering and guessing; and valuable to that degree in a smoking-klatsch, but we had to wait several days before we got the tale's sequel. Which was this.

In 1870 B. was living in London. He was a young fellow with an alert and inquiring mind and a sharp appetite for novelties. He had taken up mesmerism, as it was then called, and was doing with it many of the strange things afterward done by Charcot under its other name of hypnotism. One evening B. was exhibiting some of these marvels in the house of an eminent man of science, and had brought with him for the purpose subjects whom he had experi-mented upon before. A gentlemen present begged him to come to his house in Sydenham and give a similar exhibition before friends of his. B. said ——

"I will on this condition: that you provide a dozen persons for experiment, whom you know but who shall be strangers to me; this in order that collusion cannot be charged. I may not be able to affect any of them, but out of the dozen I can expect to affect one or two at least."

The condition was accepted, and the day appointed. But the day before the date chosen, the gentleman sent a note saying he had failed to get anybody to consent, and begging B. to bring subjects himself.

B. took with him a young man who was an easy subject and whom he had often mesmerized before. The two went upon a platform which had been arranged at the end of a drawing-room and faced a company of forty men—some young, some middle aged; some fashionable and frivolous, some of a graver stamp; some sarcastic of aspect, the others blandly unfriendly. B. noted this unpleasant atmosphere and was sorry he had not exacted the original terms. He tried to recover that lost ground by inviting the gentlemen present to provide him with subjects from their number, and said he would regard it as a great favor if his request could be complied with. He waited but got only silence—there was no other response.

He then mesmerized his young man and made him mistake salt for sugar, sugar for salt, chalk for alum, alum for chalk, water for brandy, brandy for milk, and so on; made him see ships sailing on the sea, houses on fire, battles, horse races, and all such things—and all through these performances the audience smiled contempt, and a group of young fashionables, one of whom was standing and leaning indolently against the wall, uttered low-voiced ejaculations; "Humbug!" "charlatan!" etc. It was intended that B. should hear, and he heard. He expected his host to interfere and protect him from these insults, and glanced a hint or two at him; but evidently the host was afraid. B. recognized that if he was to have any protection he must furnish it himself. He tried to locate one of those affronts and make sure of the mouth it came from but he was never quick enough. The dandy who leaned against the wall seemed to be the ring-leader, but B. was not sure of it. He went on with his demonstration, growing angrier and angrier all the while, and the offensive comments continued.

He now said, "I will now make this subject's body as rigid as iron and will ask any that doubt, to come on the platform and examine him and test him."

He stretched the young man in the air, with his head upon one table and his heels upon another and no support between, and invited the doubters to come and apply their tests. No one moved. There was an ejaculation: "Just a tuppenny juggler and his hired pal!"

This time B. spotted the utterer; it was the young fashionable who was leaning against the wall. He limbered up his subject with a few passes, then turned to the audience and said, "I was invited to come here, I did not invite myself. I was invited as a gentleman, to meet gentlemen; you best know why the host's part of the contract has not been fulfilled.

You lack the courage to come on this platform and submit to tests in your own persons, yet you have the courage—being many—to insult me, who am but one and, as you think, not able to resent it. You do not believe in mesmerism; you do not believe in the genuineness of my demonstrations; you shall have a test that will convince you. I require the person leaning against the wall to come here."

He bent his gaze upon the person, who gazed back —gazed and still gazed, B. beckoning—beckoning, drawing him, the audience watching.

"Now then—come!"

The new subject moved slowly forward, with his eyes fixed upon B.'s, and arrived upon the platform.

"Stop!" The man stopped. "Get up and stand in this chair." The man obeyed. "What do you see— the ocean?" The man nodded his head dreamily. "Is it at your feet? Do you see the waves washing in?" More nods. "Do you not notice how hot it is? Why do you wear such heavy clothes in such weather? Throw them off and take a plunge—it will do you good." The man took off his coat. "Now your vest —throw it down. Now your trousers—throw them down. Now your shirt. Now the underclothes. There —plunge! Stop!" B. turned to the house and continued ——

"Here stands one unbeliever—a Mayfair man—a society man—a swell—a smirking lady-killer—a perfumed drawing-room dandy, contemptuous of other people's feelings and sensitive about his own, proud of his prettiness, vain of his charms—here they all are before you, stark naked! As he is, so shall you be; so help me God I will now strip every coward of you to the skin!"

But he didn't. There was a wild rush and scramble, and the place was vacant in a minute. The naked man was Baron F.

•   •   •   •   •

4. Jim Wolf and the Wasps. (October 16, 1906)[3]

Uncle Remus still lives and must be over a thousand years old. Indeed I know that this must be so, because I have seen a new photograph of him in the public prints within the last month or so, and in that picture his aspects are distinctly and strikingly geological, and one can see that he is thinking about the mastodons and the plesiosaurians that he used to play with when he was young.

It is just a quarter of a century since I have seen Uncle Remus. He visited us in our home in Hartford and was reverently devoured by the big eyes of Susy and Clara, for I made a deep and awful impression upon the little creatures—who knew his book by heart through my nightly declamation of its tales to them—by revealing to them privately that he was the real Uncle Remus whitewashed so that he could come into people's houses the front way.

He was the bashfulest grown person I have ever met. When there were people about he stayed silent and seemed to suffer until they were gone. But he was lovely, nevertheless, for the sweetness and benignity of the immortal Remus looked out from his eyes, and the graces and sincerities of his character shone in his face.

[3] Published in the *North American Review* for November, 1907.

It may be that Jim Wolf was as bashful as Harris.
It hardly seems possible, yet as I look back fifty-six
years and consider Jim Wolf, I am almost persuaded
that he was. He was our long slim apprentice in my
brother's printing office in Hannibal. However, in an
earlier chapter I have already introduced him. He
was the lad whom I assisted with uninvited advice
and sympathy the night he had the memorable adventure with the cats. He was seventeen and yet he
was as much as four times as bashful as I was,
though I was only fourteen. He boarded and slept
in the house but he was always tongue-tied in the
presence of my sister, and when even my gentle
mother spoke to him he could not answer save in
frightened monosyllables. He would not enter a room
where a girl was; nothing could persuade him to do
such a thing.

Once when he was in our small parlor alone, two
majestic old maids entered and seated themselves in
such a way that Jim could not escape without passing
by them. He would as soon have thought of passing
by one of Harris's plesiosaurians, ninety feet long.
I came in presently, was charmed with the situation,
and sat down in a corner to watch Jim suffer and to
enjoy it. My mother followed, a minute later, and
sat down with the visitors and began to talk. Jim
sat upright in his chair and during a quarter of an
hour he did not change his position by a shade—
neither General Grant nor a bronze image could
have maintained that immovable pose more successfully. I mean as to body and limbs; with the face
there was a difference. By fleeting revealments of the
face I saw that something was happening—some-

thing out of the common. There would be a sudden twitch of the muscles of the face, an instant distortion which in the next instant had passed and left no trace. These twitches gradually grew in frequency but no muscle outside of the face lost any of its rigidity, or betrayed any interest in what was happening to Jim. I mean if something *was* happening to him, and I knew perfectly well that that was the case. At last a pair of tears began to swim slowly down his cheeks amongst the twitchings, but Jim sat still and let them run; then I saw his right hand steal along his thigh until halfway to his knee, then take a vigorous grip upon the cloth.

That was a wasp that he was grabbing. A colony of them were climbing up his legs and prospecting around, and every time he winced they stabbed him to the hilt—so for a quarter of an hour one group of excursionists after another climbed up Jim's legs and resented even the slightest wince or squirm that he indulged himself with in his misery. When the entertainment had become nearly unbearable, he conceived the idea of gripping them between his fingers and putting them out of commission. He succeeded with many of them but at great cost, for as he couldn't see the wasp he was as likely to take hold of the wrong end of him as he was the right; then the dying wasp gave him a punch to remember the incident by.

If those ladies had stayed all day and if all the wasps in Missouri had come and climbed up Jim's legs, nobody there would ever have known it but Jim and the wasps and me. There he would have sat until the ladies left. When they were gone we went upstairs and he took his clothes off, and his legs were a picture to look at. They looked as if they were mailed all over with shirt buttons, each with a single red hole in the center. The pain was intolerable— no, would have been intolerable, but the pain of the presence of those ladies had been so much harder to bear that the pain of the wasps' stings was quite pleasant and enjoyable by comparison.

Jim never could enjoy wasps. I remember once ——

.   .   .   .   .

(October 30, 1906)

I remember a circumstance in support of this conviction of mine; it preceded the episode which I have just recorded. In those extremely youthful days I was not aware that practical joking was a thing which, aside from being as a rule witless, is a base pastime and disreputable. In those early days I gave the matter no thought but indulged freely in practical joking without stopping to consider its moral aspects. During three-fourths of my life I have held the practical joker in limitless contempt and detestation; I have despised him as I have despised no other criminal, and when I am delivering my opinion about him the reflection that I have been a practical joker myself seems to increase my bitterness rather than to modify it.

One afternoon I found the upper part of the window in Jim's bedroom thickly cushioned with wasps. Jim always slept on the side of his bed that was against the window. I had what seemed to me a happy inspiration: I turned back the bedclothes and, at cost of one or two stings, brushed the wasps down and collected a few hundred of them on the sheet on that side of the bed, then turned the covers over them and made prisoners of them. I made a deep crease down the center of the bed to protect the front side from invasion by them, and then at night I offered to sleep with Jim. He was willing.

I made it a point to be in bed first to see if my side of it was still a safe place to rest in. It was. None of the wasps had passed the frontier. As soon as Jim was ready for bed I blew out the candle and let him climb in in the dark. He was talking as usual but I couldn't answer, because by anticipation I was suffocating with laughter, and although I gagged myself with a hatful of the sheet I was on the point of exploding all the time. Jim stretched himself out comfortably, still pleasantly chatting; then his talk began to break and become disjointed; separations intervened between his words and each separation was emphasized by a more or less sudden and violent twitch of his body, and I knew that the immigrants were getting in their work. I knew I ought to evince some sympathy, and ask what was the matter, but I couldn't do it because I should laugh if I tried. Presently he stopped talking altogether—that is on the subject which he had been pursuing, and he said, "There is something in this bed."

I knew it but held my peace.

He said, "There's thousands of them."

Then he said he was going to find out what it was. He reached down and began to explore. The wasps resented this intrusion and began to stab him all over and everywhere. Then he said he had captured one of them and asked me to strike a light. I did it, and when he climbed out of bed his shirt was black with half-crushed wasps dangling by one hind leg, and in his two hands he held a dozen prisoners that were stinging and stabbing him with energy, but his grit was good and he held them fast. By the light of the candle he identified them, and said, "Wasps!"

It was his last remark for the night. He added nothing to it. In silence he uncovered his side of the bed and, dozen by dozen, he removed the wasps to the floor and beat them to a pulp with the bootjack, with earnest and vindictive satisfaction, while I shook the bed with mute laughter—laughter which was not all a pleasure to me, for I had the sense that his silence was ominous. The work of extermination being finally completed, he blew out the light and returned to bed and seemed to compose himself to sleep—in fact he did lie stiller than anybody else could have done in the circumstances.

I remained awake as long as I could and did what I could to keep my laughter from shaking the bed and provoking suspicion, but even my fears could not keep me awake forever and I finally fell asleep and presently woke again—under persuasion of circumstances. Jim was kneeling on my breast and pounding me in the face with both fists. It hurt—but he was knocking all the restraints of my laughter loose; I could not contain it any longer and I laughed until all my body was exhausted, and my face, as I believed, battered to a pulp.

Jim never afterward referred to that episode and I had better judgment than to do it myself, for he was a third longer than I was, although not any wider.

I played many practical jokes upon him but they were all cruel and all barren of wit. Any brainless swindler could have invented them. When a person of mature age perpetrates a practical joke it is fair evidence, I think, that he is weak in the head and hasn't enough heart to signify.

. . . . .

TWO HALOS

1. "The Jumping Frog." (May 21, 1906)[1]

My experiences as an author began early in 1867.
I came to New York from San Francisco in the first
month of that year and presently Charles H. Webb,
whom I had known in San Francisco as a reporter
on *The Bulletin* and afterward editor of *The Californian*, suggested that I publish a volume of
sketches. I had but a slender reputation to publish
it on, but I was charmed and excited by the suggestion and quite willing to venture it if some indus-
trious person would save me the trouble of gathering
the sketches together. I was loath to do it myself,
for from the beginning of my sojourn in this world
there was a persistent vacancy in me where the industry ought to be.

Webb said I had some reputation in the Atlantic
states but I knew quite well that it must be of a very
attenuated sort. What there was of it rested upon
the story of "The Jumping Frog." When Artemus
Ward passed through California on a lecturing tour
in 1865 or '66, I told him the "Jumping Frog" story
in San Francisco and he asked me to write it out and
send it to his publisher, Carleton, in New York, to be
used in padding out a small book which Artemus had

[1] Published, somewhat abbreviated, in the *North American Review* for September 21, 1906.

prepared for the press and which needed some more stuffing to make it big enough for the price which was to be charged for it.

It reached Carleton in time, but he didn't think much of it and was not willing to go to the type-setting expense of adding it to the book. He did not put it in the wastebasket, but made Henry Clapp a present of it, and Clapp used it to help out the funeral of his dying literary journal, *The Saturday Press*. "The Jumping Frog" appeared in the last number of that paper, and was at once copied in the newspapers of America and England. It certainly had a wide celebrity and it still had it at the time that I am speaking of—but I was aware that it was only the frog that was celebrated. It wasn't I. I was still an obscurity.

Webb undertook to collate the sketches. He performed this office, then handed the result to me, and I went to Carleton's establishment with it. I approached a clerk and he bent eagerly over the counter to inquire into my needs; but when he found that I had come to sell a book and not to buy one, his temperature fell sixty degrees and I came near to freezing where I stood. I meekly asked the privilege of a word with Mr. Carleton, and was coldly informed that he was in his private office. Discouragements and difficulties followed, but after a while I got by the frontier and entered the Holy of Holies. Ah, now I remember how I managed it! Webb had made an appointment for me with Carleton; otherwise I never should have gotten over that frontier. Carleton rose and said brusquely and aggressively, "Well, what can I do for you?"

I reminded him that I was there by appointment to offer him my book for publication. He began to swell, and went on swelling and swelling and swelling until he had reached the dimensions of a god of about the second or third degree. Then the fountains of his great deep were broken up, and for two or three minutes I couldn't see him for the rain. It was words, only words, but they fell so densely that they darkened the atmosphere. Finally he made an imposing sweep with his right hand which comprehended the whole room and said, "Books—look at those shelves. Every one of them is loaded with books that are waiting for publication. Do I want any more? Excuse me, I don't. Good morning."

Twenty-one years elapsed before I saw Carleton again. I was then sojourning with my family at the Schweizerhof, in Lucerne. He called on me, shook hands cordially, and said at once without any preliminaries, "I am substantially an obscure person, but I have a couple of such colossal distinctions to my credit that I am entitled to immortality—to wit: I refused a book of yours and for this I stand without competitor as the prize ass of the nineteenth century."

It was a most handsome apology, and I told him so and said it was a long delayed revenge but was sweeter to me than any other that could be devised, that during the lapsed twenty-one years I had in fancy taken his life several times every year and always in new and increasingly malignant ways, but that now I was pacified, appeased, happy, even jubilant, and that thenceforth I should hold him my true and valued friend and never kill him again.

I reported my adventure to Webb and he bravely said that not all the Carletons in the universe should defeat that book, he would publish it himself on a ten per cent royalty. And so he did. He brought it out in blue and gold, and made a very pretty little book of it. I think he named it *The Celebrated Jumping Frog of Calaveras County, and Other Sketches,* price $1.25. He made the plates and printed and bound the book through a job printing house and published it through the American News Company.

In June I sailed in the *Quaker City* Excursion. I returned in November, and in Washington found a letter from Elisha Bliss of the American Publishing Company of Hartford, offering me five per cent royalty on a book which should recount the adventures of the Excursion. In lieu of the royalty I was offered the alternative of ten thousand dollars cash upon delivery of the manuscript. I consulted A. D. Richardson and he said "Take the royalty." I followed his advice and closed with Bliss. By my contract I was to deliver the manuscript in July of 1868. I wrote the book in San Francisco and delivered the manuscript within contract time. Bliss provided a multitude of illustrations for the book and then stopped. The contract date for the issue of the book went by and there was no explanation of this. Time drifted along and still there was no explanation. I was lecturing all over the country; and about thirty times a day, on an average, I was trying to answer this question: "When is your book coming out?" I got tired of inventing new answers to that question, and by and by I got horribly tired of the question itself. Whoever asked it became my enemy at once and I was usually almost eager to make that appear.

As soon as I was free of the lecture field I hastened to Hartford to make inquiries. Bliss said that the fault was not his. He wanted to publish the book but the directors of his company were staid old fogies and they were afraid of it. They had examined the book and the majority of them were of the opinion that there were places in it of a humorous character. Bliss said the house had never published a book that had a suspicion like that attaching to it, and that the directors were afraid that a departure of this kind could seriously injure the house's reputation, that he was tied hand and foot and was not permitted to carry out his contract.

One of the directors, a Mr. Drake—at least he was the remains of what had once been a Mr. Drake —invited me to take a ride with him in his buggy and I went along. He was a pathetic old relic and his ways and his talk were also pathetic. He had a delicate purpose in view and it took him some time to hearten himself sufficiently to carry it out, but at last he accomplished it. He explained the house's difficulty and distress, as Bliss had already explained it. Then he frankly threw himself and the house upon my mercy and begged me to take away *The Innocents Abroad* and release the concern from the contract. I said I wouldn't—and so ended the interview and the buggy excursion.

Then I warned Bliss that he must get to work or I should make trouble. He acted upon the warning and set up the book and I read the proofs. Then there was another long wait and no explanation. At last toward the end of July (1869, I think) I lost patience and telegraphed Bliss that if the book was not on sale in twenty-four hours I should bring suit for damages. That ended the trouble. Half a dozen copies were bound and placed on sale within the required time. Then the canvassing began, and went briskly forward. In nine months the book took the publishing house out of debt, advanced its stock from twenty-five to two hundred, and left seventy thousand dollars profit to the good. It was Bliss that told me this—but if it was true it was the first time that Bliss had told the truth in sixty-five years. He was born in 1804.

.   .   .   .   .

2. The American Publishing Company. (May 23, 1906)

But I must go back to Webb. When I got back from the *Quaker City* Excursion, in November, 1867, Webb told me that *The Jumping Frog* book had been favorably received by the press and that he believed it had sold fairly well, but that he had found it impossible to get a statement of account from the American News Company. He said the book had been something of a disaster to him, since he had manufactured it with his own private funds and was now not able to get any of the money back because of the dishonest and dodging ways of the News Company.

I was very sincerely sorry for Webb, sorry that he had lost money by befriending me, also in some degree sorry that he was not able to pay me my royalties.

I made my contract for *The Innocents Abroad* with the American Publishing Company. Then after two or three months had gone by it occurred to me that perhaps I was violating that contract, there being a clause in it forbidding me to publish books with any other firm during a term of a year or so. Of course that clause could not cover a book which had been published before the contract was made; anybody else would have known that. But I didn't know it, for I was not in the habit of knowing anything that was valuable and I was also not in the habit of asking other people for information.

It was my ignorant opinion that I was violating the Bliss contract and that I was in honor bound to suppress *The Jumping Frog* book and take it permanently out of print. So I went to Webb with the matter. He was willing to accommodate me upon these terms: that I should surrender to him such royalties as might be due me; that I should also surrender to him, free of royalty, all bound and unbound copies which might be in the News Company's hands; also that I should hand him eight hundred dollars cash; also that he should superintend the breaking up of the plates of the book, and for that service should receive such bounty as the type founders should pay for the broken plates as old type metal. Type metal was worth nine cents a pound and the weight of the plates was about forty pounds. One may perceive by these details that Webb had some talent as a trader.

After this Webb passed out of the field of my vision for a long time. But meantime chance threw me in the way of the manager of the American News

Company, and I asked him about Webb's difficulties with the concern and how they had come about. He said he didn't know of any difficulties. I then explained to him that Webb had never been able to collect anything from the company. In turn, he explained to me that my explanation was not sound. He said the company had always furnished statements to Webb at the usual intervals, and had accompanied them with the company's check to date. By his invitation I went with him to his office, and by his books and accounts he proved to me that what he had said was true. Webb had collected his dues and mine regularly from the beginning and had pocketed the money. At the time that Webb and I had settled, he was owing me six hundred dollars on royalties. The bound and unbound *Jumping Frogs* which he had inherited from me at that time had since been sold, and the result had gone into his pocket—part of it being six hundred more that should have come to me on royalties.

To sum up, I was now an author, I was an author with some little trifle of reputation, I was an author who had published a book, I was an author who had not become rich through that publication, I was an author whose first book had cost him twelve hundred dollars in unreceived royalties, eight hundred dollars in blood money, and three dollars and sixty cents smouched from old type metal. I was resolved from that moment that I would not publish with Webb any more—unless I could borrow money enough to support the luxury.

By and by when I became notorious through the publication of *The Innocents Abroad*, Webb was able to satisfy the public, first that he had discovered me, later that he had created me. It was quite generally conceded that I was a valuable asset to the American nation and to the great ranks of literature, also that for the acquisition of this asset a deep debt of gratitude was due from the nation and the ranks—to Webb.

By and by Webb and his high service were forgotten. Then Bliss and the American Publishing Company came forward and established the fact that they had discovered me, later that they had created me, therefore that some more gratitude was due. In the course of time there were still other claimants for these great services. They sprang up in California, Nevada, and around generally, and I came at last to believe that I had been more multitudinously discovered and created than any other animal that had ever issued from the Deity's hands.

Webb believed that he was a literary person. He might have gotten this superstition accepted by the world if he had not extinguished it by publishing his things. They gave him away. His prose was enchantingly puerile, his poetry was not any better, yet he kept on grinding out his commonplaces at intervals until he died, two years ago, of over-cerebration. He was a poor sort of a creature and by nature and training a fraud. As a liar he was well enough and had some success but no distinction, because he was a contemporary of Elisha Bliss and when it came to lying Bliss could overshadow and blot out a whole continent of Webbs like a total eclipse.

About 1872 I wrote another book, *Roughing It*. I had published *The Innocents* on a five per cent royalty, which would amount to about twenty-two cents per volume. Proposals were coming in now from several other good houses. One offered fifteen per cent royalty; another offered to give me *all* of the profits and be content with the advertisement which the book would furnish the house. I sent for Bliss and he came to Elmira. If I had known as much about book publishing then as I know now, I would have required of Bliss seventy-five or eighty per cent of the profits above cost of manufacture, and this would have been fair and just. But I knew nothing about the business and had been too indolent to try to learn anything about it. I told Bliss I did not wish to leave his corporation, and that I did not want extravagant terms. I said I thought I ought to have half the profit above cost of manufacture and he said with enthusiasm that that was exactly right, exactly right.

He went to his hotel and drew the contract and brought it to the house in the afternoon. I found a difficulty in it. It did not name "half profits," but named a seven and a half per cent royalty instead. I asked him to explain that. I said that that was not the understanding. He said "No, it wasn't," but that he had put in a royalty to simplify the matter— that seven and a half per cent royalty represented fully half the profit and a little more, up to a sale of a hundred thousand copies, that after that the publishing company's half would be a shade superior to mine.

I was a little doubtful, a little suspicious, and asked him if he could swear to that. He promptly put up his hand and made oath to it, exactly repeating the words which he had just used.

It took me nine or ten years to find out that that was a false oath, and that seven and a half per cent did not represent one-fourth of the profits. But in the meantime I had published several books with Bliss on seven and a half and ten per cent royalties, and of course had been handsomely swindled on all of them.

In 1879 I came home from Europe with a book ready for the press, *A Tramp Abroad*. I sent for Bliss and he came out to the house to discuss the book. I said that I was not satisfied about those royalties and that I did not believe in their "half-profit" pretenses, that this time he must put the "half profit" in the contract and make no mention of royalties—otherwise I would take the book elsewhere. He said he was perfectly willing to put it in, for it was right and just, and that if his directors opposed it and found fault with it he would withdraw from the concern and publish the book himself—fine talk, but I knew that he was master in that concern and that it would have to accept any contract that had been signed by him. This contract lay there on the billiard table with his signature attached to it. He had ridden his directors roughshod ever since the days of *The Innocents Abroad* and more than once he had told me that he had made his directors do things which they hadn't wanted to do, with the threat that if they did not comply he would leave the company's service and take me along with him.

I don't know how a grown person could ever be

so simple and innocent as I was in those days. It ought to have occurred to me that a man who could talk like that must either be a fool or convinced that I was one. However, I was the one. And so even very simple and rudimentary wisdoms were not likely to find their way into my head.

I reminded him that his company would not be likely to make any trouble about a contract which had been signed by him. Then, with one of his tooth-less smiles, he pointed out a detail which I had over-looked, to wit: the contract was with Elisha Bliss, a private individual, and the American Publishing Company was not mentioned in it.

He told me afterward that he took the contract to the directors and said that he would turn it over to the company for one-fourth of the profits of the book together with an increase of salary for himself and for Frank, his son, and that if these terms were not satisfactory he would leave the company and publish the book himself, whereupon the directors granted his demands and took the contract. The fact that Bliss told me these things with his own mouth is unassailable evidence that they were not true. Six weeks before the book issued from the press Bliss told the truth once, to see how it would taste, but it overstrained him and he died.

When the book had been out three months there was an annual meeting of the stockholders of the company and I was present, as a half-partner in the book. The meeting was held in the house of a neighbor of mine, Newton Case, a director in the company from the beginning. A statement of the company's business was read, and to me it was a revelation. Sixty-four thousand copies of the book had been sold, and my half of the profit was thirty-two thousand dollars. In 1872 Bliss had made out to me that seven and a half per cent royalty, some trifle over twenty cents a copy, represented one-half of the profits, whereas at that earlier day it hardly represented a sixth of the profits. Times were not so good now, yet it took all of fifty cents a copy to represent half.

Well, Bliss was dead and I couldn't settle with him for his ten years of swindlings. He has been dead a quarter of a century now. My bitterness against him has faded away and disappeared. I feel only compassion for him and if I could send him a fan I would.

When the balance sheets exposed to me the rascalities which I had been suffering at the hands of the American Publishing Company I stood up and delivered a lecture to Newton Case and the rest of the conspirators—meaning the rest of the directors.

· · · · ·

3. James R. Osgood. (May 24, 1906)

My opportunity was now come to right myself and level up matters with the publishing company but I didn't see it, of course. I was seldom able to see an opportunity until it had ceased to be one. I knew all about that house now and I ought to have remained with it. I ought to have put a tax upon its profits for my personal benefit, the tax to continue until the difference between royalties and half profits should in time return from the company's pocket to mine and the company's robbery of me be thus wiped

off the slate. But of course I couldn't think of anything so sane as that and I didn't. I only thought of
ways and means to remove my respectability from
that tainted atmosphere. I wanted to get my books
out of the company's hands and carry them elsewhere. After a time I went to Newton Case—in his
house as before—and proposed that the company
cancel the contracts and restore my books to me free
and unencumbered, the company retaining as a consideration the money it had swindled me out of on
*Roughing It, The Gilded Age, Sketches New and
Old,* and *Tom Sawyer.*

Mr. Case demurred at my language but I told
him I was not able to modify it, that I was perfectly
satisfied that he and the rest of the Bible Class were
aware of the fraud practiced on me in 1872 by
Bliss—aware of it when it happened and consenting
to it by silence. He objected to my calling the Board
of Directors a Bible Class. And I said then it ought
to stop opening its meetings with prayer—particularly when it was getting ready to swindle an author.
I was expecting that Mr. Case would deny the
charge of guilty knowledge and resent it, but he
didn't do it. That convinced me that my charge was
well founded, therefore I repeated it and proceeded
to say unkind things about his theological seminary.
I said, "You have put seventy-five thousand dollars
into that factory and are getting a great deal of
praise for it, whereas *my* share in that benefaction
goes unmentioned—yet I *have* a share in it, for of
every dollar that you put into it a portion was stolen
out of my pocket." He returned no thanks for these
compliments. He was a dull man and unappreciative.

Finally I tried to buy my contracts but he said it would be impossible for the Board to entertain a proposition to sell, for the reason that nine-tenths of the company's livelihood was drawn from my books and therefore its business would be worth nothing if they were taken away. At a later time Judge What's-his-name, a director, told me I was right, that the Board did know all about the swindle which Bliss had practiced upon me at the time that the fraud was committed.

As I have remarked, I ought to have remained with the company and leveled up the account. But I didn't. I removed my purity from that mephitic atmosphere and carried my next book to James R. Osgood of Boston, formerly of the firm of Field, Osgood and Company. That book was *Old Times on the Mississippi.*[2] Osgood was to manufacture the book at my expense, publish it by subscription, and charge me a royalty for his services.

Osgood was one of the dearest and sweetest and loveliest human beings to be found on the planet anywhere, but he knew nothing about subscription publishing and he made a mighty botch of it. He was a sociable creature and we played much billiards and daily and nightly had a good time. And in the meantime his clerks ran our business for us and I think that neither of us inquired into their methods or knew what they were doing. That book was a long time getting built; and when at last the final draft was made upon my purse I realized that I had paid out fifty-six thousand dollars upon that struc-

[2] This was the title used in the *Atlantic*, when the first part of the book was published in 1875. The title of the book is *Life on the Mississippi.*

ture. Bliss could have built a library for that money. It took a year to get the fifty-six thousand back into my pocket, and not many dollars followed it. So this first effort of mine to transact that kind of business on my own hook was a failure.

Osgood tried again. He published *The Prince and the Pauper*. He made a beautiful book of it but all the profit I got out of it was seventeen thousand dollars.

Next, Osgood thought he could make a success with a book in the *trade*. He had been trained to trade publishing. He was a little sore over his subscription attempts and wanted to try. I gave him *The Stolen White Elephant*, which was a collection of rubbishy sketches, mainly. I offered to bet he couldn't sell ten thousand copies in six months and he took me up, stakes five dollars. He won the money but it was something of a squeeze. However, I think I am wrong in putting that book last. I think that that was Osgood's first effort, not his third. I should have continued with Osgood after his failure with *The Prince and the Pauper* because I liked him so well, but he failed and I had to go elsewhere.

Meantime I had been having an adventure on the outside. An old and particular friend of mine unloaded a patent on me, price fifteen thousand dollars. It was worthless and he had been losing money on it a year or two, but I did not know those particulars because he neglected to mention them. He said that if I would buy the patent he would do the manufacturing and selling for me. So I took him up. Then began a cash outgo of five hundred dollars a month. That raven flew out of the Ark regularly

every thirty days, but it never got back with anything and the dove didn't report for duty. After a
time and half a time and another time, I relieved my
friend and put the patent into the hands of Charles
L. Webster, who had married a niece of mine and
seemed a capable and energetic young fellow. At a
salary of fifteen hundred a year he continued to send
the raven out monthly, with the same old result to a
penny.

At last, when I had lost forty-two thousand dollars on that patent I gave it away to a man whom I
had long detested and whose family I desired to ruin.
Then I looked around for other adventures. That
same friend was ready with another patent. I spent
ten thousand dollars on it in eight months. Then I
tried to give that patent to the man whose family I
was after. He was very grateful but he was also experienced by this time and was getting suspicious of
benefactors. He wouldn't take it and I had to let it
lapse.

Meantime, another old friend arrived with a
wonderful invention. It was an engine or a furnace
or something of the kind which would get out 99 per
cent of all the steam that was in a pound of coal. I
went to Mr. Richards of the Colt Arms Factory and
told him about it. He was a specialist and knew all
about coal and steam. He seemed to be doubtful
about this machine and I asked him why. He said,
because the amount of steam concealed in a pound
of coal was known to a fraction and that my inventor was mistaken about his 99 per cent. He
showed me a printed book of solid pages of figures,
figures that made me drunk and dizzy. He showed

me that my man's machine couldn't come within 90 per cent of doing what it proposed to do. I went away a little discouraged. But I thought that maybe the book was mistaken and so I hired the inventor to build the machine on a salary of thirty-five dollars a week, I to pay all expenses. It took him a good many weeks to build the thing. He visited me every few days to report progress and I early noticed by his breath and gait that he was spending thirty-six dollars a week on whisky, and I couldn't ever find out where he got the other dollar.

Finally, when I had spent five thousand on this enterprise the machine was finished, but it wouldn't go. It did save one per cent of the steam that was in a pound of coal, but that was nothing. You could do it with a teakettle. I offered the machine to the man whose family I was after, but without success. So I threw the thing away and looked around for something fresh. But I had become an enthusiast on steam, and I took some stock in a Hartford company which proposed to make and sell and revolutionize everything with a new kind of steam pulley. The steam pulley pulled thirty-two thousand dollars out of my pocket in sixteen months, then went to pieces and I was alone in the world again, without an occupation.

But I found one. I invented a scrapbook—and if I do say it myself, it was the only rational scrapbook the world has ever seen. I patented it and put it in the hands of that old particular friend of mine who had originally interested me in patents and he made a good deal of money out of it. But by and by, just when I was about to begin to receive a share of the money myself, his firm failed. I didn't know his firm was going to fail—he didn't say anything about it. One day he asked me to lend the firm five thousand dollars and said he was willing to pay seven per cent. As security he offered the firm's note. I asked for an endorser. He was much surprised and said that if endorsers were handy and easy to get at, he wouldn't have to come to me for the money, he could get it anywhere. That seemed reasonable and so I gave him the five thousand dollars. They failed inside of three days—and at the end of two or three years I got back two thousand dollars of the money.

That five thousand dollars had a history. Early in 1872 Joe Goodman wrote me from California that his friend and mine, Senator John P. Jones, was going to start a rival in Hartford to the Traveler's Accident Insurance Company, and that Jones wanted Joe to take twelve thousand of the stock and had said he would see that Joe did not lose the money. Joe now proposed to transfer this opportunity to me, and said that if I would make the venture Jones would protect me from loss. So I took the stock and became a director. Jones's brother-in-law, Lester, had been for a long time actuary in the Traveler's Company. He was now transferred to our company and we began business. There were five directors. Three of us attended every Board meeting for a year and a half.

At the end of eighteen months the company went to pieces and I was out of pocket twenty-three thousand dollars. Jones was in New York, tarrying for a while at a hotel which he had bought, the St. James, and I sent Lester down there to get the twenty-three thousand dollars. But he came back and reported that Jones had been putting money into so many things that he was a good deal straitened and would be glad if I would wait a while. I did not suspect that Lester was drawing upon his fancy, but it was so. He hadn't said anything to Jones about it. But his tale seemed reasonable, because I knew that Jones had built a line of artificial ice factories clear across the Southern states—nothing like it this side of the Great Wall of China. I knew that the factories had cost him a million dollars or so, and that the people down there hadn't been trained to admire ice and didn't want any and wouldn't buy any—that therefore the Chinese Wall was an entire loss and failure.

I also knew that Jones's St. James Hotel had ceased to be a profitable house because Jones, who was a big-hearted man with ninety-nine parts of him pure generosity, and that is the case to this day, had filled his hotel from roof to cellar with poor relations gathered from the four corners of the earth— plumbers, bricklayers, unsuccessful clergymen, and in fact all the different kinds of people that knew nothing about the hotel business. I was also aware that there was no room in the hotel for the public, because all its rooms were occupied by a multitude of other poor relations gathered from the four corners of the earth at Jones's invitation, and waiting for Jones to find lucrative occupations for them. I was also aware that Jones had bought a piece of the state of California with some spacious city sites on it, with room for railroads and a very fine and spacious and valuable harbor on its city front, and

that Jones was in debt for these properties. Therefore I was content to wait a while.

As the months drifted by, Lester now and then
volunteered to go and see Jones on his own hook.
His visits produced nothing. The fact is, Lester
was afraid of Jones and felt a delicacy about
troubling him with my matter while he had so many
burdens on his shoulders. He preferred to pretend
to me that he had seen Jones and had mentioned my
matter to him, whereas in truth he had never mentioned it to Jones at all. At the end of two or three
years Mr. Slee of our Elmira coal firm proposed to
speak to Jones about it and I consented. Slee visited
Jones and began in his tactful and diplomatic way
to lead up to my matter, but before he had got well
started Jones glanced up and said, "Do you mean to
say that that money has never been paid to Clemens?" He drew his check for twenty-three thousand
at once, said it ought to have been paid long ago
and that it would have been paid the moment it was
due if he had known the circumstances.

This was in the spring of 1877. With that check
in my pocket I was prepared to seek sudden fortune
again. The reader, deceived by what I have been
saying about my adventures, will jump to the conclusion that I sought an opportunity at once. I did
nothing of the kind. I was the burnt child. I wanted
nothing further to do with speculations. General
Hawley sent for me to come to the *Courant* office.
I went there with my check in my pocket. There was
a young fellow there who said that he had been a
reporter on a Providence newspaper but that he
was in another business now. He was with Graham

Bell and was agent for a new invention called the telephone. He believed there was great fortune in store for it and wanted me to take some stock. I declined. I said I didn't want anything more to do with wildcat speculation. Then he offered the stock to me at twenty-five. I said I didn't want it at any price. He became eager—insisted that I take five hundred dollars' worth. He said he would sell me as much as I wanted for five hundred dollars— offered to let me gather it up in my hands and measure it in a plug hat—said I could have a whole hatful for five hundred dollars. But I was the burnt child and I resisted all these temptations, resisted them easily, went off with my check intact, and next day lent five thousand of it on an unendorsed note to my friend who was going to go bankrupt three days later.

About the end of the year (or possibly in the beginning of 1878) I put up a telephone wire from my house down to the *Courant* office, the only telephone wire in town, and the *first* one that was ever used in a private house in the world.

That young man couldn't sell *me* any stock but he sold a few hatfuls of it to an old dry-goods clerk in Hartford for five thousand dollars. That was that clerk's whole fortune. He had been half a lifetime saving it. It is strange how foolish people can be and what ruinous risks they can take when they want to get rich in a hurry. I was sorry for that man when I heard about it. I thought I might have saved him if I had had an opportunity to tell him about my experiences.

We sailed for Europe on the 10th of April, 1878.

We were gone fourteen months, and when we got back one of the first things we saw was that clerk driving around in a sumptuous barouche with liveried servants all over it—and his telephone stock was emptying greenbacks into his premises at such a rate that he had to handle them with a shovel. It is strange the way the ignorant and inexperienced so often and so undeservedly succeed when the informed and the experienced fail.

·   ·   ·   ·   ·

4. Setting Up as a Publisher. (May 26, 1906)

As I have already remarked, I had imported my nephew-in-law, Webster, from the village of Dunkirk, New York, to conduct that original first patent-right business for me, at a salary of fifteen hundred dollars. That enterprise had lost forty-two thousand dollars for me, so I thought this a favorable time to close it up. I proposed to be my own publisher now and let young Webster do the work. He thought he ought to have twenty-five hundred dollars a year while he was learning the trade. I took a day or two to consider the matter and study it out searchingly. So far as I could see, this was a new idea. I remembered that printers' apprentices got *no* salary. Upon inquiry I found that this was the case with stone masons, brick masons, tinners, and the rest. I found that not even lawyers or apprenticed doctors got any salary for learning the trade. I remembered that on the river an apprentice pilot not only got nothing in the way of salary but he also had to pay some pilot a sum in cash which he didn't have—a large sum. It was what I had done myself. I had paid Bixby a hundred dollars and it was borrowed money. I was told by a person who said he was studying for the ministry that even Noah got no salary for the first six months—partly on account of the weather and partly because he was learning navigation.

The upshot of these thinkings and searchings of mine was that I believed I had secured something entirely new to history in Webster. And also I believed that a young backwoodsman who was starting life in New York without equipment of any kind, without proved value of any kind, without prospective value of any kind, yet able without blinking an eye to propose to learn a trade at another man's expense and charge for this benefaction an annual sum greater than any president of the United States had ever been able to save out of his pay for running the most difficult country on the planet, after Ireland, must surely be worth securing—and instantly—lest he get away. I believed that if some of his gigantic interest in No. 1 could be diverted to the protection of No. 2, the result would be fortune enough for me.

I erected Webster into a firm—a firm entitled Webster and Company, Publishers—and installed him in a couple of offices at a modest rental on the second floor of a building somewhere below Union Square, I don't remember where. For assistants he had a girl and perhaps a masculine clerk of about eight-hundred-dollar size. For a while Webster had another helper. This was a man who had long been in the subscription-book business, knew all about it,

and was able to teach it to Webster—which he did—
I paying the cost of tuition. I am talking about the
early part of 1884 now. I handed Webster a competent capital and along with it I handed him the
manuscript of *Huckleberry Finn*. Webster's function
was general agent. It was his business to appoint sub-
agents throughout the country. At that time there
were sixteen of these sub-agencies. They had canvassers under them who did the canvassing. In New
York City Webster was his own sub-agent.

Before ever any of these minor details that I am
talking about had entered into being, the careful
Webster had suggested that a contract be drawn
and signed and sealed before we made any real move.
That seemed sane, though I should not have thought
of it myself—I mean it *was* sane *because* I had
not thought of it myself. So Webster got his own
lawyer to draw the contract. I was coming to
admire Webster very much, and at this point in the
proceedings I had one of those gushing generosities
surge up in my system, and before I had thought,
I had tried to confer upon Webster a tenth interest
in the business in addition to his salary, free of
charge. Webster declined promptly—with thanks, of
course, the usual kind. That raised him another step
in my admiration. I knew perfectly well that I was
offering him a partnership interest which would pay
him two or three times his salary within the next nine
months, but he didn't know that. He was coldly and
wisely discounting all my prophecies about *Huckleberry Finn's* high commercial value. And here was
this new evidence that in Webster I had found a

jewel, a man who would not get excited; a man who would not lose his head; a cautious man; a man who would not take a risk of any kind in fields unknown to him. Except at somebody else's expense, I mean.

The contract was drawn, as I say, by a young lawyer from Dunkirk, New York, which produced him as well as Webster, and has not yet gotten over the strain. Whitford was privileged to sign himself "of the firm of Alexander and Green." Alexander and Green had a great and lucrative business and not enough conscience to damage it—a fact which came out rather prominently last year when the earthquake came which shook the entrails out of the three great life insurance companies. Alexander and Green had their offices in the Mutual Building. They kept a job lot of twenty-five lawyers on salary, and he was one of these. He was good-natured, obliging, and immensely ignorant, and was endowed with a stupidity which by the least little stretch would go around the globe four times and tie.

That first contract was all right. There was nothing the matter with it. It placed all obligations, all expenses, all liability, all responsibilities upon *me*, where they belonged.

It was a happy combination, Webster and his lawyer. The amount that the two together didn't know about anything was to me a much more awful and paralyzing spectacle than it would be to see the Milky Way get wrecked and drift off in rags and patches through the sky. When it came to courage, moral or physical, they hadn't any. Webster was afraid to venture anything in the way of business without first getting a lawyer's assurance that there was nothing jailable about it. Lawyer was consulted so nearly constantly that he was about as much a member of the staff as was the girl and the subscription expert. But as neither Webster nor he had had any personal experience of money, his lawyer was not an expensive incumbent, though he probably thought he was.

At the break of the autumn I went off with George W. Cable on a four months' reading campaign in the East and West—the last platform work which I was ever to do in this life in my own country. I resolved at the time that I would never rob the public from the platform again unless driven to it by pecuniary compulsions. After eleven years the pecuniary compulsions came and I lectured all around the globe.

Ten years have since elapsed, during which time I have only lectured for public charities and without pay. On the 19th of last month I took a public and formal leave of the platform—a thing which I had not done before—in a lecture on Robert Fulton for the benefit of the Robert Fulton Monument Fund.

I seem to be getting pretty far away from Webster and Whitford, but it's no matter. It is one of those cases where distance lends enchantment to the view. Webster was successful with *Huckleberry Finn*, and a year later handed me the firm's check for fifty-four thousand five hundred dollars, which included the fifteen thousand dollars capital which I had originally handed to him.

Once more I experienced a new birth. I have been

born more times than anybody except Krishna, I suppose.

.   .   .   .   .

5. General Grant's Publisher. (May 28, 1906)[3]

Webster conceived the idea that he had discovered me to the world but he was reasonably modest about it. He did much less cackling over his egg than Webb and Bliss had done.

It had never been my intention to publish anybody's books but my own. An accident diverted me from this wise purpose. That was General Grant's memorable book. One night in the first week of November, 1884, I had been lecturing in Chickering Hall and was walking homeward. It was a rainy night and but few people were about. In the midst of a black gulf between lamps, two dim figures stepped out of a doorway and moved along in front of me. I heard one of them say, "Do you know General Grant has actually determined to write his memoirs and publish them? He has said so today, in so many words."

That was all I heard—just those words—and I thought it great good luck that I was permitted to overhear them.

In the morning I went out and called on General Grant. I found him in his library with Col. Fred Grant, his son. The General said in substance this:

---

[3] This account of the events connected with the publication of Grant's *Memoirs* differs in many particulars, some of them important, from the far more reliable account in Volume I of the previously published *Autobiography*. The latter was written from notes soon after Grant's death. But many memoranda, letters, and notebook entries show that it also is inaccurate.

"Sit down and keep quiet until I sign a contract"—
and added that it was for a book which he was going
to write.

Fred Grant was apparently conducting a final reading and examination of the contract himself. He
found it satisfactory and said so, and his father
stepped to the table and took up the pen. It might
have been better for me, possibly, if I had let him
alone but I didn't. I said, "Don't sign it. Let Col.
Fred read it to me first."

Col. Fred read it, and I said I was glad I had
come in time to interfere. The Century Company was
the party of the second part. It proposed to pay
the General ten per cent royalty. Of course this was
nonsense—but the proposal had its source in ignorance, not dishonesty. The great Century Company knew all about magazine publishing. No one
could teach them anything about that industry. But
at that time they had had no experience of subscription publishing, and they probably had nothing
in their minds except trade publishing. They could
not even have had any valuable experience in trade
publishing, or they would not have asked General
Grant to furnish a book on the royalty commonly
granted to authors of no name or repute.

I explained that these terms would never do; that
they were all wrong, unfair, unjust. I said, "Strike
out the ten per cent and put twenty per cent in its
place. Better still, put seventy-five per cent of the
net returns in its place."

The General demurred, and quite decidedly. He
said they would never pay those terms.

I said that that was a matter of no consequence,

since there was not a reputable publisher in America who would not be very glad to pay them.

The General still shook his head. He was still desirous of signing the contract as it stood.

I pointed out that the contract as it stood had an offensive detail in it which I had never heard of in the ten per cent contract of even the most obscure author—that this contract not only proposed a ten per cent royalty for such a colossus as General Grant, but it also had in it a requirement that out of that ten per cent must come some trivial tax for the book's share of clerk hire, house rent, sweeping out the offices, or some such nonsense as that. I said he ought to have three-fourths of the profits and let the publisher pay running expenses out of his remaining fourth.

The idea distressed General Grant. He thought it placed him in the attitude of a robber—robber of a publisher. I said that if he regarded that as a crime it was because his education was limited. I said it was not a crime and was always rewarded in heaven with two halos. Would be, if it ever happened.

The General was immovable and challenged me to name the publisher that would be willing to have this noble deed perpetrated upon him. I named the American Publishing Company of Hartford. He asked if I could prove my position. I said I could furnish the proof by telegraph in six hours—three hours for my despatch to go to Hartford, three hours for Bliss's jubilant acceptance to return by the same electric gravel train—that if he needed this answer quicker I would walk up to Hartford and fetch it.

The General still stood out. But Fred Grant was

beginning to be persuaded. He proposed that the Century contract be laid on the table for twenty-four hours and that meantime the situation be examined and discussed. He said that this thing was not a matter of sentiment; it was a matter of pure business and should be examined from that point of view alone. His remark about sentiment had a bearing. The reason was this. The broking firm of Grant and Ward—consisting of General Grant, Mr. Ward (called for a time the "Little Napoleon of Finance") and Ward's confederate, Fish—had swindled General Grant out of every penny he had in the world. And at a time when he did not know where to turn for bread, Roswell Smith, head of the Century Company, offered him five hundred dollars per article for four magazine articles about certain great battles of the Civil War. The offer came to the despairing old hero like the fabled straw to the drowning man. He accepted it with gratitude and wrote the articles and delivered them. They were easily worth ten thousand dollars apiece but he didn't know it. Five hundred dollars apiece seemed to him fabulous pay for a trifle of pleasant and unlaborious scribbling.

He was now most loath to desert these benefactors of his. To his military mind and training it seemed disloyalty. If I remember rightly his first article lifted the Century's subscription list from a hundred thousand copies to two hundred and twenty thousand. This made the Century's advertisement pages, for that month, worth more than double the money they had ever commanded in any previous month. As a guess, I should say that this increase of patronage was worth, that month, eight thousand dollars. This is a safe estimate, a conservative estimate.

The doubled subscription list established in that month was destined to continue for years. It was destined to increase the magazine's advertisement income about eight or ten thousand dollars a month during six years. I have said that each of General Grant's articles was worth ten thousand dollars instead of five hundred. I could say that each of the four articles was worth twenty-five thousand dollars and still be within bounds.

I began to tout for the American Publishing Company. I argued that the company had been first in the field as applicants for a volume of Grant memoirs and that perhaps they ought to have a chance at a bid before the Century Company. This seemed to be news to General Grant. But I reminded him that once during the apparently wonderfully prosperous days of the firm of Grant and Ward I called upon him in his private office one day, helped him to consume his luncheon, and begged him to write his memoirs and give them to the American Publishing Company. He had declined at the time, and most decidedly, saying he was not in need of money and that he was not a literary person and could not write the memoirs.

I think we left the contract matter to stew for that time, and took it up again the next morning. I did a good deal of thinking during the interval. I knew quite well that the American Publishing Company would be glad to get General Grant's memoirs on a basis of three-quarters profit for him, to one-quarter for themselves. Indeed I knew quite well that there was not a publisher in the country—I mean a publisher experienced in the subscription publishing business—who would not be glad to get the book on those terms. I was fully expecting to presently hand that book to Frank Bliss and the American Publishing Company and enrich that den of reptiles—but the sober second thought came then. I reflected that the company had been robbing me for years and building theological factories out of the proceeds, and that now was my chance to feed fat the ancient grudge I bore them.

At the second conference with the General and Fred, the General exhibited some of the modesty which was so large a feature of his nature. General Sherman had published his *Memoirs* in two large volumes with Scribner's, and that publication had been a notable event. General Grant said:

"Sherman told me that his profits on that book were twenty-five thousand dollars. Do you believe I could get as much out of my book?"

I said I not only believed but I *knew* that he would achieve a vastly greater profit than that—that Sherman's book was published in the trade; that it was a suitable book for subscription distribution and ought to have been published in that way; that not many books were suitable to that method of publishing, but that the memoirs of such illustrious persons as Sherman and Grant were peculiarly adapted to that method; that a book which contained the right material for that method would harvest from eight to ten times as much profit by subscription as it could be made to produce by trade sale.

The General had his doubts that he could gather twenty-five thousand dollars profit for his memoirs. I inquired why. He said he had already applied the test and had secured the evidence and the verdict. I wondered where he could have gotten such evidence and such a verdict, and he explained. He said he had offered to sell his memoirs out and out to Roswell Smith for twenty-five thousand dollars, and that the proposition had so frightened Smith that he hardly had breath enough left in his clothes to decline with.

Then I had an idea. It suddenly occurred to me that I was a publisher myself. I had not thought of it before. I said, "Sell *me* the memoirs, General. I am a publisher. I will pay double price. I have a checkbook in my pocket; take my check for fifty thousand dollars now, and let's draw the contract."

General Grant was as prompt in declining this as Roswell Smith had been in declining the other offer. He said he wouldn't hear of such a thing. He said we were friends, and if I should fail to get the money back out of his book— He stopped there and said there was no occasion to go into particulars, he simply would not consent to help a friend run any such risk.

Then I said, "Give me the book on the terms which I have already suggested that you make with the Century people—twenty per cent royalty or in lieu of that seventy-five per cent of the profits on the publication to go to you, I to pay all running expenses such as salaries, etc., out of my fourth."

He laughed at that and asked me what my profit

out of that remnant would be. I said, a hundred thousand dollars in six months.

He was dealing with a literary person. He was aware, by authority of all the traditions, that literary persons are flighty, romantic, unpractical, and in business matters do not know enough to come in when it rains or at any other time. He did not say that he attached no value to these flights of my imagination, for he was too kindly to say hurtful things, but he might better have said it because he looked it with tenfold emphasis and the look covered the whole ground. To make conversation, I suppose, he asked me what I based this dream upon —if it had a basis.

I said, "I base it upon the difference between your literary commercial value and mine. My first two books sold a hundred and fifty thousand copies each —three dollars and a half per volume in cloth, costlier volumes at a higher price according to binding—average price of the hundred and fifty thousand, four dollars apiece. I know that your commercial value is easily four times as great as mine; therefore I know it to be a perfectly safe guess that your book will sell six hundred thousand single volumes, and that the clear profit to you will be half a million dollars and the clear profit to me a hundred thousand.

We had a long discussion over the matter. Finally General Grant telegraphed for his particular friend, George W. Childs of the Philadelphia *Ledger*, to come up to New York and furnish an opinion. Childs came. I convinced him that Webster's publishing machinery was ample and in good order. Then Childs delivered the verdict, "Give the book to Clemens." Col. Fred Grant endorsed and repeated the verdict, "Give the book to Clemens." So the contract was drawn and signed, and Webster took hold of his new job at once.

By my existing contract with Webster he merely had a salary of twenty-five hundred dollars a year. He had declined to accept, gratis, an interest in the business, for he was a cautious person and averse from running risks. I now offered him, gratis, a tenth share in the business—the contract as to other details to remain as before. Then, as a counter proposition, he modestly offered this: that his salary be increased to thirty-five hundred dollars a year; that he have ten per cent of the profits accruing from the Grant book, and that I furnish all the capital required at seven per cent.

I said I should be satisfied with this arrangement.

Then he called in his pal, Whitford, who drew the contract. I couldn't understand the contract—I never could understand any contract—and I asked my brother-in-law, General Langdon, a trained business man, to understand it for me. He read it and said it was all right. So we signed it and sealed it. I was to find out later that the contract gave Webster ten per cent of the profits on the Grant book *and* ten per cent interest in the profits of the whole business—but not any interest in such losses as might occur.

The news went forth that General Grant was going to write his memoirs and that the firm of Charles L. Webster & Co., would publish them. The announcement produced a vast sensation throughout the country. The nation was glad and this feeling poured itself heartily out in all the newspapers. On the one day, young Webster was as unknown as the unborn babe. The next day he was a notoriety. His name was in every paper in the United States. He was young, he was human, he naturally mistook this transient notoriety for fame, and by consequence he had to get his hat enlarged. His juvenile joy in his new grandeur was a pretty and pleasant spectacle to see. The first thing he did was to move out of his modest quarters and secure quarters better suited to his new importance as the most distinguished publisher in the country.

. . . . . .

(May 29, 1906)

His new quarters were on the second or third floor of a tall building which fronted on Union Square, a commercially aristocratic locality. His previous quarters had consisted of two good-sized rooms. His new ones occupied the whole floor. What Webster really needed was a cubbyhole up a back street somewhere, with room to swing a cat in—a long cat; this cubbyhole for office work. He needed no storage rooms, no cellars. The printers and binders of the great memoir took care of the sheets and the bound volumes for us and charged storage and insurance. Conspicuous quarters were not needed for that mighty book. You couldn't have hidden General Grant's publisher where the agent and the canvasser could not find him. The cubbyhole would have been sufficient for all our needs. Almost all the business would be transacted by correspondence. That correspondence would be with the sixteen general agents, none of it with their ten thousand canvassers.

However, it was a very nice spread that we made, as far as spaciousness and perspective went. These were impressive—that is, as impressive as nakedness long drawn out and plenty of it could be. It seemed to me that the look of the place was going to deceive country people and drive them away, and I suggested that we put up a protecting sign just inside the door: "Come in. It is not a rope walk."

It was a mistake to deal in sarcasms with Webster. They cut deep into his vanity. He hadn't a single intellectual weapon in his armory and could not fight back. It was unchivalrous in me to attack with mental weapons this mentally weaponless man, and I tried to refrain from it but couldn't. I ought to have been large enough to endure his vanities but I wasn't. I am not always large enough to endure my own. He had one defect which particularly exasperated me, because I didn't have it myself. When a matter was mentioned of which he was ignorant, he not only would not protect himself by remarking that he was not acquainted with the matter, but he had not even discretion enough to keep his tongue still. He would say something intended to deceive the hearers into the notion that he knew something about that subject himself—a most unlikely condition, since his ignorance covered the whole earth like a blanket and there was hardly a hole in it anywhere. Once in a drawing-room company some talk sprang up about George Eliot and her literature. I saw Webster getting ready to contribute. There was no way to hit him with a brick or a Bible or something and reduce him to unconsciousness and save him, because it would have attracted attention —and therefore I waited for his mountain to bring forth its mouse, which it did as soon as there was a vacancy between speeches. He filled that vacancy with this remark, uttered with tranquil complacency: "I've never read any of his books, on account of prejudice."

Before we had become fairly settled in the new quarters, Webster had suggested that we abolish the existing contract and make a new one. Very well, it was done. I probably never read it nor asked anybody else to read it. I probably merely signed it and saved myself further bother in that way. Under the preceding contracts Webster had been my paid servant; under the new one I was his slave, his absolute slave, and without salary. I owned nine-tenths of the business, I furnished all the capital, I shouldered all the losses, I was responsible for everything, but Webster was sole master. This new condition and my sarcasms changed the atmosphere. I could no longer give orders as before. I could not even make a suggestion with any considerable likelihood of its acceptance.

General Grant was a sick man but he wrought upon his memoirs like a well one and made steady and sure progress.

Webster throned himself in the rope walk and issued a summons to the sixteen general agents to come from the sixteen quarters of the United States and sign contracts. They came. They assembled. Webster delivered the law to them as from Mt. Sinai. They kept their temper wonderfully, marvelously. They furnished the bonds required. They signed the contracts and departed. Ordinarily they would have resented the young man's arrogances but this was not an ordinary case. The contracts were worth to each general agent a good many thousands of dollars. They knew this and the knowledge helped them to keep down their animosities.

Whitford was on hand. He was always at Webster's elbow. Webster was afraid to do anything without legal advice. He could have all the legal advice he wanted, because he had now hired Whitford by the year. He was paying him ten thousand dollars a year out of my pocket. And indeed Whitford was worth part of it—the two-hundredth part of it. It was the first time he had ever earned anything worth speaking of and he was content. The phrase "worth speaking of" is surplusage. Whitford had never earned anything. Whitford was never destined to earn anything. He did not earn the ten thousand dollars nor any part of it. In two instances his services proved a pecuniary damage to the firm. His other services were inconsequential and unnecessary. The bookkeeper could have performed them.

.   .   .   .   .

(June 1, 1906)

Whenever galley proofs or revises went to General Grant, a set came also to me. General Grant was aware of this. Sometimes I referred to the proofs casually, but entered into no particulars concerning them. By and by I learned through a member of the household that he was disturbed and disappointed because I had never expressed an opinion as to the literary quality of the memoirs. It was also suggested that a word of encouragement from me would be a help to him. I was as much surprised as Columbus's cook could have been to learn that Columbus wanted his opinion as to how Columbus was doing his navigating. It could not have occurred to me that General Grant could have any use for anybody's assistance or encouragement in any work which he might undertake to do. He was the most modest of men and this was another instance of it. He was venturing upon a new trade, an uncharted sea, and stood in need of the encouraging word, just like any creature of common clay. It was a great compliment that he should care for my opinion and should desire it, and I took the earliest opportunity to diplomatically turn the conversation in that direction and furnish it without seeming to lug it in by the ears.

By chance, I had been comparing the memoirs with Caesar's "Commentaries" and was qualified to deliver judgment. I was able to say in all sincerity that the same high merits distinguished both books —clarity of statement, directness, simplicity, unpretentiousness, manifest truthfulness, fairness and justice toward friend and foe alike, soldierly candor and frankness, and soldierly avoidance of flowery speech. I placed the two books side by side upon the same high level, and I still think that they belonged there. I learned afterward that General Grant was pleased with this verdict. It shows that he was just a man, just a human being, just an author. An author values a compliment even when it comes from a source of doubtful competency.

General Grant wrought heroically with his pen while his disease made its steady inroads upon his life, and at last his work stood completed. He was moved to Mount McGregor and there his strength passed gradually away. Toward the last he was not able to speak, but used a pencil and small slips of paper when he needed to say anything.

I went there to see him once toward the end, and he asked me with his pencil, and evidently with anxious solicitude, if there was a prospect that his book would make something for his family.

I said that the canvass for it was progressing vigorously, that the subscriptions and the money were coming in fast, that the campaign was not more than half completed yet—but that if it should stop where it was there would be two hundred thousand dollars coming to his family. He expressed his gratification, with his pencil.

When I was entering the house, the Confederate general, Buckner, was leaving it. Buckner and Grant had been fellow cadets at West Point, about 1840. I think they had served together in the Mexican War, a little later. After that war Grant (then a captain in the regular army) was ordered to a military post in Oregon. By and by he resigned and came East and found himself in New York penniless. On the street he met Buckner and borrowed fifty dollars of him. In February, 1862, Buckner was in command of the Confederate garrison of Fort Donelson. General Grant captured the fortress by assault and took fifteen thousand prisoners. After that, the two soldiers did not meet again until that day at Mount McGregor twenty-three years later.

Several visitors were present and there was a good deal of chaffing and joking, some of it at Buckner's expense.

Finally General Buckner said, "I have my full share of admiration and esteem for Grant. It dates back to our cadet days. He has as many merits and virtues as any man I am acquainted with but he has one deadly defect. He is an incurable borrower and when he wants to borrow he knows of only one limit —he wants what you've got. When I was poor he borrowed fifty dollars of me; when I was rich he borrowed fifteen thousand men."

General Grant died at Mount McGregor on the 23rd of July. In September or October the memoirs went to press. Several sets of plates were made; the printing was distributed among several great printing establishments; a great number of steam presses were kept running night and day on the book; several large binderies were kept at work binding it. The book was in sets of two volumes—large octavo. Its price was nine dollars in cloth. For costlier bindings the price was proportionately higher. Two thousand sets in tree-calf were issued at twenty-five dollars per set.

The book was issued on the 10th of December, and I turned out to be a competent prophet. In the beginning I had told General Grant that his book would sell six hundred thousand single volumes, and that is what happened. It sold three hundred thousand sets. The first check that went to Mrs. Grant was for two hundred thousand dollars; the next one, a few months later, was for a hundred and fifty thousand. I do not remember about the subsequent checks but I think that in the aggregate the book paid Mrs. Grant something like half a million dollars.

Webster was in his glory. In his obscure days his hat was number six and a quarter; in these latter days he was not able to get his head into a barrel. He loved to descant upon the wonders of the book. He liked to go into the statistics. He liked to tell that it took thirteen miles of gold leaf to print the gilt titles on the book backs; he liked to tell how many thousand tons the three hundred thousand sets weighed. Of course that same old natural thing happened: Webster thought it was *he* that sold the book. He thought that General Grant's great name helped but he regarded himself as the main reason of the book's prodigious success. This shows that Webster was merely human and merely a publisher. All publishers are Columbuses. The successful author is their America. The reflection that they—like Columbus—didn't discover what they expected to discover, and didn't discover what they started out to discover, doesn't trouble them. All they remember is that they discovered America; they forget that they started out to discover some patch or corner of India.

.   .   .   .   .

6. Failure of a Publisher. (June 2, 1906)

In the early days, when the general agents were being chosen, Webster conferred one of the best Western general agencies upon an ex-preacher, a professional revivalist whom God had deposited in Iowa for improprieties of one kind and another which had been committed by that State. All the other candidates for agencies warned Webster to keep out of that man's hands, assuring him that no sagacities of Whitford or anybody else would be able to defeat that revivalist's inborn proclivity to steal. Their persuasions went for nothing. Webster gave him the agency. We furnished him the books. He did a thriving trade. He collected a gross sum of thirty-six thousand dollars and Webster never got a cent of it.

It is no great marvel to me that Mrs. Grant got a matter of half a million dollars out of that book. The miracle is that it didn't run her into debt. It was fortunate for her that we had only one Webster. It was an unnatural oversight in me that I didn't hunt for another one.

Let me try to bring this painful business to a close. One of the things which poisoned Webster's days and nights was the aggravating circumstance that whereas he, Charles L. Webster, was the great publisher—the greatest of publishers—and my name did not appear anywhere as a member of the firm, the public persisted in regarding me as the substance of that firm and Webster the shadow. Everybody who had a book to publish offered it to me, not to Webster. I accepted several excellent books but Webster declined them every time, and he was master. But if anybody offered *him* a book, he was so charmed with the compliment that he took the book without examining it. He was not able to get hold of one that could make its living.

Joe Jefferson wrote me and said he had written his autobiography and he would like me to be the publisher. Of course I wanted the book. I sent his letter to Webster and asked him to arrange the

matter. Webster did not decline the book. He simply ignored it and brushed the matter out of his
mind. He accepted and published two or three war
books that furnished no profit. He accepted still another one: distributed the agency contracts for it,
named its price (three dollars and a half in cloth)
and also agreed to have the book ready by a certain
date, two or three months ahead. One day I went
down to New York and visited the office and asked
for a sight of that book. I asked Webster how
many thousand words it contained. He said he didn't
know. I asked him to count the words, by rough
estimate. He did it. I said, "It doesn't contain words
enough for the price and dimensions, by four-fifths.
You will have to pad it with a brick. We must start
a brickyard, and right away, because it is much
cheaper to make bricks than it is to buy them in the
market."

It set him in a fury. Any little thing like that would
have that effect. He was one of the most sensitive
creatures I ever saw, for the quality of the material
that he was made of.

He had several books on hand—worthless books
which he had accepted because they had been offered
to him instead of to me—and I found that he had
never counted the words in any of them. He had
taken them without examination. Webster was a
good general agent but he knew nothing about publishing, and he was incapable of learning anything
about it. By and by I found that he had agreed to
resurrect Henry Ward Beecher's *Life of Christ*. I
suggested that he ought to have tried for Lazarus,
because that had been tried once and we knew it

could be done. He was exasperated again. He certainly was the most sensitive creature that ever was, for his make. He had also advanced to Mr. Beecher, who was not in prosperous circumstances at the time, five thousand dollars on the future royalties. Mr. Beecher was to revamp the book—or rather I think he was to finish the book. I think he had just issued the first of the two volumes of which it was to consist when that ruinous scandal broke out and suffocated the enterprise. I think the second volume had not been written and that Mr. Beecher was now undertaking to write it. If he failed to accomplish this within a given time he was to return the money. He did not succeed and the money was eventually returned.

Webster kept back a book of mine, *A Connecticut Yankee in King Arthur's Court*, as long as he could and finally published it so surreptitiously that it took two or three years to find out that there was any such book. He suppressed a compilation made by Howells and me, *The Library of Humor,* so long and finally issued it so clandestinely that I doubt if anybody in America ever did find out that there was such a book.

William M. Laffan told me that Mr. Walters, of Baltimore, was going to have a sumptuous book made which should illustrate in detail his princely art collection; that he was going to bring the best artists from Paris to make the illustrations; that he was going to make the book himself and see to it that it was made exactly to his taste; that he was going to spend a quarter of a million dollars on it; that he wanted it issued at a great price—a price consonant with its sumptuous character, and that he wanted no penny of the proceeds. The publisher would have nothing to do but distribute the book and take the whole of the profit.

Laffan said, "There, Mark, you can make a fortune out of that without any trouble at all, and without risk or expense."

I said I would send Webster down to Baltimore at once. I tried to do it but I never succeeded. Webster never touched the matter in any way whatever. If it had been a secondhand dog that Mr. Walters wanted published, he would have only needed to apply to Webster. Webster would have broken his neck getting down to Baltimore to annex that dog. But Mr. Walters had applied to the wrong man. Webster's pride was hurt and he would not look at Mr. Walters's book. Webster had immense pride but he was short of other talents.

Webster was the victim of a cruel neuralgia in the head. He eased his pain with the new German drug, phenacetine. The physicians limited his use of it but he found a way to get it in quantity: under our free institutions anybody can poison himself that wants to and will pay the price. He took this drug with increasing frequency and in increasing quantity. It stupefied him and he went about as one in a dream. He ceased from coming to the office except at intervals, and when he came he was pretty sure to exercise his authority in ways perilous for the business. In his condition, he was not responsible for his acts.

Something had to be done. Whitford explained that there was no way to get rid of this dangerous element except by buying Webster out. But what was there to buy? Webster had always promptly collected any money that was due him. He had squandered, long ago, my share of the book's profit—a hundred thousand dollars. The business was gasping, dying. The whole of it was not worth a dollar and a half. Then what would be a fair price for me to pay for a tenth interest in it? After much consultation and much correspondence, it transpired that Webster would be willing to put up with twelve thousand dollars and step out. I furnished the check.

Webster's understudy and business manager had now been for some time a young fellow named Frederick J. Hall, another Dunkirk importation. We got all our talent from that stud farm at Dunkirk. Poor Hall meant well but he was wholly incompetent for the place. He carried it along for a time with the heroic hopefulness of youth, but there was an obstruction which was bound to defeat him sooner or later. It was this:

Stedman, the poet, had made a compilation, several years earlier, called *The Library of American Literature*—nine or ten octavo volumes. A publisher in Cincinnati had tried to make it succeed. It swallowed up that publisher, family and all. If Stedman had offered me the book I should have said "Sold by subscription and on the installment plan, there is nothing in this book for us at a royalty above four per cent, but in fact it would swamp us at any kind of royalty, because such a book would require a cash capital of several hundred thousand dollars, and we haven't a hundred thousand."

But Stedman didn't bring the book to me. He took

it to Webster. Webster was delighted and flattered. He accepted the book on an eight per cent royalty, and thereby secured the lingering suicide of Charles L. Webster and Company. We struggled along two or three years under that deadly load. After Webster's time, poor little Hall struggled along with it and got to borrowing money of a bank in which Whitford was a director—borrowing on notes endorsed by me and renewed from time to time. These notes used to come to me in Italy for renewals. I endorsed them without examining them, and sent them back. At last I found that additions had been made to the borrowings, without my knowledge or consent. I began to feel troubled. I wrote Mr. Hall about it and said I would like to have an exhaustive report of the condition of the business. The next mail brought that exhaustive report, whereby it appeared that the concern's assets exceeded its liabilities by ninety-two thousand dollars. Then I felt better. But there was no occasion to feel better, for the report ought to have read the other way. Poor Hall soon wrote to say that we needed more money and must have it right away or the concern would fail.

I sailed for New York. I emptied into the till twenty-four thousand dollars which I had earned with the pen. I looked around to see where we could borrow money. There wasn't any place. This was in the midst of the fearful panic of '93. I went up to Hartford to borrow—couldn't borrow a penny. I offered to mortgage our house and grounds and furniture for any small loan. The property had cost a hundred and sixty-seven thousand dollars, and seemed good for a small loan. Henry Robinson said,

"Clemens, I give you my word, you can't borrow three thousand dollars on that property." Very well, I knew that if that was so, I couldn't borrow it on a basketful of government bonds.

Webster and Company failed. The firm owed me about sixty thousand dollars, borrowed money. It owed Mrs. Clemens sixty-five thousand dollars, borrowed money. Also it owed ninety-six creditors an average of a thousand dollars or so apiece. The panic had stopped Mrs. Clemens's income. It had stopped my income from my books. We had but nine thousand dollars in the bank. We hadn't a penny wherewith to pay the Webster creditors. Henry Robinson said, "Hand over everything belonging to Webster and Company to the creditors, and ask them to accept that in liquidation of the debts. They'll do it. You'll see that they'll do it. They are aware that you are not individually responsible for those debts, that the responsibility rests upon the firm as a firm."

I didn't think much of that way out of the difficulty and when I made my report to Mrs. Clemens she wouldn't hear of it at all. She said, "This is my house. The creditors shall have it. Your books are your property—turn them over to the creditors. Reduce the indebtedness in every way you can think of —then get to work and earn the rest of the indebtedness, if your life is spared. And don't be afraid. We shall pay a hundred cents on the dollar yet."

It was sound prophecy. Mr. Rogers stepped in, about this time, and preached to the creditors. He said they could not have Mrs. Clemens's house— that she must be a preferred creditor and would give up the Webster notes for sixty-five thousand dollars, money borrowed of her. He said they could not have my books, that they were not an asset of Webster and Company, that the creditors could have everything that belonged to Webster and Company, that I would wipe from the slate the sixty thousand dollars I had lent to the Company, and that I would now make it my task to earn the rest of the Webster indebtedness, if I could, and pay a hundred cents on the dollar—but that this must not be regarded as a promise.

In a conversation with Mr. Rogers and a couple of lawyers, in those days, one of the men said, "Not five per cent of the men who become ruined at fifty-eight ever recover." Another said, with enthusiasm, "Five per cent! None of them ever recovers." It made me feel very sick.

That was in '94, I believe—though it may have been in the beginning of '95. However, Mrs. Clemens and Clara and I started, on the 15th of July, 1895, on our lecturing raid around the world. We lectured and robbed and raided for thirteen months. I wrote a book and published it. I sent the book money and lecture money to Mr. Rogers as fast as we captured it. He banked it and saved it up for the creditors. We implored him to pay off the smaller creditors straightway, for they needed the money, but he wouldn't do it. He said that when I had milked the world dry we would take the result and distribute it *pro rata* among the Webster people.

At the end of '98 or the beginning of '99 Mr. Rogers cabled me, at Vienna, "The creditors have all been paid a hundred cents on the dollar. There is eighteen thousand five hundred dollars left. What shall I do with it?"

I answered, "Put it in Federal Steel"—which he did, all except a thousand dollars, and took it out again in two months with a profit of a hundred and twenty-five per cent.

There—Thanks be! A hundred times I have tried to tell this intolerable story with a pen, but I never could do it. It always made me sick before I got half-way to the middle of it. But this time I have held my grip and walked the floor and emptied it all out of my system, and I hope to never hear of it again.

IN A WRITER'S WORKSHOP

1. When a Book Gets Tired. (August 30, 1906)[1]

There has never been a time in the past thirty-five years when my literary shipyard hadn't two or more half-finished ships on the ways, neglected and baking in the sun; generally there have been three or four; at present there are five. This has an unbusiness-like look but it was not purposeless, it was intentional. As long as a book would write itself I was a faithful and interested amanuensis and my industry did not flag, but the minute that the book tried to shift to *my* head the labor of contriving its situations, inventing its adventures and conducting its conversations, I put it away and dropped it out of my mind. Then I examined my unfinished properties to see if among them there might not be one whose interest in itself had revived through a couple of years' restful idleness and was ready to take me on again as amanuensis.

It was by accident that I found out that a book is pretty sure to get tired, along about the middle, and refuse to go on with its work until its powers and its interest should have been refreshed by a rest and its depleted stock of raw materials reinforced by lapse of time. It was when I had reached the middle of

[1] Published, somewhat abbreviated, in *Harper's* for August, 1922.

Tom Sawyer that I made this invaluable find. At page 400 of my manuscript the story made a sudden and determined halt and refused to proceed another step. Day after day it still refused. I was disappointed, distressed and immeasurably astonished, for I knew quite well that the tale was not finished and I could not understand why I was not able to go on with it. The reason was very simple—my tank had run dry; it was empty; the stock of materials in it was exhausted; the story could not go on without materials; it could not be wrought out of nothing.

When the manuscript had lain in a pigeonhole two years I took it out one day and read the last chapter that I had written. It was then that I made the great discovery that when the tank runs dry you've only to leave it alone and it will fill up again in time, while you are asleep—also while you are at work at other things and are quite unaware that this unconscious and profitable cerebration is going on. There was plenty of material now, and the book went on and finished itself without any trouble.

Ever since then, when I have been writing a book I have pigeonholed it without misgivings when its tank ran dry, well knowing that it would fill up again without any of my help within the next two or three years, and that then the work of completing it would be simple and easy. *The Prince and the Pauper* struck work in the middle because the tank was dry, and I did not touch it again for two years. A dry interval of two years occurred in *A Connecticut Yankee in King Arthur's Court*. A like interval had occurred in the middle of other books of mine. Two similar intervals have occurred in a story of mine

called "Which Was It?" In fact, the second interval
has gone considerably over time, for it is now four
years since that second one intruded itself. I am sure
that the tank is full again now and that I could take
up that book and write the other half of it without
a break or any lapse of interest—but I shan't do it.
The pen is irksome to me. I was born lazy, and dic-
tating has spoiled me. I am quite sure I shall never
touch a pen again; therefore that book will remain
unfinished—a pity, too, for the idea of it is (actually) new and would spring a handsome surprise
upon the reader at the end.

There is another unfinished book, which I should
probably entitle "The Refuge of the Derelicts." It
is half finished, and will remain so. There is still
another one, entitled "The Adventures of a Microbe
During Three Thousand Years—by a Microbe." It
is half finished and will remain so. There is yet another—*The Mysterious Stranger*.[2] It is more than
half finished. I would dearly like to finish it, and
it causes me a real pang to reflect that it is not to
be. These several tanks are full now, and those books

[2] Actually, he had finished *The Mysterious Stranger* a year before this date, though perhaps not aware that he had. Albert Bigelow Paine's greatest service to Mark Twain was to recognize
that the last chapter of an earlier version of the book was the
right ending for the final version which Mark had abandoned
unfinished.

In this passage Mark touches on a mysterious and agonizing
experience. "Which Was It?" (sometimes called "Which Was the
Dream?") was written in a period of frustration and failing
powers, following the catastrophes that struck him in the 1890's.
In it the theme of *The Mysterious Stranger* is present but fails to
germinate. He tried repeatedly to finish it but always failed. (See
the Easy Chair, *Harper's Magazine,* for January, 1940.) At least
one Tom Sawyer manuscript was related to the same effort. So,
very likely, was the book about the microbes, traces of which seem
to survive in an early version of *The Mysterious Stranger*.

would go gaily along and complete themselves if I
would hold the pen, but I am tired of the pen.

There was another of these half-finished stories. I
carried it as far as thirty-eight thousand words four
years ago, then destroyed it for fear I might some
day finish it. Huck Finn was the teller of the story,
and of course Tom Sawyer and Jim were the heroes
of it. But I believed that that trio had done work
enough in this world and were entitled to a permanent rest.

There are some books that refuse to be written.
They stand their ground year after year and will
not be persuaded. It isn't because the book is not
there and worth being written—it is only because
the right form for the story does not present itself.
There is only one right form for a story, and if you
fail to find that form the story will not tell itself.
You may try a dozen wrong forms but in each case
you will not get very far before you discover that
you have not found the right one—then that story
will always stop and decline to go any further. In
the story of *Joan of Arc* I made six wrong starts,
and each time that I offered the result to Mrs.
Clemens she responded with the same deadly criticism—silence. She didn't say a word but her silence
spoke with the voice of thunder. When at last I
found the right form I recognized at once that it
was the right one, and I knew what she would say.
She said it, without doubt or hesitation.

In the course of twelve years I made six attempts
to tell a simple little story which I knew would tell
itself in four hours if I could ever find the right
starting point. I scored six failures; then one day in
London I offered the text of the story to Robert Mc-

Clure and proposed that he publish that text in the magazine and offer a prize to the person who should tell it best. I became greatly interested and went on talking upon the text for half an hour; then he said, "You have told the story yourself. You have nothing to do but put it on paper just as you have told it."

I recognized that this was true. At the end of four hours it was finished, and quite to my satisfaction. So it took twelve years and four hours to produce that little bit of a story, which I have called "The Death Wafer."

To start right is certainly an essential. I have proved this too many times to doubt it. Twenty-five or thirty years ago I began a story which was to turn upon the marvels of mental telegraphy. A man was to invent a scheme whereby he could synchronize two minds, thousands of miles apart, and enable them to freely converse together through the air without the aid of a wire. Four times I started it in the wrong way and it wouldn't go. Three times I discovered my mistake after writing about a hundred pages. I discovered it the fourth time when I had written four hundred pages—then I gave it up and put the whole thing in the fire.

.   .   .   .   .

2. Humorists. (July 31, 1906)

The Western pirate of whom Duneka[3] had heard rumor has really published his book and my copy-

---

[3] F. A. Duneka was vice-president of Harper & Brothers, Mark Twain's publishers. The allusion is to a spurious reprint of *Mark Twain's Library of Humor*, an anthology edited by Howells and Charles H. Clark under Mark's supervision and first published by Mark's own firm.

right lawyer has sent me a copy of it—a great fat, coarse, offensive volume, not with my name on it as perpetrator but with its back inflamed with a big picture of me in lurid colors, placed there, of course, to indicate that I am the author of the crime. This book is a very interesting curiosity, in one way. It reveals the surprising fact that within the compass of these forty years wherein I have been playing professional humorist before the public, I have had for company seventy-eight other American humorists. Each and every one of the seventy-eight rose in my time, became conspicuous and popular, and by and by vanished. A number of these names were as familiar in their day as are the names of George Ade and Dooley today—yet they have all so completely passed from sight now that there is probably not a youth of fifteen years of age in the country whose eye would light with recognition at the mention of any one of the seventy-eight names.

This book is a cemetery; and as I glance through it I am reminded of my visit to the cemetery in Hannibal, Missouri, four years ago, where almost every tombstone recorded a forgotten name that had been familiar and pleasant to my ear when I was a boy there fifty years before. In this mortuary volume I find Nasby, Artemus Ward, Yawcob Strauss, Derby, Burdette, Eli Perkins, the "Danbury News Man," Orpheus C. Kerr, Smith O'Brien, Josh Billings, and a score of others, maybe two score, whose writings and sayings were once in everybody's mouth but are now heard of no more and are no longer mentioned. Seventy-eight seems an incredible crop of well-known humorists for one forty-year period to

have produced, and yet this book has not harvested
the entire crop—far from it. It has no mention of Ike
Partington, once so welcome and so well known; it
has no mention of Doesticks, nor of the Pfaff crowd,
nor of Artemus Ward's numerous and perishable
imitators, nor of three very popular Southern humorists whose names I am not able to recall, nor of a
dozen other sparkling transients whose light shone
for a time but has now, years ago, gone out.

Why have they perished? Because they were
merely humorists. Humorists of the "mere" sort cannot survive. Humor is only a fragrance, a decoration.
Often it is merely an odd trick of speech and of
spelling, as in the case of Ward and Billings and
Nasby and the "Disbanded Volunteer," and presently the fashion passes and the fame along with it.
There are those who say a novel should be a work of
art solely, and you must not preach in it, you must
not teach in it. That may be true as regards novels
but it is not true as regards humor. Humor must not
professedly teach, and it must not professedly preach,
but it must do both if it would live forever. By forever, I mean thirty years. With all its preaching it
is not likely to outlive so long a term as that. The
very things it preaches about, and which are novelties when it preaches about them, can cease to be
novelties and become commonplaces in thirty years.
Then that sermon can thenceforth interest no one.

I have always preached. That is the reason that
I have lasted thirty years. If the humor came of its
own accord and uninvited, I have allowed it a place
in my sermon, but I was not writing the sermon for
the sake of the humor. I should have written the

sermon just the same, whether any humor applied for admission or not. I am saying these vain things in this frank way because I am a dead person speaking from the grave. Even I would be too modest to say them in life. I think we never become really and genuinely our entire and honest selves until we are dead—and not then until we have been dead years and years. People ought to start dead, and then they would be honest so much earlier.

.   .   .   .   .

3. "1601."

Among the letters awaiting me when I got back from New York was this one:

Cleveland, June 28, 1906.

My dear Sir:

Having seen some letters of the late John Hay, copies of which I enclose, I am somewhat anxious to know the title of the piece mentioned, or whether it is printed in your published writings.

Did you know Alexander Gunn, to whom Hay's letters were addressed?

An answer at your convenience will greatly oblige,

Very truly yours,

Chas. Orr.

The letters referred to by Mr. Orr are the following:

June 21, 1880.

Dear Gunn:

Are you in Cleveland for all this week? If you will say yes by return mail I have a masterpiece to submit to your consideration which is only in my hands for a few days.

Yours, very much worritted by the depravity of Christendom,

Hay.

Letter number two discloses Hay's own high opinion of the effort and his deep concern for its safety.

June 24, 1880.

My dear Gunn:

Here it is. It was written by Mark Twain in a serious effort to bring back our literature and philosophy to the sober and chaste Elizabethan standard. But the taste of the present day is too corrupt for any thing so classic. He has not yet been able even to find a publisher. The Globe has not yet recovered from Downey's inroad, and they won't touch it.

I send it to you as one of the few lingering relics of that race of appreciative critics who know a good thing when they see it.

Read it with reverence and gratitude and send it back to me; for Mark is impatient to see once more his wandering offspring.

Yours,
Hay.

Number three makes it quite clear that Gunn had confirmed the judgment of Hay.

Washington, D. C., July 7, 1880.

My dear Gunn:

I have your letter, and the proposition which you make to pull a few proofs of the masterpiece is highly attractive, and of course highly immoral. I cannot properly consent to it, and I am afraid the great man would think I was taking an unfair advantage of his confidence. Please send back the document as soon as you can, and if, in spite of my prohibition, you take these proofs, save me one.

Very truly yours,
John Hay.

I replied to Mr. Orr as follows:

Dublin, New Hampshire
July 30, 1906.

Dear Mr. Orr:

I cannot thank you enough for sending me copies of John Hay's notes to Mr. Gunn. In the matter of humor, what an unsurpassable touch John Hay had! I may have known Alexander Gunn in those ancient days, but the name does not sound familiar to me.

The title of the piece is "1601." The piece is a supposititious conversation which takes place in Queen Elizabeth's closet in that year, between the Queen and Shakespeare, Ben Jonson, Francis Bacon, Beaumont, Sir Walter Raleigh, the Duchess of Bilgewater, and one or two others; and is not—as John Hay mistakenly supposes—"a serious effort to bring back our literature and philosophy to the sober and chaste Elizabethan standard"; no, the object was only a serious attempt to reveal to Rev. Joe Twichell the picturesqueness of parlor conversation in Elizabeth's time; therefore if there is a decent or delicate word findable in it, it is because I overlooked it. I hasten to assure you that it is *not* printed in my published writings.

1601 was so be-praised by the archeological scholars of a quarter of a century ago, that I was rather inordinately vain of it. At that time it had been privately printed in several countries, among them Japan. A sumptuous edition on large paper, rough-edged, was made by Lieut. C. E. S. Wood at West Point—an edition of 50 copies—and distributed among popes and kings and such people. In England copies of that issue were worth 20 guineas when I was there six years ago, and none to be had. I thank you again, and am,

Yours very truly,
S. L. Clemens.

Dear me, but John Hay's letters do carry me back over a long stretch of time! Joe Twichell's head was black then; mine was brown. Today both are as white and sparkly as a London footman's.

1601 was a letter which I wrote to Twichell, about 1876, from my study at Quarry Farm one summer day when I ought to have been better employed. I remember the incident very well. I had been diligently reading up for a story which I was minded to write, *The Prince and the Pauper*. I was reading ancient English books with the purpose of saturating myself with archaic English to a degree which would enable me to do plausible imitations of it in a fairly easy and unlabored way. In one of these old books I came across a brief conversation which powerfully impressed me, as I had never been impressed before, with the frank indelicacies of speech permissible among ladies and gentlemen in that ancient time. I was thus powerfully impressed because this conversation seemed real, whereas that kind of talk had not seemed real to me before. It had merely seemed Rabelaisian—exaggerated, artificial, made up by the author for his passing needs. It had not seemed to me that the blushful passages in Shakespeare were of a sort which Shakespeare had actually heard people use but were inventions of his own, liberties which he had taken with the facts under the protection of a poet's license.

But here at last was one of those dreadful conversations which commended itself to me as being absolutely real, and as being the kind of talk which ladies and gentlemen did actually indulge in in those pleasant and lamented ancient days now gone from us forever. I was immediately full of a desire to practice my archaics, and contrive one of those stir-

ring conversations out of my own head. I thought I
would practice on Twichell. I have always practiced doubtful things on Twichell from the beginning, thirty-nine years ago.

So I contrived that meeting of the illustrious personages in Queen Elizabeth's private parlor, and
started a most picturesque and lurid and scandalous
conversation between them. The Queen's cupbearer,
a dried-up old nobleman, was present to take down
the talk—not that he wanted to do it but because it
was the Queen's desire and he had to. He loathed all
those people because they were of offensively low
birth, and because they hadn't a thing to recommend
them except their incomparable brains. He dutifully
set down everything they said, and commented upon
their words and their manners with bitter scorn and
indignation. I put into the Queen's mouth, and into
the mouths of those other people, grossnesses not
to be found outside of Rabelais, perhaps. I made
their stateliest remarks reek with them, and all this
was charming to me—delightful, delicious—but
their charm was as nothing to that which was afforded me by that outraged old cupbearer's comments upon them.

It is years since I have seen a copy of *1601*. I
wonder if it would be as funny to me now as it was
in those comparatively youthful days when I wrote
it. It made a fat letter. I bundled it up and mailed
it to Twichell in Hartford. And in the fall, when we
returned to our home in Hartford and Twichell and
I resumed the Saturday ten-mile walk to Talcott
Tower and back, every Saturday, as had been our
custom for years, we used to carry that letter along.

There was a grove of hickory trees by the roadside, six miles out, and close by it was the only place in that whole region where the fringed gentian grew. On our return from the Tower we used to gather the gentians, then lie down on the grass upon the golden carpet of fallen hickory leaves and get out that letter and read it by the help of these poetical surroundings. We used to laugh ourselves lame and sore over the cupbearer's troubles. I wonder if we could laugh over them now? We were so young then! —and maybe there was not so much to laugh at in the letter as we thought there was.

However, in the winter Dean Sage came to Twichell's on a visit, and Twichell, who was never able to keep a secret when he knew it ought to be revealed, showed him the letter. Sage carried it off. He was greatly tickled with it himself, and he wanted to know how it might affect other people. He was under the seal of confidence and could not show the letter to anyone—still he wanted to try it on a dog, as the stage phrase is, and he dropped it in the aisle of the smoking car accidentally and sat down near by to wait for results. The letter traveled from group to group around the car and when he finally went and claimed it, he was convinced that it possessed literary merit. So he got a dozen copies privately printed in Brooklyn. He sent one to David Gray in Buffalo, one to a friend in Japan, one to Lord Houghton in England, and one to a Jewish Rabbi in Albany, a very learned man and an able critic and lover of old-time literatures.

1601 was privately printed in Japan and in England, and by and by we began to hear from it. The learned Rabbi said it was a masterpiece in its verities and in its imitation of the obsolete English of Elizabeth's day. And the praises delivered to me by the poet, David Gray, were very precious. He said, "Put your name to it. Don't be ashamed of it. It is a great and fine piece of literature and deserves to live, and will live. Your *Innocents Abroad* will presently be forgotten, but this will survive. Don't be ashamed; don't be afraid. Leave the command in your will that your heirs shall put on your tombstone these words, and these alone: '*He wrote the immortal 1601.*'"

When we sailed for Europe in 1891 I left those sumptuous West Point copies hidden away in a drawer of my study, where I thought they would be safe. We were gone nearly ten years, and whenever anybody wanted a copy I promised it—the promise to be made good when we should return to America. In Berlin I promised one to Rudolph Lindau, of the Foreign Office. He still lives, but I have not been able to make that promise good. I promised one to Mommsen and one to William Walter Phelps, who was our Minister at the Berlin court. These are dead, but maybe they don't miss *1601* where they are. When I went lecturing around the globe I promised *1601* pretty liberally, these promises all to be made good when I should return home.

In 1890 I had published in *Harper's Monthly* a sketch called "Luck," the particulars of which had been furnished to Twichell by a visiting English army chaplain. The next year, in Rome, an English gentleman introduced himself to me on the street and said "Do you know who the chief figure in that

'Luck' sketch is?" "No," I said, "I don't." "Well," he said, "it is Lord Wolseley—and don't you go to England if you value your scalp." In Venice another English gentleman said the same to me. These gentlemen said, "Of course Wolseley is not to blame for the stupendous luck that has chased him up ever since he came shining out of Sandhurst in that most unexpected and victorious way, but he will recognize himself in that sketch, and so will everybody else, and if you venture into England he will destroy you."

In 1900, in London, I went to the Fourth of July banquet, arriving after eleven o'clock at night at a time when the place was emptying itself. Choate was presiding. An English admiral was speaking, and some two or three hundred men were still present. I was to speak, and I moved along down behind the chairs which had been occupied by guests, toward Choate. These chairs were now empty. When I had reached within three chairs of Choate, a handsome man put out his hand and said "Stop. Sit down here. I want to get acquainted with you. I am Lord Wolseley." I was falling but he caught me, and I explained that I was often taken that way. We sat and chatted together and had a very good time— and he asked me for a copy of *1601* and I was very glad to get off so easy. I said he should have it as soon as I reached home.

We reached home the next year, and not a sign of those precious masterpieces could be found on the premises anywhere. And so all those promises remain unfulfilled to this day. Two or three days ago I found out that they have reappeared and are safe in our

house in New York. But I shall not make any of
those promises good until I shall have had an opportunity to examine that masterpiece and see whether
it really is a masterpiece or not. I have my doubts,
though I had none a quarter of a century ago. In
that day I believed *1601* was inspired.

.   .   .   .   .

4. "A Connecticut Yankee." (December 5, 1906)

A Connecticut Yankee in King Arthur's Court was
an attempt to imagine, and after a fashion set forth,
the hard conditions of life for the laboring and de-
fenseless poor in bygone times in England, and incidentally contrast these conditions with those under
which the civil and ecclesiastical pets of privilege and
high fortune lived in those times. I think I was purposing to contrast that English life, not just the
English life of Arthur's day but the English life of
the whole of the Middle Ages, with the life of modern Christendom and modern civilization—to the advantage of the latter, of course. That advantage is
still claimable and does creditably and handsomely
exist everywhere in Christendom—if we leave out
Russia and the royal palace of Belgium.

The royal palace of Belgium is still what it has
been for fourteen years, the den of a wild beast,
King Leopold II, who for money's sake mutilates,
murders, and starves half a million of friendless and
helpless poor natives in the Congo State every year,
and does it by the silent consent of all the Christian
powers except England, none of them lifting a hand
or a voice to stop these atrocities, although thirteen
of them are by solemn treaty pledged to the pro-

tecting and uplifting of those wretched natives. In fourteen years Leopold has deliberately destroyed more lives than have suffered death on all the battle-fields of this planet for the past thousand years. In this vast statement I am well within the mark, several millions of lives within the mark. It is curious that the most advanced and most enlightened century of all the centuries the sun has looked upon should have the ghastly distinction of having pro-duced this moldy and piety-mouthing hypocrite, this bloody monster whose mate is not findable in human history anywhere, and whose personality will surely shame hell itself when he arrives there—which will be soon, let us hope and trust.

The conditions under which the poor lived in the Middle Ages were hard enough, but those conditions were heaven itself as compared with those which have obtained in the Congo State for these past four-teen years. I have mentioned Russia. Cruel and piti-ful as was life throughout Christendom in the Middle Ages, it was not as cruel, not as pitiful, as is life in Russia today. In Russia, for three centuries, the vast population has been ground under the heels, and for the sole and sordid advantage, of a procession of crowned assassins and robbers who have all deserved the gallows. Russia's hundred and thirty millions of miserable subjects are much worse off today than were the poor of the Middle Ages whom we so pity. We are accustomed now to speak of Russia as medieval and as standing still in the Middle Ages but that is flattery. Russia is way back of the Middle Ages; the Middle Ages are a long way in front of her and she is not likely to catch up with them so long as the Czardom continues to exist.

.　　.　　.　　.　　.

5. *Platform Readings.* *(October 10, 1907)*

What is called a "reading," as a public platform entertainment, was first essayed by Charles Dickens, I think. He brought the idea with him from England in 1867. He had made it very popular at home and he made it so acceptable and so popular in America that his houses were crowded everywhere, and in a single season he earned two hundred thousand dollars. I heard him once during that season; it was in Steinway Hall, in December, and it made the fortune of my life—not in dollars, I am not thinking of dollars; it made the real fortune of my life in that it made the happiness of my life; on that day I called at the St. Nicholas Hotel to see my *Quaker City* Excursion shipmate, Charley Langdon, and was introduced to a sweet and timid and lovely young girl, his sister. The family went to the Dickens reading, and I accompanied them. It was forty years ago; from that day to this the sister has never been out of my mind nor heart.

Mr. Dickens read scenes from his printed books. From my distance, he was a small and slender figure, rather fancifully dressed, and striking and picturesque in appearance. He wore a black velvet coat with a large and glaring red flower in the buttonhole. He stood under a red upholstered shed behind whose slant was a row of strong lights—just such an arrangement as artists use to concentrate a strong light upon a great picture. Dickens's audience sat in a pleasant twilight, while he performed in the powerful light cast upon him from the concealed lamps. He read with great force and animation, in the lively passages, and with stirring effect. It will be understood that he did not merely read but also acted. His reading of the storm scene in which Steerforth lost his life was so vivid, and so full of energetic action, that his house was carried off its feet, so to speak.

Dickens had set a fashion which others tried to follow, but I do not remember that anyone was any more than temporarily successful in it. The public reading was discarded after a time and was not resumed until something more than twenty years after Dickens had introduced it; then it rose and struggled along for a while in that curious and artless industry called Authors' Readings. When Providence had had enough of that kind of crime the Authors' Readings ceased from troubling and left the world at peace.

Lecturing and reading were quite different things; the lecturer didn't use notes or manuscript or book, but got his lecture by heart and delivered it night after night in the same words during the whole lecture season of four winter months. The lecture field had been a popular one all over the country for many years when I entered it in 1868; it was then at the top of its popularity; in every town there was an organization of citizens who occupied themselves in the off season, every year, in arranging for a course of lectures for the coming winter; they chose their platform people from the Boston Lecture Agency list and they chose according to the town's size and ability to pay the prices. The course usually

consisted of eight or ten lectures. All that was
wanted was that it should pay expenses; that it should
come out with a money balance at the end of the
season was not required. Very small towns had to
put up with fifty-dollar men and women, with one
or two second-class stars at a hundred dollars each
as an attraction; big towns employed hundred-dollar
men and women altogether, and added John B.
Gough, or Henry Ward Beecher, or Anna Dickinson, or Wendell Phillips, as a compelling attraction;
large cities employed this whole battery of stars.
Anna Dickinson's price was four hundred dollars a
night; so was Henry Ward Beecher's; so was
Gough's, when he didn't charge five or six hundred.
I don't remember Wendell Phillips's price but it
was high.

I remained in the lecture field three seasons—long
enough to learn the trade; then domesticated myself
in my new married estate after a weary life of
wandering, and remained under shelter at home for
fourteen or fifteen years. Meantime, speculators and
money-makers had taken up the business of hiring
lecturers, with the idea of getting rich at it. In about
five years they killed that industry dead and when I
returned to the platform for a season, in 1884,
there had been a happy and holy silence for ten
years, and a generation had come to the front who
knew nothing about lectures and readings and didn't
know how to take them nor what to make of them.
They were difficult audiences, those untrained squads,
and Cable and I had a hard time with them sometimes.

Cable had been scouting the country alone for

three years with readings from his novels, and he
had been a good reader in the beginning for he had
been born with a natural talent for it, but unhappily
he prepared himself for his public work by taking
lessons from a teacher of elocution, and so by the
time he was ready to begin his platform work he
was so well and thoroughly educated that he was
merely theatrical and artificial and not half as pleasing and entertaining to a house as he had been in
the splendid days of his ignorance. I had never tried
reading as a trade and I wanted to try it. I hired
Major Pond on a percentage to conduct me over the
country, and I hired Cable as a helper at six hundred
dollars a week and expenses, and we started out on
our venture.

It was ghastly! At least in the beginning. I had
selected my readings well enough, but had not studied them. I supposed it would only be necessary to do
like Dickens—get out on the platform and read from
the book. I did that and made a botch of it. Written
things are not for speech; their form is literary; they
are stiff, inflexible, and will not lend themselves to
happy and effective delivery with the tongue—where
their purpose is to merely entertain, not instruct;
they have to be limbered up, broken up, colloquial-
ized, and turned into the common forms of unpre-
meditated talk—otherwise they will bore the house,
not entertain it. After a week's experience with the
book I laid it aside and never carried it to the platform again; but meantime I had memorized those
pieces, and in delivering them from the platform
they soon transformed themselves into flexible talk,

with all their obstructing precisenesses and formalities gone out of them for good.

One of the readings which I used was a part of an extravagant chapter in dialect from *Roughing It* which I entitled "His Grandfather's Old Ram." After I had memorized it it began to undergo changes on the platform and it continued to edit and revise itself, night after night, until by and by, from dreading to begin on it before an audience I came to like it and enjoy it. I never knew how considerable the changes had been when I finished the season's work; I never knew until ten or eleven years later, when I took up that book in a parlor in New York one night to read that chapter to a dozen friends of the two sexes who had asked for it. It *wouldn't read*— that is, it wouldn't read aloud. I struggled along with it for five minutes and then gave it up and said I should have to tell the tale as best I might from memory. It turned out that my memory was equal to the emergency; it reproduced the platform form of the story pretty faithfully, after that interval of years. I still remember that .form of it, I think, and I wish to recite it here, so that the reader may compare it with the story as told in *Roughing It*, if he pleases, and note how different the spoken version is from the written and printed version.

The idea of the tale is to exhibit certain bad effects of a good memory: the sort of memory which is too good, which remembers everything and forgets nothing, which has no sense of proportion and can't tell an important event from an unimportant one but preserves them all, states them all, and thus retards the progress of a narrative, at the same time making a tangled, inextricable confusion of it and intolerably wearisome to the listener. The historian of "His Grandfather's Old Ram" had that kind of a memory. He often tried to communicate that history to his comrades, the other surface miners, but he could never complete it because his memory defeated his every attempt to march a straight course; it persistently threw remembered details in his way that had nothing to do with the tale; these unrelated details would interest him and sidetrack him; if he came across a name or a family or any other thing that had nothing to do with his tale, he would diverge from his course to tell about the person who owned that name or explain all about that family—with the result that as he plodded on he always got further and further from his grandfather's memorable adventure with the ram, and finally went to sleep before he got to the end of the story, and so did his comrades. Once he did manage to approach so nearly to the end, apparently, that the boys were filled with an eager hope; they believed that at last they were going to find out all about the grandfather's adventure and what it was that had happened. After the usual preliminaries, the historian said:

"Well, as I was a-sayin', he bought that old ram from a feller up in Siskiyou County and fetched him home and turned him loose in the medder, and next morning he went down to have a look at him, and accident'ly dropped a ten-cent piece in the grass and stooped down—so—and was a-fumblin' around in the grass to git it, and the ram he was a-standin' up the slope taking notice; but my grandfather wasn't taking notice, because he had his back to the ram and was int'rested about the dime. Well, there he was, as I was a-sayin', down at the foot of the slope a-bendin' over—so—fumblin' in the grass, and the ram he was up there at the top of the slope, and Smith—Smith was a-standin' there—no, not jest there, a little further away—fifteen foot perhaps— well, my grandfather was a-stoopin' way down—so —and the ram was up there observing, you know, and Smith he . . . (musing) . . . the ram he bent his head down, so . . . Smith of Calaveras . . . no, no it couldn't ben Smith of Calaveras—I remem- ber now that he—b'George it was Smith of Tulare County—course it was, I remember it now perfectly plain.

"Well, Smith he stood just there, and my grand- father he stood just here, you know, and he was a-bendin' down just so, fumblin' in the grass, and when the old ram see him in that attitude he took it fur an invitation—and here he come! down the slope thirty mile an hour and his eye full of business. You see my grandfather's back being to him, and him stooping down like that, of course he—why sho! it *warn't* Smith of Tulare at all, it was Smith of Sac- ramento—my goodness, how did I ever come to get them Smiths mixed like that—why, Smith of Tulare was jest a nobody, but Smith of Sacramento—why the Smiths of Sacramento come of the best Southern blood in the United States; there warn't ever any better blood south of the line than the Sacramento Smiths. Why look here, one of them married a Whitaker! I reckon that gives you an idea of the kind of society the Sacramento Smiths could 'sociate around in; there ain't no better blood than that Whitaker blood; I reckon anybody'll tell you that.

"Look at Mariar Whitaker—there was a girl for you! Little? Why yes, she was little, but what of that? Look at the heart of her—had a heart like a bullock—just as good and sweet and lovely and generous as the day is long; if she had a thing and you wanted it, you could have it—have it and welcome; why Mariar Whitaker couldn't have a thing and another person need it and not get it—get it and welcome. She had a glass eye, and she used to lend it to Flora Ann Baxter that hadn't any, to receive company with; well, she was pretty large, and it didn't fit; it was a number seven, and she was excavated for a fourteen, and so that eye wouldn't lay still; every time she winked it would turn over. It was a beautiful eye and set her off admirable, because it was a lovely pale blue on the front side— the side you look out of—and it was gilded on the back side; didn't match the other eye, which was one of them browny-yellery eyes and tranquil and quiet, you know, the way that kind of eyes are; but that warn't any matter—they worked together all right and plenty picturesque. When Flora Ann winked, that blue and gilt eye would whirl over, and the other one stand still, and as soon as she begun to get excited that hand-made eye would give a whirl and then go on a-whirlin' and a-whirlin' faster and faster, and a-flashin' first blue and then yaller and then blue and then yaller, and when it got to whizzing and flashing like that, the oldest man in the world couldn't keep up with the expression on that side of her face. Flora Ann Baxter married a Hogadorn. I reckon that lets you understand what kind of blood she was—old Maryland Eastern Shore blood; not a better family in the United States than the Hogadorns.

"Sally—that's Sally Hogadorn—Sally married a missionary, and they went off carrying the good news to the cannibals out in one of them way-off islands round the world in the middle of the ocean somers, and they et her; et him too, which was irregular; it warn't the custom to eat the missionary, but only the family, and when they see what they had done they was dreadful sorry about it, and when the relations sent down there to fetch away the things they said so—said so right out—said they was sorry, and 'pologized, and said it shouldn't happen again; said 'twas an accident.

"Accident! now that's foolishness; there ain't no such thing as an accident; there ain't nothing happens in the world but what's ordered just so by a wiser Power than us, and it's always fur a good purpose; we don't know what the good purpose was, sometimes—and it was the same with the families that was short a missionary and his wife. But that ain't no matter, and it ain't any of our business; all that concerns us is that it was a special providence and it had a good intention. No, sir, there ain't no such thing as an accident. Whenever a thing happens that you think is an accident you make up your mind it ain't no accident at all—it's a special providence.

"You look at my Uncle Lem—what do you say to that? That's all I ask you—you just look at my Uncle Lem and talk to me about accidents! It was like this: one day my Uncle Lem and his dog was

downtown, and he was a-leanin' up against a scaffold-
ing—sick, or drunk, or somethin'—and there was
an Irishman with a hod of bricks up the ladder along
about the third story, and his foot slipped and down
he come, bricks and all, and hit a stranger fair and
square and knocked the everlasting aspirations out
of him; he was ready for the coroner in two minutes.
Now then people said it was an accident.

"Accident! there warn't no accident about it; 'twas
a special providence, and had a mysterious, noble
intention back of it. The idea was to save that Irishman. If the stranger hadn't been there that Irishman
would have been killed. The people said 'special
providence—sho! the dog was there—why didn't
the Irishman fall on the dog? Why warn't the dog
app'inted?' Fer a mighty good reason—the dog
would 'a' seen him a-coming; you can't depend on no
dog to carry out a special providence. You couldn't
hit a dog with an Irishman because—lemme see, what
was that dog's name . . . (musing) . . . oh, yes,
Jasper—and a mighty good dog too; he wa'n't no
common dog, he wa'n't no mongrel; he was a composite. A composite dog is a dog that's made up of
all the valuable qualities that's in the dog breed—
kind of a syndicate; and a mongrel is made up of the
riffraff that's left over. That Jasper was one of the
most wonderful dogs you ever see. Uncle Lem got
him of the Wheelers. I reckon you've heard of the
Wheelers; ain't no better blood south of the line than
the Wheelers.

"Well, one day Wheeler was a-meditating and
dreaming around in the carpet factory and the machinery made a snatch at him and first you know he

was a-meandering all over that factory, from the garret to the cellar, and everywhere, at such another gait as—why, you couldn't even see him; you could only hear him whiz when he went by. Well, you know a person can't go through an experience like that and arrive back home the way he was when he went. No, Wheeler got wove up into thirty-nine yards of best three-ply carpeting. The widder was sorry, she was uncommon sorry, and loved him and done the best she could fur him in the circumstances, which was unusual. She took the whole piece—thirty-nine yards—and she wanted to give him proper and honorable burial, but she couldn't bear to roll him up; she took and spread him out full length, and said she wouldn't have it any other way. She wanted to buy a tunnel for him but there wasn't any tunnel for sale, so she boxed him in a beautiful box and stood it on the hill on a pedestal twenty-one foot high, and so it was monument and grave together, and economical—sixty foot high—you could see it from everywhere—and she painted on it 'To the loving memory of thirty-nine yards best three-ply carpeting containing the mortal remainders of Millington G. Wheeler go thou and do likewise.' "

At this point the historian's voice began to wobble and his eyelids to droop with weariness, and he fell asleep; and so from that day to this we are still in ignorance; we don't know whether the old grandfather ever got the ten-cent piece out of the grass; we haven't any idea what it was that happened, or whether anything happened at all.

Upon comparing the above with the original in *Roughing It*, I find myself unable to clearly and definitely explain why the one can be effectively *re-cited* before an audience and the other can't; there is a reason but it is too subtle for adequate conveyance by the lumbering vehicle of words; I sense it but cannot express it; it is as elusive as an odor, pungent, pervasive, but defying analysis. I give it up. I merely know that the one version will recite, and the other won't.

By reciting I mean, of course, delivery from memory; neither version can be read effectively from the book. There are plenty of good reasons why this should be so, but there is one reason which is sufficient by itself, perhaps; in reading from the book you are telling another person's tale at secondhand; you are a mimic, and not the person involved; you are an artificiality, not a reality; whereas in telling the tale without the book you absorb the character and presently become the man himself, just as is the case with the actor.

The greatest actor would not be able to carry his audience by storm with a book in his hand; reading from the book renders the nicest shadings of delivery impossible. I mean those studied fictions which seem to be the impulse of the moment and which are so effective: such as, for instance, fictitious hesitancies for the right word, fictitious unconscious pauses, fictitious unconscious side remarks, fictitious unconscious embarrassments, fictitious unconscious emphases placed upon the wrong word with a deep intention back of it—these and all the other artful fictive shades which give to a recited tale the captivating naturalness of an impromptu narration can be attempted by a book reader and are attempted, but

they are easily detectable as artifice, and although the
audience may admire their cleverness and their in-
genuity as artifice, they only get at the intellect of the
house, they don't get at its heart; and so the reader's
success lacks a good deal of being complete.

When a man is reading from a book on the platform, he soon realizes that there is one powerful gun
in his battery of artifice that he can't work with an
effect proportionate to its caliber: that is the *pause*
—that impressive silence, that eloquent silence,
that geometrically progressive silence which often
achieves a desired effect where no combination of
words howsoever felicitous could accomplish it. The
pause is not of much use to the man who is reading
from a book because he cannot know what the exact
length of it ought to be; he is not the one to determine the measurement—the audience must do that
for him. He must perceive by their faces when the
pause has reached the proper length, but his eyes
are not on the faces, they are on the book; therefore
he must determine the proper length of the pause by
guess; he cannot guess with exactness and nothing
but exactness, absolute exactness, will answer.

The man who recites without the book has all the
advantage; when he comes to an old familiar remark
in his tale which he has uttered nightly for a hundred
nights—a remark preceded or followed by a pause—
the faces of the audience tell him when to end the
pause. For one audience the pause will be short, for
another a little longer, for another a shade longer
still; the performer must vary the length of the pause
to suit the shades of difference between audiences.
These variations of measurement are so slight, so

delicate, that they may almost be compared with the shadings achieved by Pratt and Whitney's ingenious machine which measures the five-millionth part of an inch. An audience is that machine's twin; it can measure a pause down to that vanishing fraction.

I used to play with the pause as other children play with a toy. In my recitals, when I went reading around the world for the benefit of Mr. Webster's creditors, I had three or four pieces in which the pauses performed an important part, and I used to lengthen them or shorten them according to the requirements of the case, and I got much pleasure out of the pause when it was accurately measured, and a certain discomfort when it wasn't. In the negro ghost story of "The Golden Arm" one of these pauses occurs just in front of the closing remark. Whenever I got the pause the right length, the remark that followed it was sure of a satisfactorily startling effect, but if the length of the pause was wrong by the five-millionth of an inch, the audience had had time in that infinitesimal fraction of a moment to wake up from its deep concentration in the grisly tale and foresee the climax, and be prepared for it before it burst upon them—and so it fell flat.

In Susy's little biography of me she tells about my proceeding to tell this ghost tale to the multitude of young lady students at Vassar College—a tale which poor Susy always dreaded—and she tells how this time she gathered her fortitude together and was resolved that she wouldn't be startled, and how all her preparations were of no avail, and how when the climax fell that multitude of girls "jumped as one man"—which is an indication that I had the pause rightly measured that time.

In "His Grandfather's Old Ram" a pause has place; it follows a certain remark, and Mrs. Clemens and Clara, when we were on our way around the world, would afflict themselves with my whole performance every night when there was no sort of necessity for it, in order that they might watch the house when that pause came; they believed that by the effect they could accurately measure the high or low intelligence of the audience. I knew better but it was not in my interest to say so. When the pause was right, the effect was sure; when the pause was wrong in length, by the five-millionth of an inch, the laughter was only mild, never a crash. That passage occurs in "His Grandfather's Old Ram" where the question under discussion is whether the falling of the Irishman on the stranger was an accident, or was a special providence. If it was a special providence, and if the sole purpose of it was to save the Irishman, why was it necessary to sacrifice the stranger? "The dog was there. Why didn't he fall on the dog? Why wa'n't the dog app'inted? Becuz *the dog would 'a' seen him a-comin'*." That last remark was the one the family waited for. A pause *after* the remark was absolutely necessary with any and all audiences because no man, howsoever intelligent he may be, can instantly adjust his mind to a new and unfamiliar, and yet for a moment or two apparently plausible, logic which recognizes in a dog an instrument too indifferent to pious restraints and too alert in looking out for his own personal interest to be safely depended upon in an emergency requiring self-sac-

rifice for the benefit of another, even when the command comes from on high.

· · · · ·

6. *The Snodgrass Letters. (September 10, 1906)*

In a chapter which I dictated five months ago, I
made a little outline sketch in which I strung together certain facts of my life and named the dates
of their occurrence. I stated that in 1849, in Hannibal, Missouri, when I was a child of fourteen, my
brother went away on a journey and I edited one
issue of his weekly newspaper for him without invitation, and when he got back it took him several weeks
to quiet down and pacify the people whom my writings had excited. That was fifty-seven years ago. I did
not meddle with a pen again, so far as I can remember, until ten years later—1859. I was a cub pilot on
the Mississippi River then, and one day I wrote a
rude and crude satire which was leveled at Captain
Isaiah Sellers, the oldest steamboat pilot on the Mississippi River, and the most respected, esteemed and
revered.

For many years he had occasionally written brief
paragraphs concerning the river and the changes
which it had undergone under his observation during
fifty years, and had signed these paragraphs "Mark
Twain" and published them in the St. Louis and New
Orleans journals. In my satire I made rude game of
his reminiscences. It was a shabby poor performance, but I didn't know it and the pilots didn't know
it. The pilots thought it was brilliant. They were
jealous of Sellers because when the gray-heads
among them pleased their vanity by detailing in the

hearing of the younger craftsmen marvels which they had seen in the long ago on the river, Sellers was always likely to step in at the psychological moment and snuff them out with wonders of his own which made their small marvels look pale and sick. However, I have told all about this in *Old Times on the Mississippi*.

The pilots handed my extravagant satire to a river reporter, and it was published in the New Orleans *True Delta*. That poor old Captain Sellers was deeply wounded. He had never been held up to ridicule before; he was sensitive, and he never got over the hurt which I had wantonly and stupidly inflicted upon his dignity. I was proud of my performance for a while and considered it quite wonderful, but I have changed my opinion of it long ago. Sellers never published another paragraph nor ever used his *nom de guerre* again.

Between 1859 and the summer of 1862 I left the pen strictly alone. I then became a newspaper reporter in Nevada, but I wrote no literature. I confined myself to writing up the inconsequential happenings of Virginia City for the *Territorial Enterprise*. I wrote no literature until 1866, when a little sketch of mine called "The Jumping Frog" was published in a perishing literary journal in New York and killed it on the spot.

Now then, if I know my own history, I never wrote and never published a line of literature until forty years ago. If I know my own history, I never had any leaning toward literature, nor any desire to meddle with it, nor had ever flourished a literary pen save by accident—and then only twice—up to forty years ago.

Now then I have arrived at that subject whose fresh new interest has sidetracked my reminiscences and postponed their completion—for the present—while I consider this new and delicious matter furnished by Saturday's mail. First in order come the following letters, two by Mr. Alden, editor of *Harper's Monthly*, and one by a Mr. Thomas Rees:

Franklin Square, New York.
September 6, 1906.

Dear Mark:

I received a few weeks ago from Mr. Thomas Rees some manuscripts offered for sale to us, purporting to be copies of "Snodgrass" papers contributed by you some fifty years ago to a newspaper published by his father. I returned them with a letter of which I send you a copy—also a copy of a letter I have just received from him. I think you should have cognizance of this correspondence.

The offer of the manuscripts was accompanied by an affadavit sworn to by Mr. Rees, Sr., attesting to your authorship.

Yours faithfully,
(signed) H. M. Alden.

Copy of Mr. Alden's letter to Mr. Thomas Rees.

August 27, 1906.

Dear Mr. Rees:

We cannot publish the "Snodgrass" letters you send us, as they have no interest to our readers as the productions of "Snodgrass," and we could not put them forth as the productions of "Mark Twain" because that would be untrue. Even the suggestion that "Snodgrass" died and was buried and arose again as "Mark Twain" would be a distinct injury to Mr. Clemens, after he had so utterly and deliberately discarded the earlier pen-name. It certainly would be a manifest impropriety. In any case I venture to suggest that Mr. Clemens should be consulted before any attempt is made to publish these things.

> Very truly yours,
> (signed) H. M. Alden.

Mr. Thomas Rees,
  Illinois State Register,
    Springfield, Illinois.

Copy of Mr. Thomas Rees's letter, Manager of the *Illinois State Register*,

> Springfield, Ill., Sept. 4, 1906.

H. M. Alden,
  C/o Harper Bros., Pubs.,
    New York City.
Dear Sir:

I acknowledge hereby the receipt of the manuscripts of the Clemens "Snodgrass" articles. Please accept my thanks for their prompt return. I notice you advise at the close of your letter reading, "In any case I venture to suggest that Mr. Clemens should be consulted before any attempt is made to publish these things." While as a matter of courtesy, in case I should conclude to publish the same, I might communicate with Mr. Clemens, I do not know that he has any rights in the premises, nor that there is anything in the ethics of the situation that call for a compliance with your advice.

Mr. Clemens wrote these articles under contract with my father and my elder brother more than half a century ago. He was paid for the same and thereby parted entirely with any right that he might have had in them at that time. They were published in a daily newspaper without being copyrighted, and thereby became public property. The only rights that I have in the premises that are not possessed by the general public, is the fact that I know where to find the text and have an affidavit of their genuineness. If I should h232232232232

l##

lay the matter of the publication of these articles before Mr. Clemens and he should request or forbid that I should publish the same, it would in no way protect him against the other eighty million people in the United States that might be disposed to take up the work. And no history of Mr. Clemens's life will be complete without at least reference to these particular articles and his former pen name.

However, I am under lasting obligations for your kind advice.

Yours respectfully,
(signed) Thomas Rees.

To me this is a most interesting thing, because it is such a naïve exposure of certain traits in human nature—traits which are in everybody, no doubt, but which only about one man in fifty millions is willing to lay bare to the public view. The rest of the fifty millions are restrained by pride from making the exposure. Did I write the rubbish with which Mr. Rees charges me? I suppose not. I have no reason to suppose that I wrote it, but I can't say, and I don't say, that I didn't write it.[4] I can only say that since by Mr. Rees's count I was only eighteen or nineteen years old at the time, it must have been a colossal event in my life, and one likely to be remembered by me for a century. I am astonished that it has left no impression, nor any sign of an impression, upon my memory. If a Far-Western lad of eighteen or nineteen had, all by himself and in his own name, *en-*

---

[4] Mark Twain is wrong here, of course. He did write the Snodgrass letters, which were eventually collected and edited by Charles Honce and published in 1928 by Pascal Covici as *The Adventures of Thomas Jefferson Snodgrass*. Mr. Rees's statements appear to have been correct throughout, and Mark's anger is a typical fulmination. He talked this way whenever he thought, however erroneously, that someone was trying to take advantage of him.

tered into a solemn contract—a contract to do or suffer anything, little or big—he would have put aside all other concerns, temporal and eternal, and made a house-to-house visitation throughout the village and told everybody, even to the cats and dogs, about it, and it would have made him celebrated.

Celebrity is what a boy or a youth longs for more than for any other thing. He would be a clown in a circus, he would be a pirate, he would sell himself to Satan, in order to attract attention and be talked about and envied. True, it is the same with every grown-up person; I am not meaning to confine this trait to the boys. But there is a distinction between the boy and the grown person—the boys are all Reeses. That is to say, they lack caution, they lack wisdom, they are innocent; they are frank, and when they have an opportunity to expose traits which they ought to hide they don't know enough to resist.

Up to the time that I was eighteen or nineteen years old, no Far-Western boy of that age had ever achieved the glory of *making a contract* about something or other and signing it. If I did it I was the only one. I hope I did it because I would like to know, even at seventy-one, that I was not commonplace even when I was a child—that I was not only not commonplace, but was the only lad in the Far West that wasn't. I cannot understand why it is that if I did it, it has left no impression upon my memory. Every boy and girl in the town would have pointed me out daily, and said with envy and admiration and malice:

"There he goes! That's the boy that *made a contract.*"

I would have hunted up stragglers, couples, groups and gangs of boys and girls every day, in order to pass them by with studied modesty and unconsciousness and hear them say:

"He's the one! He *made the contract*!"

Those happy experiences would have made a record upon my memory, I suppose. Indeed I almost know that they would have done it.

At a very much earlier age than that I was made the recipient of a considerably smaller distinction by Mrs. Horr, my schoolteacher, and I have never forgotten it for a moment since, nor ceased to be vain of it. I was only five years old, and had been under her ministrations only six months when she, inspired by something which she honestly took to be prophecy, exclaimed in the hearing of several persons that I would one day be *"President of the United States, and would stand in the presence of kings unabashed."* I carried that around personally from house to house, and was surprised and hurt to find how few people there were in that day who had a proper reverence for prophecy, and confidence in it. But no matter—the circumstance bedded in my memory for good and all. Therefore I cannot see how that much larger thing, that actual thing, that visible and palpable thing, a *contract*, an imposing and majestic contract, could have entered into my life at the maturer age of eighteen or nineteen and then flitted away forever and left no sign that it had ever been there.

When I examine the next detail I am surprised again. According to the affidavit of what is left, at this distant day, of the elder Mr. Rees, the contract required him to *pay* me for my infant literature; also that I *received the payment.* These things are unthinkable. In that day there was no man in the United States, sane or insane, who could have dreamed of such a thing as wanting an unknown lad who had never written a line of literature in his life to furnish him some literature, and not only furnish him some literature but ask him to take *pay* for it! It is true that in that ancient day everybody wrote ostensible literature. There were no exceptions then, there are none now. Everybody wrote for the local paper and was glad to get in gratis, publication was sufficient pay. There were a few persons in America, fifteen perhaps, may be twenty-five, who were so widely known as writers that they could demand remuneration of the periodicals for their output and get it, but there were no Clemenses in that clan, there were no juveniles in it, no unknown lads lost in the remotenesses of the wild and woolly West who could ask for pay for their untrained scribblings and get it.

In 1853, which is "more than fifty years ago," my brother was hit a staggering blow by a new idea, an idea that had never been thought of in the West by any person before, the idea of hiring a literary celebrity to write an original story for his Hannibal newspaper *for pay!* He wrote East and felt of the literary market, but he met with only sorrows and discouragements. He was obliged to keep within the limit of his purse, and that limit was narrowly circumscribed. What he wanted was an original story which could be continued through three issues of his weekly paper and cover a few columns of solid bourgeois each time. He offered a sum to all the American literary celebrities of that day, in turn, but, in turn, Emerson, Lowell, Holmes, and all the others declined.

At last a celebrity of about the third degree took him up—with a condition. This was a Philadelphian, Homer C. Wilbur, a regular and acceptable contributor to *Sartain's Magazine* and the other first-class periodicals. He said he could not write an original story for the sum offered, *which was five dollars,* but would translate one from the French for that sum. My brother took him up, and sent the money—I don't remember now where he got it. The story came. We made an immense noise over it. We bragged in double great primer capitals, readable at thirty yards without glasses, that we had bought it and *paid* for it, proudly naming the sum, and we ran it through four numbers of the paper, increasing the subscription list by thirty-eight copies, payable in turnips and cordwood, and it took all of three months for the excitement to quiet down.

Important as this memorable enterprise was, *no contract* passed between the parties. The whole thing was done by letters, just mere ordinary letters, fourteen or fifteen I suppose, and each person paid the other person's postage. It was a fashion of the day. Postage was ten cents, and we didn't prepay because the letter might never arrive and the money would be wasted. Nothing passed but just letters, mere ordinary letters. My brother trusted the great author, the great author trusted my brother. Signed and sealed *contracts* for periodical literature have never been known in this country, nor heard of in any other, except in the one single instance which we have under consideration this morning. The elder Rees, professional affidaviter, had the monopoly of that novelty. He wouldn't trust even an obscure child of nineteen in so stately a matter as a bucketful of literary slops, without a contract that would hold that lad and be good for fifty years.

According to the professional affidaviter, I was *paid* for those writings. If it was money, I wonder what the sum was. I know perfectly well by the Wilbur case and by the difference between Wilbur's fame and my obscurity, it couldn't have been over thirty cents for the bucketful, and I know also that it must have included the bucket. But if the pay was delivered in the universal currency of the Far West, it couldn't have been cordwood because cordwood was never hauled in smaller lots than half-cords, and a half-cord would have been worth a dollar and a quarter, and would have covered more literature than even a reckless and improvident Rees would have been willing to enter into a solemn contract for. If it was eggs, I got six dozen; if it was watermelons I got three; if it was bar soap I got five bars; if it was tallow candles I got thirty; if it was soda water I got six glasses; if it was ice cream I got three saucers—and the colic. I have no recollection of ever getting those riches. If I got any of them I know I got them in installments and wide apart; for in that day any so noble an irruption of wealth as three plates of cream, all paid down in one single installment, would have been an event so electrifying and so exalting that it would stay caked in my memory three centuries.

The common human trait which the Reeses have laid bare for inspection and which the rest of the nations of the earth carefully conceal for shame, and pretend that they do not possess, is the trait which urges a man to sacrifice all his pride, all his delicacy, all his decency, when his eye falls upon an unprotected dollar—a spectacle which sometimes takes the manhood out of him and leaves behind it nothing but the animal. Affidavits are nothing to this kind of a person; they come cheap; he would make a hundred a day for thirty cents apiece. This kind of person is gratefully ready to dig up a crime or a foolishness that has been condoned and forgotten by the merciful for fifty years, if he can get a dollar and a half out of it. It is fatal for his kind to have the luck to trace home to an esteemed and respected white-headed woman a forgotten disgrace whereby she tarnished her good name in her girlhood, for he will remorselessly expose it if there is half a handful of soiled dollars in it for him.

It is out of the breed of Reeses that the world gets its Burkes and Hares. But the Burkes and Hares are to be pitied, not reviled. They only obey the law of their nature. They did not make their nature; they are not responsible; and no humane person will permit himself to say harsh things about them. It would be impossible for me to say abusive things about these modern Burkes and Hares of the Middle West. They must have bread to eat, and their ways of acquiring it are limited. As is natural, they acquire it in those ways which give them the most pleasure, the most satisfaction, the most contentment. They dig up dead reputations and sell the rotten product for food, and eat the food. Their ancestors, Burke and Hare, dug up the dead in the cemeteries and sold the corpses for bread and ate the bread; which is another way of saying they fed upon the dead. The Reeses are only Burkes and Hares deprived of their natural trade by the obstructive modern legal conditions under which they exist.

I may have written those papers, but it is not at all likely that I did. In any case, I have no recollection of it, and must let it stand at that. But one thing I will quite confidently maintain, in spite of all the affidavits of all the Burkes and Hares, and that is that when the affidaviter says that there was a *contract*, and that I was *paid* for the work, those two statements are plain straightforward falsehoods; and what is more, and worse, they are poorly devised, unplausible, and inartistic. As works of art, even a Rees ought to be ashamed of them, I think.

.   .   .   .   .

7. *"What Is Man?" (September 4, 1907)*

Many a time in the past eight or nine years I have been strongly moved to publish that little book [*What Is Man?*], but the doubtfulness of the wisdom of doing it has always been a little stronger than the desire to do it, consequently the venture has not been made; necessarily it has not been made for, according to my own gospel, as set forth in that small book, where there are two desires in a man's heart he has no choice between the two but must obey the strongest, there being no such thing as free will in the composition of any human being that ever lived.

I have talked my gospel rather freely in conversation for twenty-five or thirty years and have never much minded whether my listeners liked it or not, but I couldn't get beyond that—the idea of actually publishing always brought me a shudder; by anticipation I couldn't bear the reproaches which would assail me from a public which had been trained from the cradle along opposite lines of thought and for that reason—which is a quite sufficient reason—would not be able to understand me.

I had early proved all this, for I laid one chapter of my gospel before the Monday Evening Club in Hartford, a quarter of a century ago, and there was not a man there who didn't scoff at it, jeer at it, revile it, and call it a lie, a thousand times a lie! That was the chapter denying that there is any such thing as personal merit; maintaining that a man is merely a machine automatically functioning without any of his help or any occasion or necessity for his help, and that no machine is entitled to praise for any of its acts of a virtuous sort nor blamable for any of its acts of the opposite sort. Incidentally, I observed that the human machine gets all its inspirations from the outside and is not capable of originating an idea of any kind in its own head; and I further remarked, incidentally, that no man ever does a duty for duty's sake but only for the sake of the satisfaction he personally gets out of doing the duty, or for the sake of avoiding the personal discomfort he would have to endure if he shirked that duty; also I indicated that there is no such thing as free will and no such thing as self-sacrifice.

The club handled me without gloves. They said I was trying to strip man of his dignity, and I said I shouldn't succeed, for it would not be possible to strip him of a quality which he did not possess. They said that if this insane doctrine of mine were accepted by the world life would no longer be worth living, but I said that that would merely leave life in the condition it was before.

Those were the brightest minds in Hartford—and indeed they were very superior minds—but my little batch of quite simple and unassailable truths could get no entrance into them, because the entrances were all stopped up with stupid misteachings handed down by stupid ancestors and docilely accepted without examination, whereas until those minds should be unstopped they would not be competent to intelligently examine my gospel and intelligently pass upon it. No mind, howsoever brilliant, is in a condition to examine a proposition which is opposed to its teachings and its heredities until, as pointed out by Lord Bacon some centuries ago, those prejudices, predilections, and inheritances shall have been swept away. I realized that night that since those able men were such children, such incompetents, in the presence of an unfamiliar doctrine, there could be but one result if my gospel should be placed before the general public: it would make not a single convert and I should be looked upon as a lunatic, besides; therefore I put aside the idea of elaborating my notions and spreading them abroad in a book.

The sorrowful effort of that night consisted partly of a skeleton sketch, but mainly of talk. Years went by and at last, in Vienna in 1898, I wrote out and completed one chapter, using the dialogue form in place of the essay form. I read it to Frank N. Doubleday, who was passing through Vienna and he wanted to take it and publish it, but I was not minded to submit it to print and criticism. I added a paragraph or a chapter now and then, as time went by, and at last in 1902 I finished it; and I further finished it in 1904 by destroying the concluding chapter, whose subject was "The Moral Sense."[5] The fact is, I couldn't even stand that chapter myself; all the other chapters were sweet and gentle, but that one was disrespectful—in fact riotous.

Again Doubleday wanted to publish but I remembered Hartford and said no. He proposed a submerged and private circulation of the little torpedo, and I acceded to that. He got two hundred and fifty copies printed for me at the De Vinne Press, and J. W. Boswell, chief of one of De Vinne's departments, took out a copyright in his own name by request, and doesn't yet know who wrote the book. Doubleday has sent ten or twelve copies to men here and in England, through Mr. Boswell (the authorship concealed, of course), and I myself have given away four copies to discreet persons. The following is the Preface to *What Is Man?*

February 1905

The studies for these papers were begun twenty-five or twenty-seven years ago; the papers were written seven years ago. I have examined them once or twice per year since and found them satisfactory. I have just examined them again and am still satisfied that they speak the truth. Every thought in them has been thought (and accepted as un-

[5] He did not destroy but only omitted this chapter. It is in the Mark Twain Papers and may be published. I don't find it riotous —or scandalous, or even amusing.

assailable truth) by millions upon millions of men—and concealed, kept private. Why did they not speak out? Because
they dreaded (and could not bear) the disapproval of the
people around them. Why have I not published? The same
reason has restrained me, I think. I can find no other.

· · · · ·

*8. "Extract from Captain Stormfield's Visit to
Heaven." (August 29, 1906)*

Several weeks ago the editor of *Harper's Bazaar*
projected a scheme for a composite story. A family
was to tell the story. The father was to begin it,
and, in turn, each member of the family was to furnish a chapter of it. There was to be a boy in the
family, and I was invited to write his chapter. I was
afraid of the scheme because I could not tell beforehand whether the boy would take an interest in it or
not. Experience has taught me long ago that if *I*
tell a boy's story, or anybody else's, it is never worth
printing; it comes from the head not the heart, and
always goes into the wastebasket. To be successful
and worth printing, the imagined boy would have to
tell his story *himself* and let me act merely as his
amanuensis. I did not tell the "Horse's Tale," the
horse told it himself through me. If he hadn't done
that it wouldn't have been told at all. When a tale
tells itself there is no trouble about it; there are no
hesitancies, no delays, no cogitations, no attempts at
invention; there is nothing to do but hold the pen
and let the story talk through it and say, after its
own fashion, what it desires to say.

Mr. Howells began the composite tale. He held
the pen and through it the father delivered his chap-

ter—therefore it was well done. A lady followed Howells and furnished the old-maid sister's chapter. This lady is of high literary distinction, she is nobly gifted, she has the ear of the nation and her novels and stories are among the best that the country has produced, but *she* did not tell those tales, she merely held the pen and they told themselves—of this I am convinced. I am also convinced of another thing, that she did not act as amanuensis for the old-maid sister but wrote the old-maid sister's chapter out of her own head, without any help from the old maid. The result is a failure. It is a piece of pure literary manufacture and has the shopmarks all over it.

I first knew Capt. Wakeman thirty-nine years ago. I made two voyages with him and we became fast friends. He was a great burly, handsome, weather-beaten, symmetrically built and powerful creature, with coal-black hair and whiskers and the kind of eye which men obey without talking back. He was full of human nature, and the best kind of human nature. He was as hearty and sympathetic and loyal and loving a soul as I have found anywhere and when his temper was up he performed all the functions of an earthquake, without the noise.

He was all sailor from head to heel; and this was proper enough, for he was born at sea and in the course of his sixty-five years he had visited the edges of all the continents and archipelagoes, but had never been on land except incidentally and spasmodically, as you may say. He had never had a day's schooling in his life but had picked up worlds and worlds of knowledge at secondhand, and none of it correct.

He was a liberal talker and inexhaustibly interesting. In the matter of a wide and catholic profanity he had not his peer on the planet while he lived. It was a deep pleasure to me to hear him do his stunts in this line. He knew the Bible by heart and was profoundly and sincerely religious. He was always studying the Bible when it was his watch below and always finding new things, fresh things, and unexpected delights and surprises in it—and he loved to talk about his discoveries and expound them to the ignorant. He believed that he was the only man on the globe that really knew the secret of the Biblical miracles. He had what he believed was a sane and rational explanation of every one of them, and he loved to teach his learning to the less fortunate.

I have said a good deal about him in my books. In one of them I have told how he brought the murderer of his colored mate to trial in the Chincha Islands before the assembled captains of the ships in port, and how when sentence had been passed he drew the line there. He had intended to capture and execute the murderer all by himself, but had been persuaded by the captains to let them try him with the due formalities and under the forms of law. He had yielded that much, though most reluctantly, but when the captains proposed to do the executing also, that was too much for Wakeman and he struck. He hanged the man himself. He put the noose around the murderer's neck, threw the bight of the line over the limb of a tree, and made his last moments a misery to him by reading him nearly into premature death with random and irrelevant chapters from the Bible.

He was a most winning and delightful creature. When he was fifty-three years old he started from a New England port, master of a great clipper ship bound around the Horn for San Francisco, and he was not aware that he had a passenger but he was mistaken as to that. He had never had a love passage but he was to have one now. When he was out from port a few weeks he was prowling about some remote corner of his ship, by way of inspection, when he came across a beautiful girl, twenty-four or twenty-five years old, prettily clothed and lying asleep with one plump arm under her neck. He stopped in his tracks and stood and gazed, enchanted. Then he said, "It's an angel—that's what it is. It's an angel. When it opens its eyes, if they are blue I'll marry it."

The eyes turned out to be blue, and the pair were married when they reached San Francisco. The girl was to have taught school there. She had her appointment in her pocket—but the Captain saw to it that that arrangement did not materialize. He built a little house in Oakland—ostensibly a house, but really it was a ship, and had all a ship's appointments, binnacle, scuppers, and everything else—and there he and his little wife lived an ideal life during the intervals that intervened between his voyages. They were a devoted pair, and worshiped each other. By and by there were two little girls, and then the nautical paradise was complete.

Captain Wakeman had a fine large imagination, and he once told me of a visit which he had made to heaven. I kept it in my mind, and a month or two later I put it on paper—this was in the first quarter of 1868, I think. It made a small book of about forty thousand words, and I called it *Captain Stormfield's Visit to Heaven.* Five or six years afterward I showed the manuscript to Howells and he said, "Publish it."

But I didn't. I had turned it into a burlesque of "The Gates Ajar," a book which had imagined a mean little ten-cent heaven about the size of Rhode Island—a heaven large enough to accommodate about a tenth of one per cent of the Christian billions who had died in the past nineteen centuries. I raised the limit; I built a properly and rationally stupendous heaven, and augmented its Christian population to ten per cent of the contents of the modern cemeteries; also, as a volunteer kindness I let in a tenth of one per cent of the pagans who had died during the preceding eons—a liberty which was not justifiable because those people had no business there, but as I had merely done it in pity, and out of kindness, I allowed them to stay. Toward the end of the book my heaven grew to such inconceivable dimensions on my hands that I ceased to apply poor little million-mile measurements to its mighty territories, and measured them by light-years only! and not only that, but a million of them linked together in a stretch.[6]

In the thirty-eight years which have since elapsed I have taken out that rusty old manuscript several times and examined it with the idea of printing it, but I always concluded to let it rest. However, I

[6] Here Mark Twain made the following footnote: "Light-year. This is without doubt the most stupendous and impressive phrase that exists in any language. It is restricted to astronomy. It describes the distance which light, moving at the rate of 186,000 miles per second, travels in our year of 52 weeks."

mean to put it into this autobiography now.[7] It is not likely to see the light for fifty years yet, and at that time I shall have been so long under the sod that I shan't care about the results.[8]

I used to talk to Twichell about Wakeman, there in Hartford, thirty years ago and more, and by and by a curious thing happened. Twichell went off on a vacation and as usual he followed his vacation custom, that is to say he traveled under an alias, so that he could associate with all kinds of disreputable characters and have a good time, and nobody be embarrassed by his presence, since they wouldn't know that he was a clergyman. He took a Pacific mail ship and started south for the Isthmus. Passenger traffic in that line had ceased almost entirely. Twichell found but one other passenger on board. He noticed that that other passenger was not a saint, so he went to foregathering with him at once, of course. After that passenger had delivered himself of about six majestically and picturesquely profane remarks Twichell (alias Peters) said, "Could it be, by chance, that you are Captain Ned Wakeman of San Francisco?"

His guess was right, and the two men were inseparable during the rest of the voyage. One day

---

[7] Here he made another footnote: "*Three hours later.* I have just burned the closing two-thirds of it." But he did not burn any of it.

[8] He changed his mind again, a year later, and published *An Extract from Captain Stormfield's Visit to Heaven* first in *Harper's* for December, 1907, and January, 1908, and then as a book. He did not publish all of it, but the fragments—at least those in the Mark Twain Papers—are unimportant and not particularly interesting. He apparently worked on the manuscript at several other times not acknowledged in the text. Note that he considered the mild burlesque shocking.

Wakeman asked Peters-Twichell if he had ever read the Bible. Twichell said a number of things in reply, things of a rambling and noncommittal character, but, taken in the sum, they left the impression that Twichell—well, never mind the impression; suffice it that Wakeman set himself the task of persuading Twichell to read that book. He also set himself the task of teaching Twichell how to understand the miracles. He expounded to him, among other miracles, the adventure of Isaac with the prophets of Baal. Twichell could have told him that it wasn't Isaac, but that wasn't Twichell's game, and he didn't make the correction. It was a delicious story, and it is delightful to hear Twichell tell it. I have printed it in full in one of my books—I don't remember which one.[9]

·   ·   ·   ·   ·

9. "The Fortifications of Paris."[10]

He [Mark Twain's infant son, Langdon Clemens] was prematurely born. We had a visitor in the house and when she was leaving she wanted Mrs. Clemens to go to the station with her. I objected. But this was a visitor whose desire Mrs. Clemens regarded as law. The visitor wasted so much precious time in taking her leave that Patrick had to drive in a gallop

[9] "Some Rambling Notes of an Idle Excursion," now a part of *Tom Sawyer Abroad and Other Stories*.

[10] This passage (under date of February 15, 1906) follows the quotation from Susy's Biography at the top of page 117, in Volume II of the published *Autobiography*. I insert it here because it shows vividly both a psychological mechanism and a psychological need that are implicit in a large part of Mark Twain's humor. "The Fortifications of Paris" is now, as "Map of Paris," reprinted in *Tom Sawyer Abroad and Other Stories*.

to get to the station in time. In those days the streets of Buffalo were not the model streets which they afterward became. They were paved with large cobblestones and had not been repaired since Columbus's time. Therefore the journey to the station was like the Channel passage in a storm. The result to Mrs. Clemens was a premature confinement, followed by a dangerous illness.

In my belief there was but one physician who could save her. That was the almost divine Mrs. Gleason of Elmira, who died at a great age two years ago after being the idol of that town for more than half a century. I sent for her and she came. Her ministrations were prosperous but at the end of a week she said she was obliged to return to Elmira because of imperative engagements. I felt *sure* that if she could stay with us three days more Livy would be out of all danger. But Mrs. Gleason's engagements were of such a nature that she could not consent to stay. This is why I placed a private policeman at the door with instructions to let no one pass out without my privity and consent. In these circumstances, poor Mrs. Gleason had no choice— therefore she stayed. She bore me no malice for this, and most sweetly said so when I saw her silken white head and her benignant and beautiful face for the last time, which was three years ago.

Before Mrs. Clemens was quite over her devastating illness Miss Emma Nye, a former schoolmate of hers, arrived from South Carolina to pay us a visit, and was immediately taken with typhoid fever. We got nurses—professional nurses of the type of that day, and of previous centuries—but we had to watch those nurses while they watched the patient, which they did in their sleep as a rule. I watched them in the daytime, Mrs. Clemens at night. She slept between medicine-times, but she always woke up at the medicine-times and went in and woke up the nurse that was on watch and saw the medicines administered. This constant interruption of her sleep seriously delayed Mrs. Clemens's recovery. Miss Nye's illness proved fatal. During the last two or three days of it, Mrs. Clemens seldom took her clothes off but stood a continuous watch. Those two or three days are among the blackest, the gloomiest, the most wretched of my long life.

The resulting periodical and sudden changes of mood in me, from deep melancholy to half-insane tempests and cyclones of humor, are among the curiosities of my life. During one of these spasms of humorous possession I sent down to my newspaper office for a huge wooden capital *M* and turned it upside down and carved a crude and absurd map of Paris upon it, and published it along with a sufficiently absurd description of it, with guarded and imaginary compliments of it bearing the signatures of General Grant and other experts.

The Franco-Prussian War was in everybody's mouth at the time and so the map would have been valuable—if it had been valuable. It wandered to Berlin, and the American students there got much satisfaction out of it. They would carry it to the big beer halls and sit over it at a beer table and discuss it with violent enthusiasm and apparent admiration, in English, until their purpose was accomplished, which was to attract the attention of any

German soldiers that might be present. When that
had been accomplished, they would leave the map
there and go off, jawing, to a little distance and wait
for results. The results were never long delayed. The
soldiers would pounce upon the map and discuss it
in German and lose their tempers over it and black-
guard it and abuse it and revile the author of it, to
the students' entire content. The soldiers were always divided in opinion about the author of it, some
of them believing he was ignorant but well-inten-
tioned, the others believing he was merely an idiot.

.   .   .   .   .

10. "The Report of My Death." (April 3, 1906)

This reminds me—nine years ago when we were
living in Tedworth Square, London, a report was
cabled to the American journals that I was dying.
I was not the one. It was another Clemens, a cousin
of mine, who was due to die but presently escaped by
some chicanery or other characteristic of the tribe of
Clemenses. The London representatives of the American papers began to flock in with American cables
in their hands, to inquire into my condition. There
was nothing the matter with me and each in his turn
was astonished, and not gratified, to find me reading
and smoking in my study and worth next to nothing
as a text for transatlantic news. One of these men
was a gentle and kindly and grave and sympathetic
Irishman, who hid his disappointment the best he
could and tried to look glad and told me that his
paper, the *Evening Sun*, had cabled him that it was
reported in New York that I was dead. What should

he cable in reply? I said, "Say the report is exaggerated."

He never smiled, but went solemnly away and sent the cable in those exact words. The remark hit the world pleasantly and to this day it keeps turning up, now and then, in the newspapers when people have occasion to discount exaggeration.

The next man was also an Irishman. He had his New York cablegram in his hand—from the New York *World*—and he was so evidently trying to get around that cable with invented softnesses and palliations that my curiosity was aroused and I wanted to see what the cable did really say. So when occasion offered I slipped it out of his hand. It said "If Mark Twain dying send five hundred words. If dead send a thousand."

VARIOUS LITERARY PEOPLE

1. Bret Harte. (June 13, 1906)[1]

How wonderful are the ways of Providence! But
I will take that up later.

About forty years ago—I was a reporter on the
Morning Call of San Francisco. I was more than
that—I was *the* reporter. There was no other. There
was enough work for one and a little over, but not
enough for two—according to Mr. Barnes's idea, and
he was the proprietor and therefore better situated
to know about it than other people.

By nine in the morning I had to be at the police
court for an hour and make a brief history of the
squabbles of the night before. They were usually between Irishmen and Irishmen, and Chinamen and
Chinamen, with now and then a squabble between
the two races for a change. Each day's evidence was
substantially a duplicate of the evidence of the day
before, therefore the daily performance was killingly
monotonous and wearisome. So far as I could see,
there was only one man connected with it who found
anything like a compensating interest in it, and that
was the court interpreter. He was an Englishman
who was glibly familiar with fifty-six Chinese dia-
lects. He had to change from one to another of them

[1] Published, much abbreviated and edited, in *Harper's Magazine* for March, 1922.

every ten minutes and this exercise was so energizing
that it kept him always awake, which was not the case
with the reporters. Next we visited the higher courts
and made notes of the decisions which had been
rendered the day before. All the courts came under
the head of "regulars." They were sources of repor-
torial information which never failed. During the rest
of the day we raked the town from end to end, gathering such material as we might, wherewith to fill our
required column—and if there were no fires to report
we started some.

At night we visited the six theaters, one after the
other: seven nights in the week, three hundred and
sixty-five nights in the year. We remained in each of
those places five minutes, got the merest passing
glimpse of play and opera, and with that for a text
we "wrote up" those plays and operas, as the phrase
goes, torturing our souls every night from the beginning of the year to the end of it in the effort to find
something to say about those performances which we
had not said a couple of hundred times before. There
has never been a time from that day to this, forty
years, that I have been able to look at even the outside of a theater without a spasm of the dry gripes,
as "Uncle Remus" calls it—and as for the inside, I
know next to nothing about that, for in all this time I
have seldom had a sight of it nor ever had a desire
in that regard which couldn't have been overcome by
argument.

After having been hard at work from nine or ten
in the morning until eleven at night scraping material
together, I took the pen and spread this muck out in
words and phrases and made it cover as much acreage

as I could. It was fearful drudgery, soulless drudgery, and almost destitute of interest. It was an awful slavery for a lazy man, and I was born lazy. I am no lazier now than I was forty years ago, but that is because I reached the limit forty years ago. You can't go beyond possibility.

Finally there was an event. One Sunday afternoon I saw some hoodlums chasing and stoning a Chinaman who was heavily laden with the weekly wash of his Christian customers, and I noticed that a policeman was observing this performance with an amused interest—nothing more. He did not interfere. I wrote up the incident with considerable warmth and holy indignation. Usually I didn't want to read in the morning what I had written the night before; it had come from a torpid heart. But this item had come from a live one. There was fire in it and I believed it was literature—and so I sought for it in the paper next morning with eagerness. It wasn't there. It wasn't there the next morning, nor the next. I went up to the composing room and found it tucked away among condemned matter on the standing galley. I asked about it. The foreman said Mr. Barnes had found it in a galley proof and ordered its extinction. And Mr. Barnes furnished his reasons—either to me or to the foreman, I don't remember which; but they were commercially sound. He said that the *Call* was like the New York *Sun* of that day : it was the washerwoman's paper—that is, it was the paper of the poor; it was the only cheap paper. It gathered its livelihood from the poor and must respect their prejudices or perish. The Irish were the poor. They were the stay and support of the *Morning Call*; without them the

Morning Call could not survive a month—and they hated the Chinamen. Such an assault as I had attempted could rouse the whole Irish hive, and seriously damage the paper. The *Call* could not afford to publish articles criticizing the hoodlums for stoning Chinamen.

I was lofty in those days. I have survived it. I was unwise, then. I am up-to-date now. Day before yesterday's New York *Sun* has a paragraph or two from its London correspondent which enables me to locate myself. The correspondent mentions a few of our American events of the past twelvemonth, such as the limitless rottenness of our great insurance companies, where theft has been carried on by our most distinguished commercial men as a profession; the exposures of conscienceless graft, colossal graft, in great municipalities like Philadelphia, St. Louis, and other large cities; the recent exposure of millionfold graft in the great Pennsylvania Railway system— with minor uncoverings of commercial swindles from one end of the United States to the other; and finally today's lurid exposure, by Upton Sinclair, of the most titanic and death-dealing swindle of them all, the Beef Trust, an exposure which has moved the President to demand of a reluctant Congress a law which shall protect America and Europe from falling, in a mass, into the hands of the doctor and the undertaker.

According to that correspondent, Europe is beginning to wonder if there is really an honest male human creature left in the United States. A year ago I was satisfied that there was no such person existing upon American soil except myself. That exception has since been rubbed out, and now it is my belief that there isn't a single male human being in America who is honest. I held the belt all along, until last January. Then I went down, with Rockefeller and Carnegie and a group of Goulds and Vanderbilts and other professional grafters, and swore off my taxes like the most conscienceless of the lot. I was a great loss to America, because I was irreplaceable. It is my belief that it will take fifty years to produce my successor. I believe the entire population of the United States—exclusive of the women—to be rotten, as far as the dollar is concerned. Understand, I am saying these things as a dead person. I should consider it indiscreet in any live one to make these remarks publicly.

But, as I was saying, I was loftier forty years ago than I am now, and I felt a deep shame in being situated as I was—slave of such a journal as the *Morning Call*. If I had been still loftier I would have thrown up my berth and gone out and starved, like any other hero. But I had never had any experience. I had *dreamed* heroism, like everybody, but I had had no practice and I didn't know how to begin. I couldn't bear to begin with starving. I had already come near to that once or twice in my life, and got no real enjoyment out of remembering about it. I knew I couldn't get another berth if I resigned. I knew it perfectly well. Therefore I swallowed my humiliation and stayed where I was. But whereas there had been little enough interest attaching to my industries, before, there was none at all now. I continued my work but I took not the least interest in it, and naturally there were results. I got to neglecting it. As I

have said, there was too much of it for one man. The
way I was conducting it now, there was apparently
work enough in it for two or three. Even Barnes
noticed that, and told me to get an assistant, on half
wages.

There was a great hulking creature down in the
counting room—good-natured, obliging, unintellec-
tual—and he was getting little or nothing a week and
boarding himself. A graceless boy of the counting-
room force who had no reverence for anybody or
anything was always making fun of this beach-
comber, and he had a name for him which somehow
seemed intensely apt and descriptive—I don't know
why. He called him Smiggy McGlural. I offered the
berth of assistant to Smiggy, and he accepted it with
alacrity and gratitude. He went at his work with ten
times the energy that was left in me. He was not intellectual but mentality was not required or needed in
a *Morning Call* reporter, and so he conducted his
office to perfection. I gradually got to leaving more
and more of the work to McGlural. I grew lazier and
lazier, and within thirty days he was doing almost
the whole of it. It was also plain that he could accomplish the whole of it, and more, all by himself, and
therefore had no real need of me.

It was at this crucial moment that that event happened which I mentioned a while ago. Mr. Barnes
discharged me. It was the only time in my life that I
have ever been discharged, and it hurts yet—although I am in my grave. He did not discharge me
rudely. It was not in his nature to do that. He was a
large, handsome man, with a kindly face and courteous ways, and was faultless in his dress. He could not

have said a rude, ungentle thing to anybody. He took me privately aside and advised me to resign. It was like a father advising a son for his good, and I obeyed.

I was on the world, now, with nowhere to go. By my Presbyterian training, I knew that the *Morning Call* had brought disaster upon itself. I knew the ways of Providence, and I knew that this offense would have to be answered for. I could not foresee when the penalty would fall nor what shape it would take, but I was as certain that it would come, sooner or later, as I was of my own existence. I could not tell whether it would fall upon Barnes or upon his newspaper. But Barnes was the guilty one, and I knew by my training that the punishment always falls upon the innocent one, consequently I felt sure that it was the newspaper that at some future day would suffer for Barnes's crime.

Sure enough! Among the very first pictures that arrived in the fourth week of April—there stood the *Morning Call* building towering out of the wrecked city, like a Washington Monument; and the body of it was all gone, and nothing was left but the iron bones! It was then that I said, "How wonderful are the ways of Providence!" I had known it would happen. I had known it for forty years. I had never lost my confidence in Providence during all that time. It was put off longer than I was expecting but it was now comprehensive and satisfactory enough to make up for that. Some people would think it curious that Providence should destroy an entire city of four hundred thousand inhabitants to settle an account of forty years standing, between a mere discharged reporter and a newspaper, but to me there was nothing strange about that, because I was educated, I was trained, I was a Presbyterian, and I knew how these things are done. I knew that in Biblical times, if a man committed a sin, the extermination of the whole surrounding nation—cattle and all—was likely to happen. I knew that Providence was not particular about the rest, so that He got somebody connected with the one He was after. I remembered that in the *Magnalia* a man who went home swearing from prayer meeting one night got his reminder within the next nine months. He had a wife and seven children, and all at once they were attacked by a terrible disease, and one by one they died in agony till at the end of a week there was nothing left but the man himself. I knew that the idea was to punish the man, and I knew that if he had any intelligence he recognized that that intention had been carried out, although mainly at the expense of other people.

In those ancient times the counting room of the *Morning Call* was on the ground floor; the office of the Superintendent of the United States Mint was on the next floor above, with Bret Harte as private secretary of the Superintendent. The quarters of the editorial staff and the reporter were on the third floor, and the composing room on the fourth and final floor. I spent a good deal of time with Bret Harte in his office after Smiggy McGlural came, but not before that. Harte was doing a good deal of writing for the *Californian*—contributing "Condensed Novels" and sketches to it and also acting as editor, I think. I was a contributor. So was Charles

H. Webb; also Prentiss Mulford; also a young lawyer named Hastings, who gave promise of distinguishing himself in literature some day. Charles Warren Stoddard was a contributor. Ambrose Bierce, who is still writing acceptably for the magazines today, was then employed on some paper in San Francisco—*The Golden Era,* perhaps. We had very good times together—very social and pleasant times. But that was after Smiggy McGlural came to my assistance; there was no leisure before that. Smiggy was a great advantage to me—during thirty days. Then he turned into a disaster.

It was Mr. Swain, Superintendent of the Mint, who discovered Bret Harte. Harte had arrived in California in the fifties, twenty-three or twenty-four years old, and had wandered up into the surface diggings of the camp at Yreka, a place which had acquired its curious name—when in its first days it much needed a name—through an accident. There was a bakeshop with a canvas sign which had not yet been put up but had been painted and stretched to dry in such a way that the word BAKERY, all but the B, showed through and was reversed. A stranger read it wrong end first, YREKA, and supposed that that was the name of the camp. The campers were satisfied with it and adopted it.

Harte taught school in that camp several months. He also edited the weekly rag which was doing duty as a newspaper. He spent a little time also in the pocket-mining camp of Jackass Gulch (where I tarried, some years later, during three months). It was at Yreka and Jackass Gulch that Harte learned to accurately observe and put with photographic exactness on paper the woodland scenery of California and the general country aspects—the stagecoach, its driver and its passengers, and the clothing and general style of the surface miner, the gambler, and their women; and it was also in these places that he learned, without the trouble of observing, all that he didn't know about mining, and how to make it read as if an expert were behind the pen. It was in those places that he also learned how to fascinate Europe and America with the quaint dialect of the miner— a dialect which no man in heaven or earth had ever used until Harte invented it. With Harte it died, but it was no loss. By and by he came to San Francisco. He was a compositor by trade, and got work in *The Golden Era* office at ten dollars a week.

.   .   .   .   .

(June 14, 1906)

Harte was paid for setting type only but he lightened his labors and entertained himself by contributing literature to the paper, uninvited. The editor and proprietor, Joe Lawrence, never saw Harte's manuscripts, because there weren't any. Harte spun his literature out of his head while at work at the case, and set it up as he spun. *The Golden Era* was ostensibly and ostentatiously a literary paper, but its literature was pretty feeble and sloppy and only exhibited the literary forms, without really being literature. Mr. Swain, the Superintendent of the Mint, noticed a new note in that *Golden Era* orchestra—a new and fresh and spirited note that rose above that orchestra's mumbling confusion and was recognizable as music. He asked Joe Lawrence who the performer was, and Lawrence told him. It seemed to Mr. Swain a shame that Harte should be wasting himself in such a place and on such a pittance so he took him away, made him his private secretary, on a good salary, with little or nothing to do, and told him to follow his own bent and develop his talent. Harte was willing and the development began.

Bret Harte was one of the pleasantest men I have ever known. He was also one of the unpleasantest men I have ever known. He was showy, meretricious, insincere; and he constantly advertised these qualities in his dress. He was distinctly pretty, in spite of the fact that his face was badly pitted with smallpox. In the days when he could afford it—and in the days when he couldn't—his clothes always exceeded the fashion by a shade or two. He was always conspicuously a little more intensely fashionable than the fashionablest of the rest of the community. He had good taste in clothes. With all his conspicuousness there was never anything really loud nor offensive about them. They always had a single smart little accent, effectively located and that accent would have distinguished Harte from any other of the ultra-fashionables. Oftenest it was his necktie. Always it was of a single color, and intense. Most frequently, perhaps, it was crimson—a flash of flame under his chin; or it was indigo blue and as hot and vivid as if one of those splendid and luminous Brazilian butterflies had lighted there. Harte's dainty self-complacencies extended to his carriage and gait. His carriage was graceful and easy, his gait was of the mincing sort, but was the right gait for him, for an unaffected one would not have harmonized with the rest of the man and the clothes.

He hadn't a sincere fiber in him. I think he was incapable of emotion, for I think he had nothing to feel with. I think his heart was merely a pump and had no other function. I am almost moved to say I *know* it had no other function. I knew him intimately in the days when he was private secretary on the second floor and I a fading and perishing reporter on the third, with Smiggy McGlural looming doomfully in the near distance. I knew him intimately when he came east five years later, in 1870, to take the editorship of the proposed *Lakeside Magazine*, in Chicago, and crossed the continent through such a prodigious blaze of national interest and excitement that one might have supposed he was the Viceroy of India on a progress, or Halley's comet come again after seventy-five years of lamented absence.

I knew him pretty intimately thenceforth until he crossed the ocean to be consul, first at Crefeldt in Germany and afterwards in Glasgow. He never returned to America. When he died, in London, he had been absent from America and from his wife and daughters twenty-six years.

This is the very Bret Harte whose pathetics, imitated from Dickens, used to be a godsend to the farmers of two hemispheres on account of the freshets of tears they compelled. He said to me once with a cynical chuckle that he thought he had mastered the art of pumping up the tear of sensibility. The idea conveyed was that the tear of sensibility was oil, and that by luck he had struck it.

Harte told me once, when he was spending a business-fortnight in my house in Hartford, that his fame was an accident—an accident that he much regretted for a while. He said he had written "The Heathen Chinee" for amusement; then had thrown it into the wastebasket; that presently there was a call for copy to finish out the *Overland Monthly* and let it get to press. He had nothing else, so he fished the "Chinee" out of the basket and sent that. As we all remember, it created an explosion of delight whose reverberations reached the last confines of Christendom and Harte's name, from being obscure to invisibility in the one week, was as notorious and as visible in the next as if it had been painted on the sky in letters of astronomical magnitude. He regarded this fame as a disaster, because he was already at work on such things as "The Luck of Roaring Camp," a loftier grade of literature, a grade which he had been hoping to presently occupy with distinction in the sight of the world.

"The Heathen Chinee" did obstruct that dream but not for long. It was presently replaced by the finer glory of "The Luck of Roaring Camp," "Tennessee's Partner," and those other felicitous imitations of Dickens. In the San Franciscan days Bret Harte was by no means ashamed when he was praised as being a successful imitator of Dickens; he was proud of it. I heard him say, myself, that he thought he was the best imitator of Dickens in America, a remark which indicates a fact, to wit: that there were a great many people in America at that time who were ambitiously and undisguisedly imitating

Dickens. His long novel, *Gabriel Conroy,* is as much like Dickens as if Dickens had written it himself.

It is a pity that we cannot escape from life when we are young. When Bret Harte started east in his newborn glory thirty-six years ago, with the eyes of the world upon him, he had lived all of his life that was worth living. He had lived all of his life that was to be respectworthy. He had lived all of his life that was to be worthy of his *own* respect. He was entering upon a miserable career of poverty, debt, humiliation, shame, disgrace, bitterness, and a world-wide fame which must have often been odious to him, since it made his poverty and the shabbiness of his character conspicuous beyond the power of any art to mercifully hide them.

There was a happy Bret Harte, a contented Bret Harte, an ambitious Bret Harte, a hopeful Bret Harte, a bright, cheerful, easy-laughing Bret Harte, a Bret Harte to whom it was a bubbling and effervescent joy to be alive. That Bret Harte died in San Francisco. It was the corpse of that Bret Harte that swept in splendor across the continent; that refused to go to the Chicago banquet given in its honor because there had been a breach of etiquette—a carriage had not been sent for it; that resumed its eastward journey behind the grand scheme of the *Lakeside Monthly* in sorrowful collapse; that undertook to give all the product of its brain for one year to the *Atlantic Monthly* for ten thousand dollars—a stupendous sum in those days—furnished nothing worth speaking of for the great pay, but collected and spent the money before the year was out, and then began a dismal and harassing death-in-life of borrowing from men and living on women which was to cease only at the grave.

. . . . .

(February 4, 1907)

In these days things are happening which bring Bret Harte to my mind again; they rake up memories of him which carry me back thirty and forty years. He had a curious adventure once, when he was a young chap new to the Pacific Coast and floating around seeking bread and butter. He told me some of his experiences of that early day. For a while he taught a school in the lively gold-mining camp of Yreka, and at the same time he added a trifle to his income by editing the little weekly local journal for the pair of journeymen typesetters who owned it.

His duties as editor required him to read proof. Once a galley slip was laid before him which consisted of one of those old-time obituaries which were so dismally popular all over the United States when we were still a soft-hearted and sentimental people. There was half a column of the obituary and it was built upon the regulation plan; that is to say, it was made up of superlatives—superlatives wherewith the writer tried to praise Mrs. Thompson, the deceased, to the summit of her merit, the result being a flowery, overheated, and most extravagant eulogy, and closing with that remark which was never missing from the regulation obituary: "Our loss is her eternal gain."

In the proof Harte found this observation: "Even in Yreka her chastity was conspicuous." Of course that word was a misprint for "charity," but Harte didn't think of that; he knew a printer's mistake had been made and he also knew that a reference to the manuscript would determine what it was; therefore he followed proofreader custom and with his pen indicated in the usual way that the manuscript must be examined. It was a simple matter and took only a moment of his time; he drew a black line under the word chastity, and in the margin he placed a question mark enclosed in parentheses. It was a brief way of saying, "There is something the matter with this word; examine the manuscript and make the necessary correction." But there is another proofreader law which he overlooked. That law says that when a word is not emphatic enough you must draw a line under it, and this will require the printer to reinforce it by putting it in italics.

When Harte took up the paper in the morning and looked at that obituary he took only one glance; then he levied on a mule that was not being watched and cantered out of town, knowing well that in a very little while there was going to be a visit from the widower, with his gun. In the obituary the derelict observation now stood in this form: "Even in Yreka her *chastity* was conspicuous (?)"—a form which turned the thing into a ghastly and ill-timed sarcasm!

I am reminded, in a wide roundabout way, of another of Harte's adventures, by a remark in a letter lately received from Tom Fitch, whom Joe Goodman crippled in the duel—for Tom Fitch is still alive, although inhabiting Arizona. After wandering for years and years all about the planet, Fitch has gone back to his early loves, the sand, the sagebrush,

and the jackass rabbit; and these things, and the old-
time ways of the natives, have refreshed his spirit
and restored to him his lost youth. Those friendly
people slap him on the shoulder and call him—well,
never mind what they call him; it might offend your
ears, but it does Fitch's heart good. He knows its
deep meanings; he recognizes the affection that is
back of it, and so it is music to his spirit, and he is
grateful.

When "The Luck of Roaring Camp" burst upon
the world Harte became instantly famous; his name
and his praises were upon every lip. One day he had
occasion to go to Sacramento. When he went ashore
there he forgot to secure a berth for the return trip.
When he came down to the landing, in the late afternoon, he realized that he had made a calamitous
blunder; apparently all Sacramento was proposing
to go down to San Francisco; there was a queue of
men which stretched from the purser's office down
the gangplank, across the levee, and up the street
out of sight.

Harte had one hope: inasmuch as in theaters,
operas, steamboats, and steamships, half a dozen
choice places are always reserved to be conferred
upon belated clients of distinction, perhaps his name
might procure for him one of those reserved places,
if he could smuggle his card to the purser; so he
edged his way along the queue and at last stood
shoulder to shoulder with a vast and rugged miner
from the mountains, who had his revolvers in his
belt, whose great slouch hat overshadowed the whisk-
ered face of a buccaneer, and whose raiment was
splashed with clay from his chin down to his boot

tops. The queue was drifting slowly by the purser's wicket, and each member of it was hearing, in his turn, the fatal words: "No berths left; not even floor space." The purser was just saying it to the truculent big miner when Harte passed his card in. The purser exclaimed, passing a key, "Ah, Mr. Bret Harte, glad to see you, sir! Take the whole stateroom, sir."

The bedless miner cast a scowl upon Harte which shed a twilight gloom over the whole region and frightened that author to such a degree that his key and its wooden tag rattled in his quaking hand; then he disappeared from the miner's view and sought seclusion and safety behind the lifeboats and such things on the hurricane deck. But nevertheless the thing happened which he was expecting—the miner soon appeared up there and went peering around; whenever he approached dangerously near, Harte shifted his shelter and hid behind a new one. This went on without unhappy accident for half an hour, but at last failure came: Harte made a miscalculation; he crept cautiously out from behind a lifeboat and came face to face with the miner! He felt that it was an awful situation, a fatal situation but it was not worth while to try to escape, so he stood still and waited for his doom. The miner said, sternly, "Are you Bret Harte?"

Harte confessed it in a feeble voice.

"Did you write that 'Luck of Roaring Camp'?"

Harte confessed again.

"Sure?"

"Yes"—in a whisper.

The miner burst out, fervently and affectionately,

"*Son* of a ———! Put it there!" and he gripped Harte's hand in his mighty talons and mashed it.

Tom Fitch knows that welcome phrase, and the love and admiration that purge it of its earthiness and make it divine.

In the early days I liked Bret Harte, and so did the others, but by and by I got over it; so also did the others. He couldn't keep a friend permanently. He was bad, distinctly bad; he had no feeling, and he had no conscience. His wife was all that a good woman, a good wife, a good mother, and a good friend, can be; but when he went to Europe as consul he left her and his little children behind, and never came back again from that time until his death, twenty-six years later.

He was an incorrigible borrower of money; he borrowed from all his friends; if he ever repaid a loan the incident failed to pass into history. He was always ready to give his note but the matter ended there. We sailed for Europe on the 10th of April, 1878, and on the preceding night there was a banquet to Bayard Taylor, who was going out in the same ship as our minister to Germany. At that dinner I met a gentleman whose society I found delightful, and we became very friendly and communicative. He fell to talking about Bret Harte, and it soon appeared that he had a grievance against him. He had so admired Harte's writings that he had greatly desired to know Harte himself.

The acquaintanceship was achieved and the borrowing began. The man was rich and he lent gladly. Harte always gave his note, and of his own motion, for it was not required of him. Harte had then been

in the East about eight years, and these borrowings
had been going on during several of those years; in
the aggregate they amounted to about three thousand dollars. The man told me that Harte's notes
were a distress to him, because he supposed that
they were a distress to Harte.

.   .   .   .   .

Then he had what he thought was a happy idea:
he compacted the notes into a bale and sent them
to Harte on the 24th of December '77 as a Christmas present; and with them he sent a note begging
Harte to allow him this privilege because of the
warm and kind and brotherly feeling which prompted
it. Per next day's mail Harte fired the bale back at
him, accompanying it with a letter which was all
afire with insulted dignity, and which formally and
by irrevocable edict permanently annulled the existing friendship. But there was nothing in it about
paying the notes sometime or other.[2]

When Harte made his spectacular progress across
the continent in 1870, he took up his residence at
Newport, Rhode Island, that breeding place—that
stud farm, so to speak—of aristocracy; aristocracy
of the American type; that auction mart where the
English nobilities come to trade hereditary titles for
American girls and cash. Within a twelvemonth he
had spent his ten thousand dollars and he shortly
thereafter left Newport, in debt to the butcher, the
baker, and the rest, and took up his residence with
his wife and his little children in New York. I will

[2] This agrees with what Mark had told Colonel Higginson eighteen months before this dictation. See *Letters and Journals of
Thomas Wentworth Higginson*, p. 330.

remark that during Harte's sojourns in Newport and Cohasset he constantly went to dinners among the fashionables where he was the only male guest whose wife had not been invited. There are some harsh terms in our language but I am not acquainted with any that is harsh enough to properly characterize a husband who will act like that.

When Harte had been living in New York two or three months he came to Hartford and stopped over night with us. He said he was without money, and without a prospect; that he owed the New York butcher and baker two hundred and fifty dollars and could get no further credit from them; also he was in debt for his rent and his landlord was threatening to turn his little family into the street. He had come to me to ask for a loan of two hundred and fifty dollars. I said that that would relieve only the butcher and baker part of the situation, with the landlord still hanging over him; he would better accept five hundred, which he did. He employed the rest of his visit in delivering himself of sparkling sarcasms about our house, our furniture, and the rest of our domestic arrangements.

Howells was saying yesterday that Harte was one of the most delightful persons he had ever met and one of the wittiest. He said that there was a charm about him that made a person forget, for the time being, his meannesses, his shabbinesses and his dishonesties, and almost forgive them. Howells is right about Harte's bright wit but he had probably never made a search into the character of it. The character of it spoiled it; it possessed no breadth and no variety; it consisted solely of sneers and sarcasms;

when there was nothing to sneer at, Harte did not flash and sparkle and was not more entertaining than the rest of us.

Once he wrote a play with a perfectly delightful Chinaman in it—a play which would have succeeded if anyone else had written it; but Harte had earned the enmity of the New York dramatic critics by freely and frequently charging them with being persons who never said a favorable thing about a new play except when the favorable thing was bought and paid for beforehand. The critics were waiting for him, and when his own play was put upon the stage they attacked it with joy, they abused it and derided it remorselessly.[3] It failed, and Harte believed that the critics were answerable for the failure. By and by he proposed that he and I should collaborate in a play in which each of us should introduce several characters and handle them. He came to Hartford and remained with us two weeks. He was a man who could never persuade himself to do a stroke of work until his credit was gone, and all his money, and the wolf was at his door; then he could sit down and work harder—until temporary relief was secured—than any man I have ever seen.

To digress for a moment. He came to us once just upon the verge of Christmas, to stay a day and finish a short story for the New York *Sun* called "Faithful Blossom"[4]—if my memory serves me. He was to have a hundred and fifty dollars for the story in any case, but Mr. Dana had said he should have two hundred and fifty if he finished it in time for

---

[3] Probably "Two Men of Sandy Bar."
[4] "Thankful Blossom."

Christmas use. Harte had reached the middle of his story, but his time limit was now so brief that he could afford no interruptions, wherefore he had come to us to get away from the persistent visits of his creditors.

He arrived about dinner time. He said his time was so short that he must get to work straightway after dinner; then he went on chatting in serenity and comfort all through dinner, and afterward by the fire in the library until ten o'clock; then Mrs. Clemens went to bed, and my hot whisky punch was brought; also a duplicate of it for Harte. The chatting continued. I generally consume only one hot whisky, and allow myself until eleven o'clock for this function; but Harte kept on pouring and pouring, and consuming and consuming, until one o'clock; then I excused myself and said good night. He asked if he could have a bottle of whisky in his room. We rang up George and he furnished it. It seemed to me that he had already swallowed whisky enough to incapacitate him for work but it was not so; moreover, there were no signs upon him that his whisky had had a dulling effect upon his brain.

He went to his room and worked the rest of the night, with his bottle of whisky and a big wood fire for comfort. At five or six in the morning he rang for George; his bottle was empty, and he ordered another; between then and nine he drank the whole of the added quart, and then came to breakfast not drunk, not even tipsy, but quite himself and alert and animated. His story was finished; finished within the time limit, and the extra hundred dollars was secured. I wondered what a story would be like that had been completed in circumstances like these; an hour later I was to find out.

At ten o'clock the young girls' club—by name The Saturday Morning Club—arrived in our library. I was booked to talk to the lassies, but I asked Harte to take my place and read his story. He began it but it was soon plain that he was like most other people—he didn't know how to read; therefore I took it from him and read it myself. The last half of that story was written under the unpromising conditions which I have described; it is a story which I have never seen mentioned in print and I think it is quite unknown, but it is my conviction that it belongs at the very top of Harte's literature.

To go back to that other visit. The next morning after his arrival we went to the billiard room and began work upon the play.[5] I named my characters and described them; Harte did the same by his. Then he began to sketch the scenario, act by act, and scene by scene. He worked rapidly and seemed to be troubled by no hesitations or indecisions; what he accomplished in an hour or two would have cost me several weeks of painful and difficult labor, and would have been valueless when I got through. But Harte's work was good and usable; to me it was a wonderful performance.

Then the filling in began. Harte set down the dialogue swiftly, and I had nothing to do except when one of my characters was to say something; then Harte told me the nature of the remark that was required, I furnished the language and he jotted it down. After this fashion we worked two or three

[5] "Ah Sin."

or four hours every day for a couple of weeks, and produced a comedy that was good and would act. His part of it was the best part of it but that did not disturb the critics; when the piece was staged they praised my share of the work with a quite suspicious prodigality of approval, and gave Harte's share all the vitriol they had in stock. The piece perished.

All that fortnight at our house Harte made himself liberally entertaining at breakfast, at luncheon, at dinner, and in the billiard room—which was our workshop—with smart and bright sarcasms leveled at everything on the place; and for Mrs. Clemens's sake I endured it all until the last day; then, in the billiard room, he contributed the last feather; it seemed to be a slight and vague and veiled satirical remark with Mrs. Clemens for a target; he denied that she was meant, and I might have accepted the denial if I had been in a friendly mood but I was not, and was too strongly moved to give his reasonings a fair hearing. I said in substance this:

"Harte, your wife is all that is fine and lovable and lovely, and I exhaust praise when I say she is Mrs. Clemens's peer—but in all ways you are a shabby husband to her, and you often speak sarcastically, not to say sneeringly, of her, just as you are constantly doing in the case of other women; but your privilege ends there; you must spare Mrs. Clemens. It does not become you to sneer at all; you are not charged anything here for the bed you sleep in, yet you have been very smartly and wittily sarcastic about it, whereas you ought to have been more reserved in that matter, remembering that you have

not owned a bed of your own for ten years; you have
made sarcastic remarks about the furniture of the
bedroom and about the table ware and about the
servants and about the carriage and the sleigh and
the coachman's livery—in fact about every detail of
the house and half of its occupants; you have spoken
of all these matters contemptuously, in your un-
wholesome desire to be witty, but this does not become you; you are barred from these criticisms by
your situation and circumstances; you have a talent
and a reputation which would enable you to support
your family most respectably and independently if
you were not a born bummer and tramp; you are
a loafer and an idler, and you go clothed in rags,
with not a whole shred on you except your inflamed
red tie, and *it* isn't paid for; nine-tenths of your income is borrowed money—money which, in fact, is
stolen, since you never intended to repay any of it;
you sponge upon your hard-working widowed sister
for bread and shelter in the mechanics' boarding-
house which she keeps; latterly you have not ventured to show your face in her neighborhood because
of the creditors who are on watch for you. Where
have you lived? Nobody knows. Your own people
do not know. But I know. You have lived in the
Jersey woods and marshes, and have supported yourself as do the other tramps; you have confessed it
without a blush; you sneer at everything in this
house, but you ought to be more tender, remembering that everything in it was honestly come by and
has been paid for."

Harte owed me fifteen hundred dollars at that
time; later he owed me three thousand. He offered

me his note, but I was not keeping a museum and
didn't take it.

．　．　．　．　．

Harte's indifference concerning contracts and engagements was phenomenal. He could be blithe and
gay with a broken engagement hanging over him;
he could even joke about the matter; if that kind
of a situation ever troubled him, the fact was not
discoverable by anybody. He entered into an engagement to write the novel, *Gabriel Conroy,* for my
Hartford publisher, Bliss. It was to be published by
subscription. With the execution of the contract,
Bliss's sorrows began. The precious time wasted
along; Bliss could get plenty of promises out of
Harte but no manuscript—at least no manuscript
while Harte had money or could borrow it. He
wouldn't touch the pen until the wolf actually had
him by the hind leg; then he would do two or three
days' violent work and let Bliss have it for an advance of royalties.

About once a month Harte would get into des-
perate straits; then he would dash off enough manuscript to set him temporarily free and carry it to
Bliss and get a royalty advance. These assaults upon
his prospective profits were never very large, except
in the eyes of Bliss; to Bliss's telescopic vision a
couple of hundred dollars that weren't due, or hadn't
been earned, were a prodigious matter. By and by
Bliss became alarmed. In the beginning he had recognized that a contract for a full-grown novel from
Bret Harte was a valuable prize, and he had been
indiscreet enough to let his good fortune be trum-

peted about the country. The trumpeting could have been valuable for Bliss if he had been dealing with a man addicted to keeping his engagements; but he was not dealing with that kind of a man, therefore the influence of the trumpeting had died down and vanished away long before Harte had arrived at the middle of his book; that kind of an interest once dead is dead beyond resurrection.

Finally Bliss realized that *Gabriel Conroy* was a white elephant. The book was nearing a finish, but, as a subscription book, its value had almost disappeared. He had advanced to Harte thus far—I think my figures are correct—thirty-six hundred dollars,[6] and he knew that he should not be able to sleep much until he could find some way to make that loss good; so he sold the serial rights in *Gabriel Conroy* to one of the magazines for that trifling sum—and a good trade it was, for the serial rights were not really worth that money, and the book rights were hardly worth the duplicate of it.

I think the sense of shame was left out of Harte's constitution. He told me once, apparently as an incident of no importance—a mere casual reminiscence —that in his early days in California when he was a blooming young chap with the world before him and bread and butter to seek, he kept a woman who

---

[6] The final rupture between Harte and Mark Twain appears to have taken place when "Ah Sin" was produced, after a long friction some of whose content has been indicated in this text. On March 1, 1877, Harte wrote a savage letter to Mark (which is still unpublished), making a number of charges against him and conveying a greater number of insults. By this letter, however, it appears that Bliss had advanced six thousand dollars on *Gabriel Conroy*. Harte accuses Bliss of falsifying his royalty statements and suggests that he did so in Mark's interest and with Mark's collusion.

was twice his age—no, the woman kept him. When he was consul in Great Britain, twenty-five or thirty years later, he was kept, at different times, by a couple of women—a connection which has gone into history, along with the names of those women. He lived in their houses, and in the house of one of them he died.

I call to mind an incident in my commerce with Harte which reminds me of one like it which happened during my sojourn on the Pacific Coast. When Orion's thoughtful carefulness enabled my Hale and Norcross stock speculation to ruin me, I had three hundred dollars left and nowhere in particular to lay my head. I went to Jackass Gulch and cabined for a while with some friends of mine, surface miners. They were lovely fellows; charming comrades in every way and honest and honorable men; their credit was good for bacon and beans, and this was fortunate because their kind of mining was a peculiarly precarious one; it was called pocket-mining and so far as I have been able to discover, pocket-mining is confined and restricted on this planet to a very small region around about Jackass Gulch.

A "pocket" is a concentration of gold dust in one little spot on the mountainside; it is close to the surface; the rains wash its particles down the mountainside, and they spread, fan-shape, wider and wider as they go. The pocket-miner washes a pan of dirt, finds a speck or two of gold in it, makes a step to the right or the left, washes another pan, finds another speck or two, and goes on washing to the right and to the left until he knows when he has reached both limits of the fan by the best of circumstantial evidence, to wit—that his pan-washings furnish no longer the speck of gold. The rest of his work is easy—he washes along up the mountainside, tracing the narrowing fan by his washings, and at last he reaches the gold deposit. It may contain only a few hundred dollars, which he can take out with a couple of dips of his shovel; also it may contain a concentrated treasure worth a fortune. It is the fortune he is after, and he will seek it with a never-perishing hope as long as he lives.

These friends of mine had been seeking that fortune daily for eighteen years; they had never found it but they were not at all discouraged; they were quite sure they would find it some day. During the three months that I was with them they found nothing, but we had a fascinating and delightful good time trying. Not long after I left, a greaser (Mexican) came loafing along and found a pocket with a hundred and twenty-five thousand dollars in it on a slope which our boys had never happened to explore. Such is luck! And such the treatment which honest, good perseverance gets so often at the hands of unfair and malicious Nature!

Our clothes were pretty shabby but that was no matter; we were in the fashion; the rest of the slender population were dressed as we were. Our boys hadn't had a cent for several months and hadn't needed one, their credit being perfectly good for bacon, coffee, flour, beans and molasses. If there was any difference, Jim[7] was the worst dressed of the three of us; if there was any discoverable difference in the matter of age, Jim's shreds were the oldest;

[7] Jim Gillis.

but he was a gallant creature, and his style and bearing could make any costume regal. One day we were in the decayed and naked and rickety inn when a couple of musical tramps appeared; one of them played the banjo and the other one danced unscientific clog-dances and sang comic songs that made a person sorry to be alive. They passed the hat and collected three or four dimes from the dozen bankrupt pocket-miners present. When the hat approached Jim he said to me, with his fine millionaire air, "Let me have a dollar."

I gave him a couple of halves. Instead of modestly dropping them into the hat, he pitched them into it at the distance of a yard, just as in the ancient novels milord the Duke doesn't hand the beggar a benefaction, but "tosses" it to him or flings it at his feet—and it is always a "purse of gold." In the novel, the witnesses are always impressed; Jim's great spirit was the spirit of the novel; to him the half-dollars were a purse of gold; like the Duke he was playing to the gallery, but the parallel ends there. In the Duke's case, the witnesses knew he could afford the purse of gold, and the largest part of their admiration consisted in envy of the man who could throw around purses of gold in that fine and careless way. The miners admired Jim's handsome liberality but they knew he couldn't afford what he had done, and that fact modified their admiration. Jim was worth a hundred of Bret Harte, for he was a man, and a whole man. In his little exhibition of vanity and pretense he exposed a characteristic which made him resemble Harte, but the resemblance began and ended there.

I come to the Harte incident now. When our play
was in a condition to be delivered to Parsloe, the
lessee of it, I had occasion to go to New York, and
I stopped at the St. James Hotel, as usual. Harte
had been procrastinating; the play should have been
in Parsloe's hands a day or two earlier than this,
but Harte had not attended to it. About seven in
the evening he came into the lobby of the hotel,
dressed in an ancient gray suit so out of repair that
the bottoms of his trousers were frazzled to a fringe;
his shoes were similarly out of repair and were sodden with snow-slush and mud, and on his head and
slightly tipped to starboard rested a crumpled little
soft hat which was a size or two too small for him;
his bright little red necktie was present, and rather
more than usually cheery and contented and conspicuous. He had the play in his hand. Parsloe's
theatre was not three minutes' walk distant; I supposed he would say, "Come along—let's take the
play to Parsloe."

But he didn't; he stepped up to the counter, offered his parcel to the clerk, and said with the manner of an earl, "It is for Mr. Parsloe—send it to
the theater."

The clerk looked him over austerely and said,
with the air of a person who is presenting a check-
mating difficulty, "The messenger's fee will be ten
cents."

Harte said, "Call him."

Which the clerk did. The boy answered the call,
took the parcel and stood waiting for orders. There
was a certain malicious curiosity visible in the clerk's

face. Harte turned toward me, and said, "Let me have a dollar."

I handed it to him. He handed it to the boy and said, "Run along."

The clerk said, "Wait, I'll give you the change."

Harte gave his hand a ducal wave and said, "Never mind it. Let the boy keep it."

.   .   .   .   .

Edward Everett Hale wrote a book which made a great and pathetic sensation when it issued from the press in the lurid days when the Civil War was about to break out and the North and South were crouched for a spring at each other's throats. It was called *The Man Without a Country*. Harte, in a mild and colorless way, was that kind of a man—that is to say, he was a man without a country; no, not man —man is too strong a term; he was an invertebrate without a country. He hadn't any more passion for his country than an oyster has for its bed; in fact not so much and I apologize to the oyster. The higher passions were left out of Harte; what he knew about them he got from books. When he put them into his own books they were imitations; often good ones, often as deceptive to people who did not know Harte as are the actor's simulation of passions on the stage when he is not feeling them but is only following certain faithfully studied rules for their artificial reproduction.

On the 7th of November, 1876—I think it was the 7th—he suddenly appeared at my house in Hartford and remained there during the following day, election day. As usual, he was tranquil; he was serene; doubtless the only serene and tranquil voter in the United States; the rest—as usual in our country—were excited away up to the election limit, for that vast political conflagration was blazing at white heat which was presently to end in one of the Republican party's most cold-blooded swindles of the American people, the stealing of the presidential chair from Mr. Tilden, who had been elected, and the conferring of it upon Mr. Hayes, who had been defeated.

I was an ardent Hayes man but that was natural, for I was pretty young at the time. I have since convinced myself that the political opinions of a nation are of next to no value, in any case, but that what little rag of value they possess is to be found among the old, rather than among the young. I was as excited and inflamed as was the rest of the voting world, and I was surprised when Harte said he was going to remain with us until the day after the election; but not much surprised, for he was such a careless creature that I thought it just possible that he had gotten his dates mixed. There was plenty of time for him to correct his mistake, and I suggested that he go back to New York and not lose his vote. But he said he was not caring about his vote; that he had come away purposely, in order that he might avoid voting and yet have a good excuse to answer the critics with.

Then he told me why he did not wish to vote. He said that through influential friends he had secured the promise of a consulate from Mr. Tilden and the same promise from Mr. Hayes, that he was going to be taken care of no matter how the contest might go, and that his interest in the election began and ended there. He said he could not afford to vote for either of the candidates, because the other candidate might find it out and consider himself privileged to cancel his pledge. It was a curious satire upon our political system! Why should a president care how an impending consul had voted? Consulships are not political offices; naturally and properly a consul's qualifications should begin and end with fitness for the post; and in an entirely sane political system the question of a man's political complexion could have nothing to do with the matter. However, the man who was defeated by the nation was placed in the presidential chair and the man without a country got his consulship.

Harte had no feeling, for the reason that he had no machinery to feel with. John McCullough, the tragedian, was a man of high character; a generous man, a lovable man, and a man whose truthfulness could not be challenged. He was a great admirer of Harte's literature, and in the early days in San Francisco he had had a warm fondness for Harte himself; as the years went by this fondness cooled to some extent, a circumstance for which Harte was responsible. However, in the days of Harte's consulship McCullough's affection for him had merely undergone a diminution; it had by no means disappeared; but by and by something happened which abolished what was left of it. John McCullough told me all about it.

One day a young man appeared in his quarters in New York and said he was Bret Harte's son, and had just arrived from England with a letter of in-

troduction and recommendation from his father—
and he handed the letter to McCullough. McCullough greeted him cordially, and said, "I was expecting you, my boy. I know your errand, through a
letter which I have already received from your
father; and by good luck I am in a position to satisfy
your desire. I have just the place for you, and you
can consider yourself on salary from today, and
now."

Young Harte was eloquently grateful, and said,
"I knew you would be expecting me, for my father
promised me that he would write you in advance."

McCullough had Harte's letter in his pocket but
he did not read it to the lad. In substance it was this:

"My boy is stage-struck and wants to go to you
for help, for he knows that you and I are old friends.
To get rid of his importunities, I have been obliged
to start him across the water equipped with a letter
strongly recommending him to your kindness and
protection, and begging you to do the best you can
to forward his ambition, for my sake. I was obliged
to write the letter, I couldn't get out of it, but the
present letter is to warn you beforehand to pay no
attention to the other one. My son is stage-struck,
but he isn't of any account, and will never amount
to anything; therefore don't bother yourself with
him; it wouldn't pay you for your lost time and
sympathy."

John McCullough stood by the boy and pushed his
fortunes on the stage and was the best father the lad
ever had.

I have said more than once in these pages that
Harte had no heart and no conscience, and I have

also said that he was mean and base. I have not said, perhaps, that he was treacherous, but if I have omitted that remark I wish to add it now.

All of us at one time or another blunder stupidly into indiscreet acts and speeches; I am not an exception; I have done it myself. About a dozen years ago, I drifted into the Players Club one night and found half a dozen of the boys grouped cozily in a private corner sipping punches and talking. I joined them and assisted. Presently Bret Harte's name was mentioned and straightway that mention fired a young fellow who sat at my elbow, and for the next ten minutes he talked as only a person can talk whose subject lies near his heart. Nobody interrupted; everybody was interested. The young fellow's talk was made up of strong and genuine enthusiasms; its subject was praise—praise of Mrs. Harte and her daughters. He told how they were living in a little town in New Jersey, and how hard they worked, and how faithfully, and how cheerfully, and how contentedly, to earn their living—Mrs. Harte by teaching music, the daughters by exercising the arts of drawing, embroidery, and such things—I meantime listening as eagerly as the rest, for I was aware that he was speaking the truth and not overstating it.

But presently he diverged into eulogies of the ostensible head of that deserted family, Bret Harte. He said that the family's happiness had one defect in it; the absence of Harte. He said that their love and their reverence for him was a beautiful thing to see and hear; also their pity of him on account of his enforced exile from home. He also said that Harte's own grief, because of this bitter exile, was beautiful to contemplate; that Harte's faithfulness in writing by every steamer was beautiful, too; that he was always longing to come home in his vacations but his salary was so small that he could not afford it; nevertheless, in his letters he was always promising himself this happiness in the next steamer or the next one after that one; and that it was pitiful to see the family's disappointment when the named steamers kept on arriving without him; that his self-sacrifice was an ennobling spectacle; that he was man enough and fine enough to deny himself in order that he might send to the family every month, for their support, that portion of his salary which a more selfish person would devote to the Atlantic voyage.

Up to this time I had "stood the raise," as the poker players say, but now I broke out and called the young fellow's hand—as the poker players also say. I couldn't help it. I saw that he had been misinformed. It seemed to be my duty to set him right.

I said, "Oh, that be hanged! There's nothing in it. Bret Harte has deserted his family, and that is the plain English of it. Possibly he writes to them, but I am not weak enough to believe it until I see the letters; possibly he is pining to come home to his deserted family, but no one that knows him will believe that. But there is one thing about which I think there can be no possibility of doubt—and that is, that he has never sent them a dollar, and has never intended to send them a dollar. Bret Harte is the most contemptible, poor little soulless blatherskite that exists on the planet today ———"

I had been dimly aware, very vaguely aware, by fitful glimpses of the countenances around me, that something was happening. It was I that was happening, but I didn't know it.

But when I had reached the middle of that last sentence somebody seized me and whispered into my ear, with energy, "For goodness sake shut up! This young fellow is Steele. He's engaged to one of the daughters."

·　·　·　·　·

2. *The Memorial to Thomas Bailey Aldrich. (July 3, 1908)*[8]

Last Monday Albert Bigelow Paine personally conducted me to Boston, and next day to Portsmouth, New Hampshire, to assist at the dedication of the Thomas Bailey Aldrich Memorial Museum.

As text and basis I will here introduce a few simple statistics. The late Thomas Bailey Aldrich was born in his grandfather's house in the little town of Portsmouth, New Hampshire, seventy-two or seventy-three years ago. His widow has lately bought that house and stocked it with odds and ends that once belonged to the child Tom Aldrich, and to the schoolboy Tom Aldrich, and to the old poet Tom Aldrich, and turned the place into a memorial museum in honor of Aldrich and for the preservation of his fame. She has instituted an Aldrich Memorial

[8] The following excerpt is from page 2539 of the type script. See Introduction.
"At this point I desire to give notice to my literary heirs, assigns, and executors, that they are to suppress, for seventy-five years, what I am now about to say about that curious function. It is not that I am expecting to say anything that shall really need suppressing, but that I want to talk without embarrassment and speak with freedom—freedom, comfort, appetite, relish."
A marginal note in pencil by Albert Bigelow Paine reads: "Not to be used for 75 years from 1908."

Museum Corporation under the laws of the State of New Hampshire, and has turned the museum over to this corporation which is acting for the City of Portsmouth, the ultimate heir of the benefaction, and she has injected the mayor of Portsmouth and other important people into that corporation to act as advertisement and directors. A strange and vanity-devoured, detestable woman! I do not believe I could ever learn to like her except on a raft at sea with no other provisions in sight.

The justification for an Aldrich Memorial Museum for pilgrims to visit and hallow with their homage may exist, but to me it seems doubtful. Aldrich was never widely known; his books never attained to a wide circulation; his prose was diffuse, self-conscious, and barren of distinction in the matter of style; his fame as a writer of prose is not considerable; his fame as a writer of verse is also very limited, but such as it is it is a matter to be proud of. It is based not upon his output of poetry as a whole but upon half a dozen small poems which are not surpassed in our language for exquisite grace and beauty and finish. These gems are known and admired and loved by the one person in ten thousand who is capable of appreciating them at their just value.

It is this sprinkling of people who would reverently visit the memorial museum if it were situated in a handy place. They would amount to one visitor per month, no doubt, if the museum were in Boston or New York, but it isn't in those places—it is in Portsmouth, New Hampshire, an hour and three-quarters from Boston by the Boston and Maine Railway, which still uses the cars it employed in its early

294 MARK TWAIN IN ERUPTION

business fifty years ago; still passes drinking water around per teapot and tin cup, and still uses soft coal and vomits the gritty product of it into those venerable cars at every window and crack and joint. A memorial museum of George Washington relics could not excite any considerable interest if it were located in that decayed town and the devotee had to get to it over the Boston and Maine.

When it came to making fun of a folly, a silliness, a windy pretense, a wild absurdity, Aldrich the brilliant, Aldrich the sarcastic, Aldrich the ironical, Aldrich the merciless, was a master. It was the greatest pity in the world that he could not be at that memorial function in the Opera House at Portsmouth to make fun of it. Nobody could lash it and blight it and blister it and scarify it as he could. However, I am overlooking one important detail: he could do all this, and would do it with enthusiasm, if it were somebody else's foolish memorial, but it would not occur to him to make fun of it if the function was in his own honor, for he had very nearly as extensive an appreciation of himself and his gifts as had the late Edmund Clarence Stedman, who believed that the sun merely rose to admire his poetry and was so reluctant to set at the end of the day and lose sight of it, that it lingered and lingered and lost many minutes diurnally, and was never able to keep correct time during his stay in the earth. Stedman was a good fellow; Aldrich was a good fellow; but vain?—bunched together they were as vain as I am myself, which is saying all that can be said under that head without being extravagant.

For the protection of the reader I must confess

that I am perhaps prejudiced. It is possible that I would never be able to see anything creditable in anything Mrs. Aldrich might do. I conceived an aversion for her the first time I ever saw her, which was thirty-nine years ago, and that aversion has remained with me ever since. She is one of those people who are profusely affectionate, and whose demonstrations disorder your stomach. You never believe in them; you always regard them as fictions, artificialities, with a selfish motive back of them. Aldrich was delightful company, but we never saw a great deal of him because we couldn't have him by himself.

. . . . .

(July 8, 1908)

I had not inquired into the amount of travel which would be required. It came near being great, for I had supposed we must go to New York and reship thence to Boston, which would have made a hard day of it, considering the character of the weather. And a long day—a very long day—twelve hours between getting out of bed at home and stepping into the hotel in Boston. But by accident we found out that we could change cars at South Norwalk and save four hours, so we reached Boston at two in the afternoon after a dusty and blistering and rather fatiguing journey. We were to go to Portsmouth next day, June 30th. Printed cards had been distributed by mail to the invited guests containing transportation information. Whereby it appeared that the nine o'clock express for Portsmouth would have a couple of special cars sacred to the guests.

To anybody but me, to any reasonable person, to

any unprejudiced person, the providing of special
cars by the surviving rich Aldriches would have
seemed so natural a thing, so properly courteous a
thing—in fact so necessary and unavoidable a politeness—that the information would have excited no
comment but would have been unemotionally received as being a wholly matter-of-course thing; but
where prejudice exists it always discolors our
thoughts and feelings and opinions. I was full of
prejudice, and so I resented this special train. I said
to myself that it was out of character; that it was for
other people, ordinary people, the general run of
the human race, to provide the simple courtesy of a
special train on an occasion like this and pay the cost
of it, but it was not for Mrs. Aldrich to do such a
thing; it was not for Mrs. Aldrich to squander
money on politeness to guests, eleemosynarily rich
as she is.

It irritated me, disappointed me, affronted me, to
see her rising above herself under the elevating influence of a high family occasion; in my malice I
wanted to find some way to account for it that would
take the credit out of it, and so I said to myself that
she, the great advertiser, the persistent advertiser,
the pushing and scrabbling and tireless advertiser,
was doing this gaudy thing for the sake of spreading it around in the newspapers and getting her com-
pensation out of it as an advertisement. That seemed
a sort of plausible way of accounting for it, but I was
so deeply prejudiced that it did not pacify me; I
could not reconcile myself to seeing her depart from
herself and from her traditions and be hospitable at
her own expense—still, she was defeating me, and I

had to confess it and take the medicine. However, in my animosity I said to myself that I would not allow her to collect glory from me at an expense to her of two dollars and forty cents, so I made Paine buy tickets to Portsmouth and return. That idea pleased me; indeed there is more real pleasure to be gotten out of a malicious act, where your heart is in it, than out of thirty acts of a nobler sort.

But Paine and I went into one of the two special cars in order to chat with their occupants, who would be male and female authors—friends, some of them, the rest acquaintances. It was lucky that we went in there, the result was joyous. I was sitting where I could carry on a conversational yell with all the males and females at the northern end of the car, when the conductor came along, austere and digni-fied as is the way of his breed of animals, and began to collect tickets! Several of the guests in my neigh-borhood I knew to be poor, and I saw—not with any real pleasure—a gasp of surprise catch in their throats and a pathetic look of distress exhibit itself in their faces. They pulled out of their pockets and their reticules the handsomely engraved card of in-vitation, along with the card specifying the special train, and offered those credentials to the unsym-pathetic conductor and explained that they were *in-vited* to the mortuary festival and did not have to pay. The smileless conductor-devil said with his cold and hollow Boston and Maine Railway bark, that he hadn't any orders to pass anybody, and he would trouble them for transportation cash.

The incident restored my Mrs. Aldrich to me un-damaged and just the same old thing she had always been, undeodorized and not a whiff of her missing. Here she was, rich, getting all the glory inseparable from the act of indulging in the imposing grandeur of a special train, and in the valuable advertising for herself incident to it, and then stepping aside and leaving her sixty hard-worked bread-winners to pay the bill for her. I realized that I had gotten back my lost treasure, the real Mrs. Aldrich, and that she was "all there," as the slang-mongers phrase it.

There was another detail of this sorrowful incident that was undeniably pitiful; persons unused to the luxurious Pullman car and accustomed to travel in the plebian common car, have the fashion of sticking their fare tickets in the back of the seat in front of them, where the conductor can see them as he goes along; on a New England railway the conductor goes along every few minutes, glances at the exposed tickets, punches some holes in them, and keeps that up all day, until the ticket has at last ceased to be a ticket and consists only of holes; but in the meantime the owner of the ticket has been at peace, he has been saved the trouble of pulling a ticket out of his vest pocket every two or three minutes.

Now then, these special-train guests, naturally thinking that their engraved invitation card was intended to serve as a pay ticket, had stuck it in the back of the seats in front of them so that the conductor could turn it into a colander with his punch and leave the owner unmolested; and now when they pointed out these cards to him with a confident and self-complacent and slightly rebuking air, and he responded by his countenance with a pointedly irrev-

erent though silent scoff, those people were visibly
so ashamed, so humiliated, that I think Mrs. Aldrich herself would have been almost sorry for them.
I was noble enough to be sorry for them—so sorry
that I almost wished I hadn't seen it. There were
sixty guests, ten or fifteen of them from New York,
the rest from Boston or thereabouts, and the entire
transportation bill could have been covered by a hundred and fifty dollars, yet that opulent and stingy
woman was graceless enough to let that much-sacri-
ficing company of unwealthy literary people pay the
bill out of their own pockets.

Every now and then in the special train some
lamb, undergoing the slaughter, would inquire of
some other lamb who this train was in charge of;
there was never a lamb that could answer that question; manifestly the special train was not in charge
of anybody; there was nobody at the Boston Station
to tell any guest where to go or which were the special cars; there was nobody on board the train to see
that the tin-pot boy came around, now and then, in
the awful swelter of that scorching day; at Portsmouth there was nobody to take charge of any guests
save the governor's party and about a dozen others.
The Madam's motorcar, which is a sumptuous and
costly one, was there to fetch the governor—free of
charge, I heard.

At the Opera House about three-fourths of the
special-train guests were sent to seats among the
general audience, while the governor and staff and
several more or less notorious authors were mar-
shaled into the green room to wait until the house
should be full and everything ready for the solemni-

ties to begin. The mayor of Portsmouth was there too, a big, hearty, muscular animal, just the ideal municipal mayor of this present squalid century. Presently we marched in onto the stage, receiving the noisy welcome which was our due. Howells and I followed the mayor and the governor and his staff, and the rest of the literary rabble followed us. We sat down in a row stretching across the stage, Howells sitting with me near the center in a short willow sofa.

He glanced down the line and murmured, "What an old-time, pleasant look it has about it! If we were blacked and had sharp-pointed long collars that projected slanting upward past our eyebrows like railway bars, it would be complete; and if Aldrich were here he would want to break out in the old introductory formula of happy memory and say breezily, 'How is you tonight, Brer Bones? How is you feelin', Brer Tamborine? How's yo' symptoms seem to segashuate dis ebenin'?'"

After a time the mayor stepped to the front and thundered forth a vigorous and confident speech in which he said many fine and deservedly complimentary things about Aldrich, and described the gentle and dreamy and remote Portsmouth of Aldrich's boyhood of sixty years ago and compared it with the booming Portsmouth of today. He didn't use that word; it would have been injudicious; he only implied it. The Portsmouth of today doesn't boom; it is calm, quite calm, and asleep. Also he told about the gathering together of the Aldrich mementoes and the stocking of Aldrich's boyhood home with part of them, and the stocking of a fireproof building in the yard with the rest of them, and the placing of the whole generous deposit in the hands of an Aldrich Museum Corporation, with the privilege of saving it for posterity at the expense of the city.

.   .   .   .   .

(July 9, 1908)

Governor Guild, talking at ease, made a graceful and animated speech, a speech well suited to the occasion, it having been faultlessly memorized. The delivery was free from halts and stumbles and hesitations. A person who is to make a speech at any time or anywhere, upon any topic whatever, owes it to himself and to his audience to write the speech out and memorize it, if he can find the time for it. In the days when I was still able to memorize a speech I was always faithful to that duty—for my own sake, not the hearers'. A speech that is well memorized can, by trick and art, be made to deceive the hearer completely and make him reverently marvel at the talent that can enable a man to stand up unprepared and pour out perfectly phrased felicities as easily and as comfortably and as confidently as less gifted people talk lusterless commonplaces. I am not talking morals now, I am merely talking sense. It was a good beginning—those well-memorized speeches, the mayor's and the governor's; they were happy, interesting, animated, effective.

Then the funeral began. Mourner after mourner crept to the front and meekly and weakly and sneakingly read the poem which he had written for the occasion; and read it confidentially as a rule, for the voice of the true poet, even the voice of the third-rate poet, is seldom able to carry to the middle benches. Pretty soon I was glad I had come in black clothes; at home they had fitted me out in that way, warning me that the occasion was not of a festive character, but mortuary, and I must dress for sorrow, not for the weather. They were odiously hot and close and suffocating and steamy and sweaty, those black clothes there on that sad platform, but they fitted the poetry to a dot; they fitted the wailing deliveries to a dot; they fitted the weary, hot faces of the audience to another dot; and I was glad my outfit was in harmony with the general suffering.

Poet after poet got up and crawled to the desk and pulled out his manuscript and lamented; and this went on and on and on, till the very solemnness of the thing began to become ludicrous. In my lifetime I have not listened to so much manuscript-reading before upon any occasion. I will not deny that it was good manuscript, and I will concede that none of it was bad; but no poet who isn't of the first class knows how to read, and so he is an affliction to everybody but himself when he tries it.

Even Col. Higginson, inconceivably old as he is and inured to platform performances for generations and generations, stood up there, bent by age to the curve of a parenthesis, and piped out his speech from manuscript, doing it with the ghostly and creaky remnant of a voice that long ago had rung like a tocsin when he charged with his regiment and led it to bloody victories. Howells's speech was brief, and naturally, and necessarily felicitously, worded, for fine thought and perfect wording are a natural gift with Howells, and he had it by heart and delivered it well; but he read his poem from manuscript. He did it gracefully and well, then added it to the pile and came back to his seat by my side, glad it was over and looking like a pardoned convict. Then I abolished my prepared and vaguely and ineffectually memorized solemnities and finished the day's performance with twelve minutes of lawless and unconfined and desecrating nonsense.

The memorial function was over. It was dreary; it was devilish; it was hard to endure; there were two sweltering hours of it, but I would not have missed it for twice the heat and exhaustion and Boston and Maine travel it cost, and the cinders I swallowed.

.   .   .   .   .

3. Murat Halstead and Bayard Taylor. (July 7, 1908)

Murat Halstead is dead. He was a most likable man. He lived to be not far short of eighty, and he devoted about sixty years to diligent, hard slaving at editorial work. His life and mine make a curious contrast. From the time that my father died, March 24, 1847, when I was past eleven years old, until the end of 1856, or the first days of 1857, I worked— not diligently, not willingly, but fretfully, lazily, repiningly, complainingly, disgustedly, and always shirking the work when I was not watched. The statistics show that I was a worker during about ten years. I am approaching seventy-three, and I believe I have never done any work since—unless I may call two or three years of lazy effort as reporter on the Pacific Coast by that large and honorable name—

and so I think I am substantially right in saying that when I escaped from the printing office fifty or fifty-one years ago I ceased to be a worker and ceased permanently.

Piloting on the Mississippi River was not work to me; it was play—delightful play, vigorous play, adventurous play—and I loved it; silver mining in the Humboldt Mountains was play, only play, because I did not do any of the work; my pleasant comrades did it and I sat by and admired; my silver mining in Esmeralda was not work, for Higbie and Robert Howland did it and again I sat by and admired. I accepted a job of shoveling tailings in a quartz mill there, and that was really work and I had to do it myself, but I retired from that industry at the end of two weeks, and not only with my own approval but with the approval of the people who paid the wages. These mining experiences occupied ten months and came to an end toward the close of September, 1862.

I then became a reporter in Virginia City, Nevada, and later in San Francisco, and after something more than two years of this salaried indolence I retired from my position on the *Morning Call*, by solicitation. Solicitation of the proprietor. Then I acted as San Franciscan correspondent of the Virginia City *Enterprise* for two or three months; next I spent three months in pocket-mining at Jackass Gulch with the Gillis boys; then I went to the Sandwich Islands and corresponded thence for the Sacramento *Union* five or six months; in October, 1866, I broke out as a lecturer, and from that day to this I have always been able to gain my living without doing any work; for the writing of books and magazine matter was always play, not work. I enjoyed it; it was merely billiards to me.

I wonder why Murat Halstead was condemned to sixty years of editorial slavery and I let off with a lifetime of delightful idleness. There seems to be something most unfair about this—something not justifiable. But it seems to be a law of the human constitution that those that deserve shall not have and those that do not deserve shall get everything that is worth having. It is a sufficiently crazy arrangement, it seems to me.

On the 10th of April, a little more than thirty years ago, I sailed for Germany in the steamer *Holsatia* with my little family—at least we got ready to sail, but at the last moment concluded to remain at our anchorage in the Bay to see what the weather was going to be. A great many people came down in a tug to say good-by to the passengers, and at dark, when we had concluded to go to sea, they left us.

When the tug was gone it was found that Murat Halstead was still with us; he had come to say good-by to his wife and daughter; he had to remain with us, there was no alternative. We presently went to sea. Halstead had no clothing with him except what he had on, and there was a fourteen-day voyage in front of him. By happy fortune there was one man on board who was as big as Halstead, and only that one man; he could get into that man's clothes but not into any other man's in that company. That lucky accident was Bayard Taylor; he was an unusually large man and just the size of Halstead, and he had an abundance of clothes and was glad to share them with Halstead, who was a close friend of his of long standing.

Toward midnight I was in the smoking cabin with them and then a curious fact came out; they had not met for ten years, and each was surprised to see the other looking so bulky and hearty and so rich in health; each had for years been expecting to hear of the other's death; for when they had last parted both had received death sentences at the hands of the physician. Heart disease in both cases, with death certain within two years. Both were required to lead a quiet life, walk and not run, climb no stairs when not obliged to do it, and above all things avoid surprises and sudden excitements, if possible. They understood that a single sudden and violent excitement would be quite sufficient for their needs and would promptly end their days, and so for ten years these men had been creeping and never trotting nor running; they had climbed stairs at gravel-train speed only and they had avoided excitements diligently and constantly—and all that time they were as hearty as a pair of elephants and could not understand why they continued to live.

Then something happened. And it happened to both at about the same time. The thing that happened was a sudden and violent surprise followed immediately by another surprise—surprise that they didn't fall dead in their tracks. These surprises happened about a week before the *Holsatia* sailed. Halstead was editor and proprietor of the Cincinnati *Commercial*, and was sitting at his editorial desk at midnight, high up in the building, when a mighty explosion occurred, close by, which rocked the building to its foundations and shivered all its glass, and before Halstead had time to reflect and not let the explosion excite him, he had sailed down six flights of stairs in thirty-five seconds and was standing panting in the street trying to say, "Thy will be done," and deadly afraid that that was what was going to happen. But nothing happened, and from that time forth he had been an emancipated man, and now for a whole week had been making up for ten years' lost time, hunting for excitements and devouring them like a famished person.

Bayard Taylor's experience had been of the like character. He turned a corner in the country and crossed a railway track just in time for an express train to nip a corner off the seat of his breeches and blow him into the next county by compulsion of the hurricane produced by the onrush of the train. He mourned and lamented, thinking that the fatal surprise had come at last; then he put his hand on his heart and got another surprise, for he found that it was still beating. He rose up and dusted himself off and became jubilant and gave praise and went off like Halstead to hunt up some more excitements and make up for ten years' lost time.

Bayard Taylor was on his way to Berlin as our new minister to Germany; he was a genial, lovable, simple-hearted soul, and as happy in his new dignity as ever a new plenipotentiary was since the world began. He was a poet and had written voluminously in verse, and had also made the best of all English translations of Goethe's "Faust." But all his poetry is forgotten now except two very fine songs, one about the Scotch soldiers singing "Annie Laurie" in the trenches before Sebastopol, and the other the tremendously inspiriting love song of an Arab lover to his sweetheart. No one has gathered together his odds and ends and started a memorial museum with them, and if he is still able to think and reflect he is glad of it.

He had a prodigious memory and one night while we were walking the deck he undertook to call up out of the deeps of his mind a yard-long list of queer and quaint and unrelated words which he had learned, as a boy, by reading the list twice over, for a prize, and had easily won it for the reason that the other competitors after studying the list an hour were not able to recite it without making mistakes. Taylor said he had not thought of that list since that time, but was sure he could reproduce it after half an hour's digging in his mind. We walked the deck in silence during the half hour, then he began with the first word and sailed glibly through without a halt and also without a mistake, he said.

He had a negro manservant with him who came on board dressed up in the latest agony of the fashion and looking as fine as a rainbow; then he disappeared and we never saw him again for ten or twelve days; then he came on deck drooping and meek, subdued, subjugated, the most completely wilted and disreputable looking flower that was ever seen outside of a conservatory or inside of it either. The mystery was soon explained. The sea had gotten his works out of order the first day on board, and he went to the ship's doctor to acquire a purge. The doctor gave him fourteen large pills and told him, in German, to take one every three hours till he found relief; but he didn't understand German, so he took the whole fourteen at one dose, with the result above recorded.

·   ·   ·   ·   ·

4. Kipling. (August 11, 1906)[9]

This morning's cables contain a verse or two from Kipling, voicing his protest against a liberalizing new policy of the British government which he fears will deliver the balance of power in South Africa into the hands of the conquered Boers. Kipling's name, and Kipling's words always stir me now, stir me more than do any other living man's. But I remember a time, seventeen or eighteen years back, when the name did not suggest anything to me and only the words moved me. At that time Kipling's name was beginning to be known here and there, in spots, in India, but had not traveled outside of that empire. He came over and traveled about America, maintaining himself by correspondence with Indian journals. He wrote dashing, free-handed, brilliant letters but no one outside of India knew about it.

On his way through the State of New York he stopped off at Elmira and made a tedious and blistering journey up to Quarry Farm in quest of me. He ought to have telephoned the farm first; then he would have learned that I was at the Langdon homestead, hardly a quarter of a mile from his hotel. But he was only a lad of twenty-four and properly impulsive and he set out without inquiring on that dusty and roasting journey up the hill. He found Susy Crane and my little Susy there, and they came

[9] Published, in part, in Paine, *Biography*, pp. 880-81.

as near making him comfortable as the weather and
the circumstances would permit.

.   .   .   .   .

(August 13, 1906)

The group sat on the veranda and while Kipling
rested and refreshed himself he refreshed the others
with his talk, talk of a quality which was well above
what they were accustomed to, talk which might be
likened to footprints, so strong and definite was the
impression which it left behind. They often spoke
wonderingly of Kipling's talk afterward, and they
recognized that they had been in contact with an extraordinary man, but it is more than likely that they
were the only persons who had perceived that he was
extraordinary. It is not likely that they perceived his
full magnitude, it is most likely that they were Eric
Ericsons who had discovered a continent but did not
suspect the horizonless extent of it. His was an unknown name and was to remain unknown for a year
yet, but Susy kept his card and treasured it as an interesting possession. Its address was Allahabad.

No doubt India had been to her an imaginary
land up to this time, a fairyland, a dreamland, a land
made out of poetry and moonlight for the Arabian
Nights to do their gorgeous miracles in; and doubtless Kipling's flesh and blood and modern clothes
realized it to her for the first time and solidified it.
I think so because she more than once remarked
upon its incredible remoteness from the world that
we were living in, and computed that remoteness and
pronounced the result with a sort of awe, fourteen
thousand miles, or sixteen thousand, whichever it
was. Kipling had written upon the card a compliment

to me. This gave the card an additional value in Susy's eyes, since as a distinction it was the next thing to being recognized by a denizen of the moon.

Kipling came down that afternoon and spent a couple of hours with me, and at the end of that time I had surprised him as much as he had surprised me, and the honors were easy. I believed that he knew more than any person I had met before, and I knew that he knew I knew less than any person he had met before—though he did not say it and I was not expecting that he would. When he was gone, Mrs. Langdon wanted to know about my visitor. I said, "He is a stranger to me but he is a most remarkable man—and I am the other one. Between us, we cover all knowledge; he knows all that can be known, and I know the rest."

He was a stranger to me and to all the world, and remained so for twelve months, then he became suddenly known and universally known. From that day to this he has held this unique distinction: that of being the only living person, not head of a nation, whose voice is heard around the world the moment it drops a remark, the only such voice in existence that does not go by slow ship and rail but always travels first-class by cable.

About a year after Kipling's visit in Elmira, George Warner came into our library one morning in Hartford, with a small book in his hand, and asked me if I had ever heard of Rudyard Kipling. I said, "No."

He said I would hear of him very soon, and that the noise he was going to make would be loud and continuous. The little book was the *Plain Tales* and he left it for me to read, saying it was charged with a new and inspiriting fragrance and would blow a refreshing breath around the world that would revive the nations. A day or two later he brought a copy of the London *World* which had a sketch of Kipling in it, and a mention of the fact that he had traveled in the United States. According to this sketch he had passed through Elmira. This remark, added to the additional fact that he hailed from India, attracted my attention—also Susy's. She went to her room and brought his card from its place in the frame of her mirror, and the Quarry Farm visitor stood identified.

I am not acquainted with my own books but I know Kipling's—at any rate I know them better than I know anybody else's books. They never grow pale to me; they keep their color; they are always fresh. Certain of the ballads have a peculiar and satisfying charm for me. To my mind, the incomparable Jungle Books must remain unfellowed permanently. I think it was worth the journey to India to qualify myself to read *Kim* understandingly and to realize how great a book it is. The deep and subtle and fascinating charm of India pervades no other book as it pervades *Kim*; *Kim* is pervaded by it as by an atmosphere. I read the book every year and in this way I go back to India without fatigue—the only foreign land I ever daydream about or deeply long to see again.

.   .   .   .   .

5. *Elinor Glyn.* (*January 13, 1908*)

Two or three weeks ago Elinor Glyn called on me one afternoon and we had a long talk, of a distinctly unusual character, in the library. It may be that by the time this chapter reaches print she may be less well known to the world than she is now, therefore I will insert here a word or two of information about her. She is English. She is an author. The newspapers say she is visiting America with the idea of finding just the right kind of a hero for the principal character in a romance which she is purposing to write. She has come to us upon the stormwind of a vast and sudden notoriety.

The source of this notoriety is a novel of hers called *Three Weeks*. In this novel the hero is a fine and gifted and cultivated young English gentleman of good family, who imagines he has fallen in love with the ungifted, uninspired, commonplace daughter of the rector. He goes to the Continent on an outing, and there he happens upon a brilliant and beautiful young lady of exceedingly foreign extraction, with a deep mystery hanging over her. It transpires later that she is the childless wife of a king or kinglet, a coarse and unsympathetic animal whom she does not love.

She and the young Englishman fall in love with each other at sight. The hero's feeling for the rector's daughter was pale, not to say colorless, and it is promptly consumed and extinguished in the furnace fires of his passion for the mysterious stranger —passion is the right word, passion is what the pair of strangers feel for each other, what they recognize as real love—the only real love, the only love worthy to be called by that great name—whereas the feeling which the young man had for the rector's daughter is perceived to have been only a passing partiality.

The queenlet and the Englishman flit away privately to the mountains and take up sumptuous quarters in a remote and lonely house there—and then business begins. They recognize that they were highly and holily created for each other and that their passion is a sacred thing, that it is their master by divine right, and that its commands must be obeyed. They get to obeying them at once and they keep on obeying them and obeying them, to the reader's intense delight and disapproval, and the process of obeying them is described, several times, almost exhaustively, but not quite—some little rag of it being left to the reader's imagination, just at the end of each infraction, the place where his imagination is to take up and do the finish being indicated by stars.

The unstated argument of the book is that the laws of Nature are paramount and properly take precedence of the interfering and impertinent restrictions obtruded upon man's life by man's statutes.

Mme. Glyn called, as I have said, and she was a picture! Slender, young, faultlessly formed and incontestably beautiful—a blonde with blue eyes, the incomparable English complexion, and crowned with a glory of red hair of a very peculiar, most rare, and quite ravishing tint. She was clad in the choicest stuffs and in the most perfect taste. There she is, just a beautiful girl; yet she has a daughter fourteen years old. She isn't winning; she has no charm but the charm of beauty, and youth, and grace, and intelligence and vivacity; she *acts* charm, and does it well, exceedingly well in fact, but it does not convince, it doesn't stir the pulse, it doesn't go to the heart, it leaves the heart serene and unemotional. Her English hero would have prodigiously admired her; he would have loved to sit and look at her and hear her talk, but he would have been able to get away from that lonely house with his purity in good repair, if he wanted to.

I talked with her with daring frankness, frequently calling a spade a spade instead of coldly symbolizing it as a snow shovel; and on her side she was equally frank. It was one of the damnedest conversations I have ever had with a beautiful stranger of her sex, if I do say it myself that shouldn't. She wanted my opinion of her book and I furnished it. I said its literary workmanship was excellent, and that I quite agreed with her view that in the matter of the sexual relation man's statutory regulations of it were a distinct interference with a higher law, the law of Nature. I went further and said I couldn't call to mind a written law of any kind that had been promulgated in any age of the world in any statute book or any Bible for the regulation of man's conduct in *any* particular, from assassination all the way up to Sabbath-breaking, that wasn't a violation of the law of Nature, which I regarded as the highest of laws, the most peremptory and absolute of all laws—Nature's laws being in my belief plainly and simply the laws of God, since He instituted them, He and no other, and the said laws, by authority of this divine origin taking precedence of all the statutes of man. I said that her pair of indelicate lovers were obeying the law of their make and disposition; that therefore they were obeying the clearly enunciated law of God, and in His eyes must manifestly be blameless.

Of course what she wanted of me was support and defense—I knew that but I said I couldn't furnish it. I said we were the servants of convention; that we could not subsist, either in a savage or a civilized state, without conventions; that we must accept them and stand by them, even when we disapproved of them; that while the laws of Nature, that is to say the laws of God, plainly made every human being a law unto himself, we must steadfastly refuse to obey those laws, and we must as steadfastly stand by the conventions which ignore them, since the statutes furnish us peace, fairly good government, and stability, and therefore are better for us than the laws of God, which would soon plunge us into confusion and disorder and anarchy, if we should adopt them. I said her book was an assault upon certain old and well-established and wise conventions, and that it would not find many friends, and indeed would not deserve many.

She said I was very brave, the bravest person she had ever met (gross flattery which could have beguiled me when I was very very young), and she implored me to publish these views of mine, but I said, "No, such a thing is unthinkable." I said that if I, or any other wise, intelligent, and experienced person, should suddenly throw down the walls that protect and conceal his *real* opinions on almost any subject under the sun, it would at once be perceived that he had lost his intelligence and his wisdom and ought to be sent to the asylum. I said I had been revealing to her my private sentiments, *not* my public ones;

that I, like all the other human beings, expose to the world only my trimmed and perfumed and carefully barbered public opinions and conceal carefully, cautiously, wisely, my private ones.

I explained that what I meant by that phrase "public opinions" was *published* opinions, opinions spread broadcast in print. I said I was in the common habit, in private conversation with friends, of revealing every private opinion I possessed relating to religion, politics, and men, but that I should never dream of *printing* one of them, because they are individually and collectively at war with almost everybody's public opinion, while at the same time they are in happy agreement with almost everybody's private opinion. As an instance, I asked her if she had ever encountered an intelligent person who privately believed in the Immaculate Conception[10]— which of course she hadn't; and I also asked her if she had ever seen an intelligent person who was daring enough to publicly deny his belief in that fable and print the denial. Of course she hadn't encountered any such person.

I said I had a large cargo of most interesting and important private opinions about every great matter under the sun, but that they were not for print. I reminded her that we all break over the rule two or three times in our lives and fire a disagreeable and unpopular private opinion of ours into print, but we never do it when we can help it, we never do it except when the desire to do it is too strong for us and overrides and conquers our cold, calm, wise judg-

---

[10] Throughout Mark Twain's writing, he confuses the doctrine of the Immaculate Conception with that of the Virgin Birth of Christ.

ment. She mentioned several instances in which I had come out publicly in defense of unpopular causes, and she intimated that what I had been saying about myself was not perhaps in strict accordance with the facts; but I said they were merely illustrations of what I had just been saying, that when I publicly attacked the American missionaries in China and some other iniquitous persons and causes, I did not do it for any reason but just the one: that the inclination to do it was stronger than my diplomatic instincts, and I had to obey and take the consequences. But I said I was not moved to defend her book in public; that it was not a case where inclination was overpowering and unconquerable, and that therefore I could keep diplomatically still and should do it.

The lady was young enough, and inexperienced enough, to imagine that whenever a person has an unpleasant opinion in stock which could be of educational benefit to Tom, Dick, and Harry, it is his *duty* to come out in print with it and become its champion. I was not able to get that juvenile idea out of her head. I was not able to convince her that we never do *any* duty for the duty's sake but only for the mere personal satisfaction we get out of doing that duty. The fact is, she was brought up just like the rest of the world, with the ingrained and stupid superstition that there is such a thing as *duty for duty's sake,* and so I was obliged to let her abide in her darkness. She believed that when a man held a private unpleasant opinion of an educational sort, which would get him hanged if he published it, he ought to publish it anyway and was a coward if he didn't. Take it all around, it was a very pleasant conversation, and glaringly unprintable, particularly those considerable parts of it which I haven't had the courage to more than vaguely hint at in this account of our talk.

Some days afterward I met her again for a moment, and she gave me the startling information that she had written down every word I had said, just as I had said it, without any softening and purifying modifications, and that it was "just splendid, just wonderful." She said she had sent it to her husband, in England. Privately I didn't think that that was a very good idea, and yet I believed it would interest him. She begged me to let her publish it and said it would do infinite good in the world, but I said it would damn me before my time and I didn't wish to be useful to the world on such expensive conditions.[11]

[11] There is a brief note on this interview in Elinor Glyn's autobiography, *Romantic Adventure,* 1937, p. 144.

THE LAST VISIT TO ENGLAND[1]

1. White and Red.

There was to be a dinner of high dignity that night at one of the colleges. I was to occupy a place at the high table with the Chancellor, the heads of colleges, Ambassador Reid, and some other distinguished personages, and respond to a toast. I had asked and received permission to stay at home until the banquet should be over and speechmaking time at hand. I had been asking and acquiring this privilege in America for six years and valued it beyond price. A banquet is probably the most fatiguing thing in the world except ditchdigging. It is the insanest of all recreations. The inventor of it overlooked no detail that could furnish weariness, distress, harassment, and acute and long-sustained misery of mind and body.

These sorrows begin with the assembling of the clans half an hour before the dinner. During all that half-hour one must stand on his feet with the crowd, amid a persecuting din of conversation, and must shake hands and exchange banalities and "I am so glad to see you, sirs" with apparently seven millions

[1] Mark Twain's visit to England in 1907 to receive the Litt.D. from Oxford is covered exhaustively in the dictations. Paine has used so much of this material in the *Biography*, however, that I am printing only a small part. These dictations are dated in July and August of 1907.

of fellow sufferers. Then the banquet begins and there is an hour and a half of that. It is an hour and a half of nerve-wrecking clamor, of intolerable clattering and clashing of knives and forks and plates, of shrieking and shouting commonplaces at one's elbow-mates, and of listening to the like shriekings and shoutings from them in return; and when there is a band—and there usually is—the pandemonium is complete and there is nothing to approach it but hell on a Sunday night.

During that awful hour and a half the faces of certain of the men are a study, and are pathetically interesting. These are the men who have been damned—that is to say, they are under sentence to make speeches. The faces of these are drawn and troubled, and exhibit a distressed preoccupation. Such of the damned as have come with memorized speeches are trying to say them over privately and talk to their neighbors at the same time, and also at the same time try to look interested in what the neighbors are saying. The result is a curious and piteous jumble of expressions and vacancies in the faces, an exhibition which compels the deep and sincere compassion of any beholder who has been of the damned himself and knows what it is like. The other men under sentence are the men who have not been appointed to speak, but who know they are likely to be called upon and who are now trying their best to think up something to say; if they are not succeeding they are no better off than those others, as far as comfort goes. It is unquestionably best to stay away from the banquet until the feeding and the racket are over and the time arrived for the speaking to begin; and so, as I have said, I had long ago adopted the policy of staying away until the banquet should be over and the speechmaking ready to begin. This judicious policy has saved my life, I suppose.

That banquet at the College was to begin at seven o'clock. At eight nobody was able to tell me what kind of clothes I ought to wear; some said evening dress, others said the scarlet gown. We sent a messenger to the College to inquire, and he came back and said evening dress. It was an error. I was fairly within the place before I noticed that it was just one wide and flaming conflagration of crimson gowns— a kind of human prairie on fire. I had to pass through the center of it in my black clothes, and I had never in my life felt so painfully and offensively and humiliatingly conspicuous before; and then I had to stand at the high table and look out over that fire and try to keep my mind on my business and make a speech. I could not have been in the least degree more uncomfortable if I had been stark naked. I called to mind a phrase which I had used ten years before when describing a great court function in the imperial palace at Vienna, a scene of dazzling color and splendor and gorgeousness, through the midst of which the American minister in black evening dress plowed his way, far and away the most conspicuous figure in that sea of flashing glories. I said he looked as out of place as a Presbyterian in hell. I was looking the same way now, and I knew how odiously showy and uncomfortable he must have felt.

Was it my conspicuousness that distressed me? Not at all. It was merely that I was not beautifully conspicuous but uglily conspicuous—it makes all the difference in the world. If I had been clothed from helmet to spurs in plate armor of virgin gold and shining like the sun, I should have been entirely at ease, utterly happy, perfectly satisfied with myself; to be so thunderingly conspicuous, but at the same time so beautifully conspicuous, would have caused me not a pang—on the contrary it would have filled me with joy, pride, vanity, exaltation. When I appear clothed in white, a startling accent in the midst of a somber multitude in midwinter, the most conspicuous object there, I am not ashamed, not ill at ease, but serene and content, because my conspicuousness is not of an offensive sort; it is not an insult and cannot affront any eye nor affront anybody's sense of propriety. My red gown was brought to me just as I was leaving the place—oh, infamously too late!

·   ·   ·   ·   ·

2. Marie Corelli.

I met Marie Corelli at a small dinner party in Germany fifteen years ago and took a dislike to her at once, a dislike which expanded and hardened with each successive dinner course until when we parted at last, the original mere dislike had grown into a very strong aversion. When I arrived in England, I found a letter from her awaiting me at Brown's Hotel. It was warm, affectionate, eloquent, persuasive; under its charm the aversion of fifteen years melted away and disappeared. It seemed to me that that aversion must have been falsely based; I thought I must certainly have been mistaken in the woman, and I felt a pang or two of remorse. I answered her letter at once—her love letter I may say—answered it with a love letter. Her home is in Shakespeare's Stratford. She at once wrote again, urging me in the most beguiling language to stop there and lunch with her when I should be on my way to London, on the 29th. It looked like an easy matter; the travel connected with it could not amount to much, I supposed, therefore I accepted by return mail.

I had now—not for the first time, nor the thousandth—trampled upon an old and wise and stern maxim of mine, to wit: "Supposing is good, but finding out is better." The supposing was finished, the letter was gone; it was now time to find out. Ashcroft[2] examined the timetables and found that I would leave Oxford at eleven o'clock the 29th, leave Stratford at midafternoon, and not reach London until about half past six. That is to say, I would be seven and a half hours in the air, so to speak, with no rest for the sole of my foot and a speech at the Lord Mayor's to follow! Necessarily I was aghast; I should probably arrive at the Lord Mayor's banquet in a hearse.

Ashcroft and I then began upon a hopeless task —to persuade a conscienceless fool to mercifully retire from a self-advertising scheme which was dear to her heart. She held her grip; anyone who knew her could have told us she would. She came to Oxford on the 28th to make sure of her prey. I begged her to let me off, I implored, I supplicated; I pleaded my white head and my seventy-two years and the likelihood that the long day in trains that would stop

[2] Mark Twain's secretary on the trip to England.

every three hundred yards and rest ten minutes would break me down and send me to the hospital. It had no effect. By God I might as well have pleaded with Shylock himself! She said she could not release me from my engagement; it would be quite impossible; and added, "Consider my side of the matter a little. I have invited Lady Lucy and two other ladies, and three gentlemen; to cancel the luncheon now would inflict upon them the greatest inconvenience; without doubt they have declined other invitations to accept this one; in my own case I have canceled three social engagements on account of this matter."

I said, "Which is the superior disaster: that your half-dozen guests be inconvenienced, or the Lord Mayor's three hundred? And if you have already canceled three engagements and thereby inconvenienced three sets of guests, canceling seems to come easy to you, and it looks as if you might add just one more to the list, in mercy to a suffering friend."

It hadn't the slightest effect; she was as hard as nails. I think there is no criminal in any jail with a heart so unmalleable, so unmeltable, so unfazeable, so flinty, so uncompromisingly hard as Marie Corelli's. I think one could hit it with a steel and draw a spark from it.

She is about fifty years old but has no gray hairs; she is fat and shapeless; she has a gross animal face; she dresses for sixteen, and awkwardly and unsuccessfully and pathetically imitates the innocent graces and witcheries of that dearest and sweetest of all ages; and so her exterior matches her interior and harmonizes with it, with the result—as I think—that she is the most offensive sham, inside and out, that misrepresents and satirizes the human race today. I would willingly say more about her but it would be futile to try; all the adjectives seem so poor and feeble and flabby, this morning.

So we went to Stratford by rail, with a car change or two, we not knowing that one could save time and fatigue by walking. She received us at Stratford station with her carriage and was going to drive us to Shakespeare's church, but I canceled that; she insisted but I said that day's program was already generous enough in fatigues without adding another. She said there would be a crowd at the church to welcome me and they would be greatly disappointed, but I was loaded to the chin with animosity and childishly eager to be as unpleasant as possible, so I held my ground, particularly as I was well acquainted with Marie by this time and foresaw that if I went to the church I should find a trap arranged for a speech; my teeth were already loose from incessant speaking, and the very thought of adding a jabber at this time was a pain to me; besides, Marie, who never wastes an opportunity to advertise herself, would work the incident into the newspapers and I who could not waste any possible opportunity of disobliging her naturally made the best of this one.

She said she had been purchasing the house which the founder of Harvard College had once lived in and was going to present it to America—another advertisement. She wanted to stop at that dwelling and show me over it, and she said there would be a crowd there. I said I didn't want to see the damned house. I didn't say it in those words but in that vicious spirit, and she understood; even her horses understood and were shocked, for I saw them shudder. She pleaded and said we need not stop for more than a moment, but I knew the size of Marie's moments by now, when there was an advertisement to be had, and I declined. As we drove by I saw that the house and the sidewalk were full of people— which meant that Marie had arranged for another speech. However, we went by, bowing in response to the cheers, and presently reached Marie's house, a very attractive and commodious English home.

I said I was exceedingly tired and would like to go immediately to a bedchamber and stretch out and get some rest, if only for fifteen minutes. She was voluble with tender sympathy and said I should have my desire at once; but deftly steered me into the drawing-room and introduced me to her company. That being over, I begged leave to retire, but she wanted me to see her garden and said it would take only a moment. We examined her garden, I praising it and damning it in the one breath—praising with the mouth and damning with the heart. Then she said there was another garden, and dragged me along to look at it. I was ready to drop with fatigue but I praised and damned as before, and hoped I was through now and might be suffered to die in peace; but she beguiled me to a grilled iron gate and pulled me through it into a stretch of waste ground where stood fifty pupils of a military school, with their master at their head—arrangement for another advertisement.

She asked me to make a little speech and said the boys were expecting it. I complied briefly, shook hands with the master and talked with him a moment, then—well then we got back to the house. I got a quarter of an hour's rest, then came down to the luncheon. Toward the end of it that implacable woman rose in her place, with a glass of champagne in her hand, and made a speech! With me for a text, of course. Another advertisement, you see—to be worked into the newspapers. When she had finished I said, "I thank you very much"—and sat still. This conduct of mine was compulsory, therefore not avoidable; if I had made a speech, courtesy and custom would have required me to construct it out of thanks and compliments, and there was not a rag of that kind of material lurking anywhere in my system.

We reached London at half past six in the evening in a pouring rain, and half an hour later I was in bed—in bed and tired to the very marrow; but the day was at an end, at any rate, and that was a comfort. This was the most hateful day my seventy-two years have ever known.

I have now exposed myself as being a person capable of entertaining and exhibiting a degraded and brutally ugly spirit, upon occasion, and in making this exposure I have done my duty by myself and by my reader—notwithstanding which I claim and maintain that in any other society than Marie Corelli's my spirit is the sweetest that has ever yet descended upon this planet from my ancestors, the angels.

I spoke at the Lord Mayor's banquet that night, and it was a botch.

·   ·   ·   ·   ·

3. *Winston Churchill.*

Ashcroft's next note says: "*Sunday, June 30th.* Dined with Sir Gilbert and Lady Parker."

It was a large company, with a sprinkling of titles, and also with a sprinkling of men and women distinguished for achievement; but the whole scene is abolished from my memory by one wonderful face, just as the stars sparkling upon the horizon are swallowed up in the glory of the rising sun and extinguished. I am referring in this prodigious way to the face of a young woman. By the figure which I have used I have intended to indicate that this young creature's beauty was of the sort which is called dazzling; it is the right word; that face dazzled all the other faces to extinction, and just blazed and blazed in a splendid solitude; and in that solitude it still goes on blazing in my memory to this day. Lady —Lady something—but the name has gone from me; names and faces will not stay with me; that name has departed but I should know the face again anywhere.

The style was English, her features were English, the complexion was English, the set of the head was English, the poise was English, the character was English, the dignity was English—all high-born English; but over it all, and pervading it and suffusing it with that subtle something which we call charm, was a friendly and outreaching good fellowship and an easy and natural and unstudied grace of manner and carriage which was American—rare everywhere, and infrequent, but most frequent among our people, I think. I explained to her what I thought of her, and said England ought to be proud of such a product; but she smiled like a complimented angel, and rippled out a musical little laugh, and said she was an American product and destitute of English blood.

It was a very pleasant surprise. Later, at another

dinner party, this pleasant surprise was repeated, where I mistook a couple of titled American ladies for English women; they were women whose looks, whose ways, and the set and style of whose upholstery was distinctly English. Those two ladies were grieved and disappointed; for they had hoped and believed that they had kept their beloved nationality unmodified and unalloyed by time and changed relations, and that it was visible on their outsides. These ladies had been living in England five years, and one cannot remain so long in an unaccustomed atmosphere without taking color from it.

There was talk of that soaring and brilliant young statesman, Winston Churchill, son of Lord Randolph Churchill and nephew of a duke. I had met him at Sir Gilbert Parker's seven years before, when he was twenty-three years old, and had met him and introduced him to his lecture audience a year later in New York, when he had come over to tell of the lively experiences he had had as a war correspondent in the South African war, and in one or two wars on the Himalayan frontier of India.

Sir Gilbert Parker said, "Do you remember the dinner here seven years ago?"

"Yes," I said, "I remember it."

"Do you remember what Sir William Vernon Harcourt said about you?"

"No."

"Well, you didn't hear it. You and Churchill went up to the top floor to have a smoke and a talk, and Harcourt wondered what the result would be. He said that whichever of you got the floor first would keep it to the end, without a break; he believed that

you, being old and experienced, would get it and that
Churchill's lungs would have a half-hour's rest for
the first time in five years. When you two came down,
by and by, Sir William asked Churchill if he had had
a good time, and he answered eagerly, 'Yes.' Then
he asked you if you had had a good time. You hesi-
tated, then said without eagerness, 'I have had a
smoke.' "

· · · · · ·

4. Sidney Lee.

From Ashcroft's notes: "*Monday, July 1*. Dined
with Sidney Lee at the Garrick Club, and called at
Mrs. Macmillan's, to see Lady Jersey, on the way
home."

It was a distinguished company at the dinner, and
once more I encountered J. M. Barrie; also once
more he sat on the other side of the table and out of
conversing distance. The same thing happened in
London twice, seven years ago, and once in New
York since then. I have never had five minutes' talk
with him that wasn't broken off by an interruption;
after the interruption he always dissolves mysteri-
ously and disappears. I should like to have one good
unbroken talk with that gifted Scot some day before
I die.

The Garrick was familiar to me; I had often fed
there in bygone years as guest of Henry Irving,
Toole, and other actors—all dead now. It could
have been there, but I think it was at Bateman's,
thirty-five years ago, that I told Irving and Wills,
the playwright, about the whitewashing of the fence
by Tom Sawyer, and thereby captured a chapter on

cheap terms; for I wrote it out when I got back to the hotel while it was fresh in my mind.[3]

Sidney Lee's dinner was in a room which I was sure I had not seen for thirty-five years, yet I recognized it and could dreamily see about me the forms and faces of the small company of that long forgotten occasion. Anthony Trollope was the host, and the dinner was in honor of Joaquin Miller, who was on the top wave of his English notoriety at that time. There were three other guests: one is obliterated, but I remember two of them, Tom Hughes and Levison-Gower. No trace of that obliterated guest remains with me—I mean the *other* obliterated guest, for I was an obliterated guest also. I don't remember that anybody ever addressed a remark to either of us; no, that is a mistake—Tom Hughes addressed remarks to us occasionally; it was not in his nature to forget or neglect any stranger. Trollope was voluble and animated, and was but vaguely aware that any other person was present excepting him of the noble blood, Levison-Gower. Trollope and Hughes addressed their talk almost altogether to Levison-Gower, and there was a deferential something about it that almost made me feel that I was at a religious service; that Levison-Gower was the acting deity, and that the illusion would be perfect if somebody would do a hymn or pass the contribution box. All this was most curious and unfamiliar and interesting. Joaquin Miller did his full share of the talking, but he was a discordant note, a disturber and degrader of the solemnities. He was affecting the pic-

[3] This is discussed in my introduction to the Limited Editions Club's edition of *Tom Sawyer*, 1939.

turesque and untamed costume of the wild Sierras at the time, to the charmed astonishment of conventional London, and was helping out the effects with the breezy and independent and aggressive manners of that faraway and romantic region. He and Trollope talked all the time and both at the same time, Trollope pouring forth a smooth and limpid and sparkling stream of faultless English, and Joaquin discharging into it his muddy and tumultuous mountain torrent, and— Well, there was never anything just like it except the Whirlpool Rapids under Niagara Falls.

It was long ago, long ago! and not even an echo of that turbulence was left in this room where it had once made so much noise and display. Trollope is dead; Hughes is dead; Levison-Gower is dead; doubtless the obliterated guest is dead; Joaquin Miller is white-headed and mute and quiet in his dear mountains.

·   ·   ·   ·   ·

I had not seen Sidney Lee since 1902, when he made a flying visit to our side of the ocean and was banqueted by Andrew Carnegie, one night, in his new palace at 92nd Street and Fifth Avenue. He is not now a bashful man but is as much at his ease in company as is anybody, whereas when he came to America that time there was only one other man on our soil who could successfully compete with him in bashfulness, and that was Joel Uncle Remus Harris. Sidney Lee's bashfulness spread out and covered the whole northern half of the United States, and

Harris's crowded the southern half; there was no room in the republic for another man of this pattern.

There were twenty men at Carnegie's; in the drawing-room before dinner, they were introduced to Mr. Lee one by one, and they were all struck by his extreme bashfulness. They were strangely bashful themselves at the dinner, yet there was no man present who had not been a long time before the public and accustomed to foregathering with all sorts of people under all sorts of conditions. That dinner afforded the strangest and most unaccountable exhibitions of timidity I have ever witnessed; I have never seen anything like it among grown-up men, either before or since then, in my long pilgrimage. Was Mr. Lee the cause of it? Or was it Mrs. Carnegie? I have asked myself that conundrum many a time, but have never yet been able to answer it to my satisfaction. Mrs. Carnegie was the only lady present. I took her out and sat at her right, at the center of the table; opposite me, across the table, sat Mr. Carnegie with Mr. Lee at his right; next to Lee sat John Burroughs, the naturalist; next to Burroughs sat Carl Schurz, great soldier and statesman; next to Schurz sat Melville Stone, head of the Associated Press of the planet; next to Stone sat Horace White, old and famous and able journalist. At Carnegie's left sat Mr. Howells; at Mr. Howells's left sat Gilder, of the *Century*; and so on—I will not try to name the rest of the assemblage.

When the feast was finished and the black coffee and cigars installed, Mr. Carnegie—smiley and complacent little man!—rose in his place to speak. His smiliness, his complacency, his ease, his confidence—

supports which had never failed him in his life before upon such an occasion—withered quickly away and vanished before he had uttered a word; it was a new and surprising and most interesting thing to see. Carnegie was in a bad stage fright; everybody saw it, yet nobody was entirely able to believe it, I suppose.

When he began to speak, the words came hesitatingly—gaspingly, one may fairly say—and with disastrous spaces between; he at once began to advertise his fright and his nervousness by that couple of age-worn indications which the distressed novice has unconsciously resorted to at banquets since the beginning of time: first he took up his wineglasses one at a time, as a player takes up chessmen, and made a new arrangement of them on the cloth; then he took them up again, one at a time, and grouped them in a new way; again he took them up, and again changed the grouping—all this with a painful attention to detail that was most uncomfortable to witness, so charged was it with doubt and miserable anxiety; next he resorted to that other ancient sign, the fussing with his napkin. He folded it, kneaded it with his knuckles; he turned it around this way, then that way, then the other way, always kneading it and always stammering incoherently along.

There was but four feet of tablecloth between him and me, yet his voice was so weak and his syllables so mumbled, so slurred, and so vacantly delivered, that I did not catch any more than half the words of any sentence; and when he sat down I was wholly ignorant of the matter of his speech, and even of the purpose of it. I knew he was introducing Mr. Lee, because I knew his speech could have no object other than that, but I got not a thing out of his remarks that I could not have gotten out of them if he had delivered them with the sign language of the deaf and dumb—a language with which I have no acquaintance. I noticed another thing: his hand quaked and quivered all the time that he was fumbling with his glasses and his napkin.

Sidney Lee got up and shivered—stood shivering the most of a minute, but not all of it—uttered three or four quite inaudible sentences, and sat down still alive but not noticeably so.

Mr. Carnegie got up and performed again with napkin and glasses, and with palsied lips and extinguished voice, and resumed his seat. I had not caught a word that I could understand. Apparently he had been introducing John Burroughs, for Burroughs got up and began to rock on his base and quiver and swallow the dry swallow which indicates distress and which compels the compassion of all witnesses. What he said was confused and disjointed, and marred with hesitations and repetitions, but one could at least hear it. He wandered hopelessly and helplessly for a minute or two, hunting for a text, skirmishing for an idea; then I spoke across and came to his rescue with the suggestion that he discard the conventions and step boldly out upon familiar ground and talk shop. I said that in a time gone by he had published an article in which he had offered the theory, with reservations, that the reason an oak forest always grew up in the place previously occupied by a pine forest when the pine forest had been removed, was because the squirrels had used the carpet of pine-needles as a hiding place for acorns, and had forgotten them and left them there, with the result that when the pines were removed the sun had a chance to warm the acorns and make them sprout—and asked him to say whether he had since established the correctness of his theory. This text turned his language loose and he had no further trouble with his speech.

Carl Schurz, that marvelously ready and fluent and felicitous handler of our great English tongue on its highest planes, followed Burroughs and furnished us another surprise. He had never been frightened before, in all the history of his long and illustrious public career, but he was frightened now; all his noble and charming and exquisite phrasing was gone, and he stumbled pathetically along over a bumping corduroy road of disjointed commonplaces and poverties of expression, and soon reached the edge of his difficult world and fell over it and subsided, a defeated man.

Melville Stone rose, stammered, wandered, straggled, got lost, and was quickly vanquished and added to the muster roll of the failures.

The very same fate befell Horace White.

Then Howells got up and bent over the table with his left hand supporting his curve, while he arranged and rearranged his wineglasses with his right, and gasped and stuttered and dripped disconnected and puerile words all around; next he turned to his napkin for help and heavily bore down upon it and pitilessly rolled it, unrolled it, and rolled it again, and presently cut an uncompleted sentence in two with something like a despairing gasp and wilted into his seat, a target for everybody's heartfelt compassion.

Gilder followed, and failed; when he got through, any stranger could have told by the look of his napkin that it had been helping a scared man make a speech.

Mr. Hornblower, a celebrated advocate, followed Gilder. He tried to talk—indeed he made what could be justly called a heroic effort to do it—but he soon gave it up. He said he would frankly confess that his trouble was that he was frightened; that he was frightened to speechlessness; that he could not divine why, and was wholly unable to account for his curious and novel condition, but that the fact remained as stated: he was frightened and couldn't go on. He said he could not remember ever having had a like experience since he had made his success at the bar. Then he sat down looking thankful that his ordeal was over.

I forgot to say that I followed Sidney Lee—but the omission is of no consequence; I was in the conflict before that deadly and mysterious contagion of fright had got well started, and so I escaped infection.

·   ·   ·   ·   ·

5. *The Holy Grail.*

Secretary's note: "Mr. Clemens called on Lady Stanley, widow of the explorer, in the afternoon."

In fact, that was one of my earliest calls. Lady Stanley was as eager and impulsive as ever and as free from any concealment of her feelings as she was when I first knew her, a proud and happy young bride, so many years ago. Stanley has been dead three years and a half, but I think all her days and nights are spent in worship of him, and I believe he is almost as present to her as he was in life.

She is an intense spiritualist and has long lived in the atmosphere of that cult. Mrs. Myers, her widowed sister, was the wife of the late president of the British Psychical Society, who was a chief among spiritualists. To me, who take no interest in otherworldly things and am convinced that we know nothing whatever about them and have been wrongly and uncourteously and contemptuously left in total ignorance of them, it is a pleasure and a refreshment to have converse with a person like Lady Stanley, who uncompromisingly believes in them; and not only believes in them but considers them important. She was as exactly and as comprehensively happy and content in her beliefs as I am in my destitution of them, and I perceived that we could exchange places and both of us be precisely as well off as we were before; for when all is said and done, the one sole condition that makes spiritual happiness and preserves it is the absence of doubt. Lady Stanley and I, and the black savage who worships a tar baby in the African jungle and is troubled by no religious doubts or misgivings, are just equals, and equally fortunately situated; either of us could change places with either of the others and be fully as well off as before; the trade would cost neither party the value of a farthing.

Lady Stanley wanted to convert me to her beliefs and her faith, and there has been a time when I would have been eager to convert her to my position, but that time has gone by; I would not now try to unsettle any person's religious faith, where it was untroubled by doubt—not even the savage African's. I have found it pretty hard to give up missionarying —that least excusable of all human trades—but I was obliged to do it because I could not continue to exercise it without private shame while publicly and privately deriding and blaspheming the other missionaries.

I found that Stanley had left behind him an uncompleted autobiography. It sets forth freely and frankly the details of his childhood and youth and early manhood, then stops with his adventures in our Civil War, if I remember rightly. Lady Stanley is preparing it for publication, and I was surprised and also greatly gratified to find that she was not purposing to suppress certain facts that used to sift around in whispers in Stanley's lifetime—to wit, that he was of humble origin and was born in a workhouse. No doubt there was a time when she would have been glad to see these things suppressed and forgotten but she has risen above that; she lives upon a higher and worthier plane now; she perhaps realizes that those humble beginnings are matter for pride now, when one remembers how high the peerless explorer climbed in spite of them.

I will mix my dates again—this in order to bring into immediate juxtaposition a couple of curiosities in the way of human intellectual gymnastics. Lady Stanley believes that Stanley's spirit is with her all the time and talks with her about her ordinary daily concerns—a thing which is to me unthinkable. I wonder if it would be unthinkable to Archdeacon Wilberforce, also? I do not know, but I imagine that that would be the case. I imagine that the Immaculate Conception and the rest of the impossibilities recorded in the Bible would have no difficulties for him, because in those cases he has been trained from the cradle to believe the unbelievable and is so used to it that it comes natural and handy to him—but that kind of teaching is no preparation for acceptance of other unbelievable things, to whose examination one comes with an untwisted and unprejudiced mind. Wilberforce is educated, cultured, and has a fine and acute mind, and he comes of an ancestry similarly equipped; therefore he is competent to examine new marvels with an open mind, and I think the chances are that he rejects the claims of spiritualism with fully as much confidence as he accepts Immaculate Conception. Is it possible that Mr. Wilberforce has been trained from the cradle up to believe in the Holy Grail? It does not seem likely; yet he does believe in it and not only believes in it but believes he has it in his possession.

If I had had this astonishing fact at secondhand I could not have believed it, and would not have believed it even if I had gotten it from the twelve apostles in writing, with every signature vouched for by a notary public. I should have said that to an educated, cultured, highly intellectual man who believes he has held the Holy Grail in his hand, complete and unquestioning belief in Munchausens, and in all other conceivable extravagances, must come easy.

The text for what I am talking about now I find in this note of Ashcroft's: "*Sunday, June 23*. In the afternoon Mr. Clemens visited Archdeacon Wilberforce, 20 Dean's Yard, Westminster. Sir William Crookes, Sir James Knowles, Mrs. Myers (widow of the author of *Human Personality and Its Survival of Bodily Death*) and perhaps seventy-five or a hundred others were there."

As soon as I entered I was told by the Archdeacon that a most remarkable event had occurred—that the long lost Holy Grail had at last been found and that there could be no mistake whatever about its identity! I could not have been more startled if a gun had gone off at my ear. For a moment, or at least half a moment, I supposed that he was not in earnest; then that supposition vanished; manifestly he was in earnest—indeed he was eagerly and excitedly in earnest. He leading, we plowed through the crowd to the center of the drawing-room, where Sir William Crookes, the renowned scientist, was standing. Sir William is a spiritualist. We closed in upon Sir William, Mrs. Myers accosting me and joining us. Mr. Wilberforce then told me the rest of the story of the Holy Grail, and it was apparent that Sir William already knew all about it and was, moreover, a believer in the marvel. In brief, the story was that a young grain merchant, a Mr. Pole, had recently been visited in a vision by an angel who commanded him to go to a certain place outside the ancient Glastonbury Abbey, and said that upon digging in that place he would find the Holy Grail. Mr. Pole obeyed. He sought out the indicated spot and dug there, and under four feet of packed and solid earth he found the relic. All this had happened a week or ten days before this present conversation of June 23d.

The Holy Grail was in the house. A proper spirit

of reverence forbade its exhibition to a crowd but
Mr. Wilberforce offered to grant me a private view
of it, therefore I followed him and Sir William;
Mrs. Myers joined us. When we arrived at the room
where the relic was, we found there the finder of it
and one man—a guardian of the place, this latter
seemed to be. Mr. Pole brought a wooden box of a
quite humble and ordinary sort, and took from it a
loose bundle of white linen cloth, handling it carefully, and gave it into Mr. Wilberforce's hands, who
proceeded to unwind its envelope—not hastily but
with cautious pains and impressively; the pervading
silence was itself impressive and I was affected by it.
Stillness and solemnity have a subduing power of
their own, let the occasion be what it may. This
power had time and opportunity to deepen and
gather force, degree by degree, for the linen bandage
was of considerable length. At last the sacred vessel,
which tradition asserts received the precious blood of
the crucified Christ, lay exposed to view.

In the belief of two persons present, this was the
very vessel which was brought by night and secretly
delivered to Nicodemus nearly nineteen centuries
ago, after the Creator of the universe had delivered
up His life on the cross for the redemption of the
human race; the very cup which the stainless Sir
Galahad had sought with knightly devotion in far
fields of peril and adventure, in Arthur's time, fourteen hundred years ago; the same cup which princely
knights of other bygone ages had laid down their
lives in long and patient efforts to find, and had
passed from life disappointed—and here it was at
last, dug up by a Liverpool grain broker at no cost

of blood or travel and apparently no purity required of him above the average purity of the twentieth-century dealer in cereal futures; not even a stately name required—no Sir Galahad, no Sir Bors de Ganis, no Sir Lancelot of the Lake—nothing but a mere Mr. Pole; given name not known, probably Peterson. No armor of shining steel required; no plumed helmet, no emblazoned shield, no death-dealing spear, no formidable sword endowed with fabulous powers: in fact no armor at all, and no weapons, but just a plebeian pick and shovel. Here, right under our very eyes, was the Holy Grail, re-nowned for nineteen hundred years—the longed-for, the prayed-for, the sought-for, the most illustrious relic the world has ever known; and there, within touch of our hand, stood its rescuer, Peterson Pole, whom God preserve! It was an impressive moment.

To be exact, it was not a cup at all; it was not a vase; it was not a goblet. It was merely a saucer—a saucer of green glass enclosing a saucer of white silver. Both surfaces of the saucer were adorned with small flower figures in soft colors pierced with openwork, and through these piercings the impris-oned silver saucer could be seen. In size and shape and shallowness, this saucer was like any other saucer. It may have been a cup, or a beaker, or a grail, once, but if so time has shriveled it.

Mr. Wilberforce said that it was the true Holy Grail; that there was no room for the slightest doubt about it; that no vessel like it was now in existence anywhere; that its age could not be short of four thousand years; that its place of concealment, under four feet of solid earth, was another indication of its antiquity, since it takes many centuries to form four feet of solid earth. It was evident that Sir William Crookes, who as a scientist will accept no alleged revelation of science until it has been submitted to the most exacting and remorseless tests—and has stood the tests and stands absolutely proven—was quite satisfied with these juvenile guessings and empty reasonings, and fully believed in the genuineness of this Holy Grail, and did not even doubt the authenticity of that angel of indigestion that brought the news to the grain broker.

I am glad to have lived to see that half-hour—that astonishing half-hour. In its particular line it stands alone in my life's experiences; having no fellow, and nothing, indeed, that even remotely resembles it. I have long suspected that man's claim to be the reasoning animal was a doubtful one, but this episode has swept that doubtfulness away; I am quite sure now that often, very often, in matters concerning religion and politics a man's reasoning powers are not above the monkey's. Mrs. Myers has lived in an atmosphere of spiritualism for many years, and subscribes to that cult's claims; still the Holy Grail was too large a mouthful for her; she indicated this in a private remark to me.

If this had been an American episode, the newspapers would have rung with laughter from one end of the country to the other, whether the sponsor of the Grail was at the bottom of the Church or at its summit—but Mr. Wilberforce is a great *English* Church dignitary, the episode is English also, and that makes all the difference. We followed custom, and kept still. So did the English press. Two or three weeks after the 23d a brief account of the finding of the Holy Grail was published in a London paper, along with the names involved, and this account was cabled over and published in the American papers; there the matter dropped, without comment on either side of the ocean; I have not seen nor heard of a single reference to it from that day to this.

MISCELLANY

A great man is lost to the country; a great man and great citizen, the greatest citizen we had and the only statesman left to us, after the death of Senator Hoar of Massachusetts. I speak of Grover Cleveland, twice President of the United States, who died yesterday. He was a very great president, a man who not only properly appreciated the dignity of his high office but added to its dignity. The contrast between President Cleveland and the present occupant of the White House is extraordinary; it is the contrast between an archangel and the Missing Link. Mr. Cleveland was all that a president ought to be; Mr. Roosevelt is all that a president ought not to be—he covers the entire ground.

It is said that Mr. Cleveland has left but little for his family to live on. His widow ought to have a life pension of twenty-five thousand dollars but she will not get it. If she were the bastard of a bounty jumper and had a vote to sell, Roosevelt and Congress would tumble and scramble over each other in their eagerness to confer the pension and buy that vote.

◇◇◇◇◇

I met Mr. [Horace] Greeley only once and then

by accident. It was in 1871, in the (old) *Tribune*
office. I climbed one or two flights of stairs and went
to the wrong room. I was seeking Colonel John Hay
and I really knew my way and only lost it by my
carelessness. I rapped lightly on the door, pushed it
open and stepped in. There sat Mr. Greeley, busy
writing, with his back to me. I think his coat was off.
But I knew who it was, anyway. It was not a pleasant
situation, for he had the reputation of being pretty
plain with strangers who interrupted his train of
thought. The interview was brief. Before I could pull
myself together and back out, he whirled around and
glared at me through his great spectacles and said:

"Well, what in hell do *you* want!"

"I was looking for a gentlem——"

"Don't keep them in stock—clear out!"

I could have made a very neat retort but didn't,
for I was flurried and didn't think of it till I was
downstairs.

◇◇◇◇◇

When a United States Court has convicted a man
of being a pirate—that is to say, a thief—it is perhaps time for him to resign the superintendency of
his Sunday school and tone down some other of his
lurid pieties; unless, as is more than likely in Mr.
John Wanamaker's case, he uses these arts and offices
merely as advertisements for his mercantile business.
It is now time—and also just and right—to secure
to this odorous pilgrim this extra distinction, which
he has laboriously and indisputably earned—to wit:
that he is the only individual in a population of 60,-
000,000 who is known to have picked the pockets of

the heirs of the dead General Grant. The soldier fought death, hour by hour, in pain and weariness, to earn money to leave behind as a livelihood for his family; and before they had got a penny of it, this occasional moral instructor of youth in the Philadelphia Business College had his scrofulous hands on it. John Wanamaker helped himself first; the family had to wait. Whenever he prays from the platform of his Sunday school hereafter, it will be a good idea for him to always fetch out this incident and explain it to the Throne. It may not do any real good, but it will amuse the angels.

S. L. C. of the firm of Pubs. of G. G.'s P. M.[1]

◇◇◇◇◇

(October 31, 1908)

So Butters[2] has escaped. I seem to have no luck lately. My case is like Wm. C. Prime's. Prime was a gushing pietist; religion was his daily tipple; he was always under the influence of religion. Seldom actually and solidly drunk with holiness but always on the verge of it, always dizzy, boozy, twaddlesome. But there was another and a pleasanter side to him: when he wasn't praying, when he wasn't praising God intemperately, he was damning to the nethermost hell three or four men whom he hated with his whole heart, and imploring the Throne of Grace to keep them alive so that he could go on

[1] This was written at the time of Mark Twain's suit against Wanamaker in 1886 or 1887. He seems to have intended to discourse about it in the *Autobiography*, but did not.
[2] Henry Butters.

hating and damning them and be happy. Chiefest of these was Mr. Lincoln's great Secretary of War, Edwin M. Stanton.

When Stanton died in 1869, Prime was doing the Nile with his brother-in-law, the distinguished philologist of Hartford, Hammond Trumbull. One day when the dahabeah was tied up to the bank near Luxor, Prime was ashore lounging up and down in the rich gloaming and pouring out ecstasies of pious gratitude to the Creator for permitting His worm to see this sumptuous loveliness while yet in the flesh. An ascending dahabeah handed Trumbull the sad news of our nation's bereavement. He stepped ashore to break it to Prime. Then he stopped and respectfully waited, for Prime was doing an attitude— doing it in his best theatrical style, with one eye furtively cocked toward Heaven to see if it was being noticed up there. And he was working off his panegyric and stacking up his grateful adorations mountains high. He finished with an eloquent burst and a self-satisfied nod of the head, as who should say, "There—put that in your archives." Then Trumbull told him.

There was a sudden change. Prime shook his fist at the sky and shouted venomously:

"You've taken him—taken my all and left me a pauper! Humbly and faithfully have I served You from the cradle up, and *this* is what I get for it!"

Butters has escaped, and now I likewise am poor indeed. He has been my pet aversion, my heart's detested darling, for nearly seven years; and now for no sufficient reason, no even plausible excuse, he is taken from me. I would rather have lost thirty uncles.[3]

◇◇◇◇◇

(October 3, 1907)[4]

In some ways I was always honest; even from my earliest years I could never bring myself to use money which I had acquired in questionable ways; many a time I tried, but principle was always stronger than desire. Six or eight months ago, Lieut.-Gen. Nelson A. Miles was given a great dinner party in New York, and when he and I were chatting together in the drawing-room before going out to dinner he said, "I've known you as much as thirty years, isn't it?"

I said, "Yes, that's about it, I think."

He mused a moment or two and then said, "I wonder we didn't meet in Washington in 1867; you were there at that time, weren't you?"

I said, "Yes, but there was a difference; I was not known then; I had not begun to bud—I was an obscurity; but you had been adding to your fine Civil War record; you had just come back from your brilliant Indian campaign in the Far West, and had been rewarded with a brigadier-generalship in the regular army, and everybody was talking about you and praising you. If you had met me, you wouldn't be able to remember it now—unless some unusual circumstance of the meeting had burnt it into your memory. It is forty years ago, and people don't remember nobodies over a stretch of time like that."

I didn't wish to continue the conversation along that line, so I changed the subject. I could have

[3] See Introduction.
[4] Published in the *North American Review* for December, 1907.

proven to him without any trouble that we did meet in Washington in 1867, but I thought it might embarrass one or the other of us, so I didn't do it. I remember the incident very well. This was the way of it:

I had just come back from the *Quaker City* Excursion, and had made a contract with Elisha Bliss of Hartford to write a book about it. I was out of money, and I went down to Washington to see if I could earn enough there to keep me in bread and butter while I should write the book. I came across William Swinton,[5] brother of the historian, and together we invented a scheme for our mutual sustenance; we became the fathers and originators of what is a common feature in the newspaper world now, the syndicate. We became the old original first Newspaper Syndicate on the planet; it was on a small scale but that is usual with untried new enterprises. We had twelve journals on our list; they were all weeklies, all obscure and poor and all scattered far away among the back settlements. It was a proud thing for those little newspapers to have a Washington correspondence, and a fortunate thing for us that they felt in that way about it. Each of the twelve took two letters a week from us, at a dollar per letter; each of us wrote one letter per week and sent off six duplicates of it to these benefactors, thus

[5] This agrees with the *Autobiography*, I, 323. Paine makes it John Swinton, not William, *Biography,* p. 359. I have been unable to establish which it was—if, in fact, it was either. Both Swintons might be called historians, but at the time Mark speaks of John was chief of the editorial staff of the *New York Times.* William, who had recently been a war correspondent, was much more likely to have been in Washington.

acquiring twenty-four dollars a week to live on, which was all we needed in our cheap and humble quarters.

Swinton was one of the dearest and loveliest human beings I have ever known, and we led a charmed existence together, in a contentment which knew no bounds. Swinton was refined by nature and breeding; he was a gentleman by nature and breeding; he was highly educated; he was of a beautiful spirit; he was pure in heart and speech. He was a Scotchman, and a Presbyterian; a Presbyterian of the old and genuine school, being honest and sincere in his religion and loving it and finding serenity and peace in it. He hadn't a vice, unless a large and grateful sympathy with Scotch whisky may be called by that name. I didn't regard it as a vice, because he was a Scotchman, and Scotch whisky to a Scotchman is as innocent as milk is to the rest of the human race. In Swinton's case it was a virtue and not an economical one. Twenty-four dollars a week would really have been riches to us if we hadn't had to support that jug; because of the jug we were always sailing pretty close to the wind, and any tardiness in the arrival of any part of our income was sure to cause some inconvenience.

I remember a time when a shortage occurred; we had to have three dollars, and we had to have it before the close of the day. I don't know now how we happened to want all that money at one time; I only know we had to have it. Swinton told me to go out and find it, and he said he would also go out and see what he could do. He didn't seem to have any doubt that we would succeed, but I knew that that was his religion working in him; I hadn't the same confidence; I hadn't any idea where to turn to raise all that bullion and I said so. I think he was ashamed of me, privately, because of my weak faith. He told me to give myself no uneasiness, no concern; and said in a simple, confident and unquestioning way, "The Lord will provide." I saw that he fully believed the Lord would provide, but it seemed to me that if he had had my experience— But never mind that; before he was done with me his strong faith had had its influence, and I went forth from the place almost convinced that the Lord really would provide.

I wandered around the streets for an hour, trying to think up some way to get that money, but nothing suggested itself. At last I lounged into the big lobby of the Ebbitt House, which was then a new hotel, and sat down. Presently a dog came loafing along. He paused, glanced up at me and said with his eyes, "Are you friendly?" I answered with my eyes that I was. He gave his tail a grateful wag and came forward and rested his jaw on my knee and lifted his brown eyes to my face in a winningly affectionate way. He was a lovely creature, as beautiful as a girl, and he was made all of silk and velvet. I stroked his smooth brown head and fondled his drooping ears, and we were a pair of lovers right away. Pretty soon Brig.-Gen. Miles, the hero of the land, came strolling by in his blue and gold splendors with everybody's admiring gaze upon him. He saw the dog and stopped, and there was a light in his eye which showed that he had a warm place in his heart for dogs like this gracious creature; then he came forward and patted the dog and said,

"He is very fine—he is a wonder; would you sell him?"

I was greatly moved; it seemed a marvelous thing to me, the way Swinton's prediction had come true.

I said, "Yes."

The General said, "What do you ask for him?"

"Three dollars."

The General was manifestly surprised. He said, "Three dollars? Only three dollars? Why that dog is a most uncommon dog; he can't possibly be worth less than fifty. If he were mine, I wouldn't take a hundred for him. I'm afraid you are not aware of his value. Reconsider your price if you like, I don't wish to wrong you."

But if he had known me he would have known that I was no more capable of wronging him than he was of wronging me. I responded with the same quiet decision as before,

"No, three dollars. That is his price."

"Very well, since you insist upon it," said the General, and he gave me three dollars and led the dog away, and disappeared upstairs.

In about ten minutes a gentle-faced, middle-aged gentleman came along, and began to look around here and there and under tables and everywhere, and I said to him, "Is it a dog you are looking for?"

His face had been sad, before, and troubled; but it lit up gladly now, and he answered, "Yes—have you seen him?"

"Yes," I said, "he was here a minute ago, and I saw him follow a gentleman away. I think I could find him for you if you would like me to try."

I have seldom seen a person look so grateful, and

there was gratitude in his voice, too, when he conceded that he would like me to try. I said I would do it with great pleasure but that as it might take a little time I hoped he would not mind paying me something for my trouble. He said he would do it most gladly—repeating that phrase "most gladly,"—and asked me how much.

I said, "Three dollars."

He looked surprised, and said, "Dear me, it is nothing! I will pay you ten, quite willingly."

But I said, "No, three is the price," and I started for the stairs without waiting for any further argument, for Swinton had said that that was the amount that the Lord would provide and it seemed to me that it would be sacrilegious to take a penny more than was promised.

I got the number of the General's room from the office clerk, as I passed by his wicket, and when I reached the room I found the General there caressing his dog, and quite happy. I said, "I am sorry, but I have to take the dog again."

He seemed very much surprised and said, "Take him again? Why, he is my dog; you sold him to me, and at your own price."

"Yes," I said, "it is true—but I have to have him, because the man wants him again."

"What man?"

"The man that owns him; he wasn't my dog."

The General looked even more surprised than before, and for a moment he couldn't seem to find his voice; then he said, "Do you mean to tell me that you were selling another man's dog—and knew it?"

"Yes, I knew it wasn't my dog."

"Then why did you sell him?"

I said, "Well, that is a curious question to ask. I sold him because you wanted him. You offered to buy the dog; you can't deny that. I was not anxious to sell him—I had not even thought of selling him —but it seemed to me that if it could be any accommodation to you ——"

He broke me off in the middle, and said, "*Accommodation* to me? It is the most extraordinary spirit of accommodation I have ever heard of—the idea of your selling a dog that didn't belong to you ——"

I broke him off there and said, "There is no relevancy about this kind of argument; you said yourself that the dog was probably worth a hundred dollars. I only asked you three; was there anything unfair about that? You offered to pay more, you know you did. I only asked you three; you can't deny it."

"Oh, what in the world has that to do with it! The crux of the matter is that you didn't own the dog—can't you see that? You seem to think that there is no impropriety in selling property that isn't yours provided you sell it cheap. Now then——"

I said, "Please don't argue about it any more. You can't get around the fact that the price was perfectly fair, perfectly reasonable—considering that I didn't own the dog—and so arguing about it is only a waste of words. I have to have him back again because the man wants him; don't you see that I haven't any choice in the matter? Put yourself in my place. Suppose you had sold a dog that didn't belong to you; suppose you——"

"Oh," he said, "don't muddle my brains any more

with your idiotic reasonings! Take him along, and give me a rest."

So I paid back the three dollars and led the dog downstairs and passed him over to his owner, and collected three for my trouble.

I went away then with a good conscience, because I had acted honorably; I never could have used the three that I sold the dog for, because it was not rightly my own, but the three I got for restoring him to his rightful owner was righteously and properly mine, because I had earned it. That man might never have gotten that dog back at all, if it hadn't been for me. My principles have remained to this day what they were then. I was always honest; I know I can never be otherwise. It is as I said in the beginning—I was never able to persuade myself to use money which I had acquired in questionable ways.

Now then, that is the tale. Some of it is true.

❖❖❖❖❖

(*May* 26, 1907)

Through Mr. Paine I learn that Jim Gillis is dead. He died, aged seventy-seven, in California about two weeks ago, after a long illness. Mr. Paine went with Mr. Goodman to see him but Jim was too ill to see anyone. Steve Gillis's end is also near at hand and he lies cheerfully and tranquilly waiting. He is up in the sylvan Jackass Gulch country, among the other Gillises whom I knew so well something more than forty years ago—George and Billy, brothers of Steve and Jim. Steve and George and

Billy have large crops of grandchildren, but Jim remained a bachelor to the end.

I think Jim Gillis was a much more remarkable person than his family and his intimates ever suspected. He had a bright and smart imagination and it was of the kind that turns out impromptu work and does it well, does it with easy facility and without previous preparation, just builds a story as it goes along, careless of whither it is proceeding, enjoying each fresh fancy as it flashes from the brain and caring not at all whether the story shall ever end brilliantly and satisfactorily or shan't end at all. Jim was born a humorist and a very competent one. When I remember how felicitous were his untrained efforts, I feel a conviction that he would have been a star performer if he had been discovered, and had been subjected to a few years of training with a pen. A genius is not very likely to ever discover himself; neither is he very likely to be discovered by his intimates; in fact I think I may put it in stronger words and say it is impossible that a genius—at least a literary genius—can ever be discovered by his intimates; they are so close to him that he is out of focus to them and they can't get at his proportions; they cannot perceive that there is any considerable difference between his bulk and their own. They can't get a perspective on him, and it is only by a perspective that the difference between him and the rest of their limited circle can be perceived.

St. Peter's cannot be impressive for size to a person who has always seen it close at hand and has never been outside of Rome; it is only the stranger, approaching from far away in the Campagna, who sees Rome as an indistinct and characterless blur, with the mighty cathedral standing up out of it all lonely and unfellowed in its majesty. Thousands of geniuses live and die undiscovered—either by themselves or by others. But for the Civil War, Lincoln and Grant and Sherman and Sheridan would not have been discovered, nor have risen into notice. I have touched upon this matter in a small book which I wrote a generation ago and which I have not published as yet—*Captain Stormfield's Visit to Heaven*. When Stormfield arrived in heaven he was eager to get a sight of those unrivaled and incomparable military geniuses, Caesar, Alexander and Napoleon, but was told by an old resident of heaven that they didn't amount to much there as military geniuses, that they ranked as obscure corporals only by comparison with a certain colossal military genius, a shoemaker by trade, who had lived and died unknown in a New England village and had never seen a battle in all his earthly life. He had not been discovered while he was in the earth, but heaven knew him as soon as he arrived there, and lavished upon him the honors which he would have received in the earth if the earth had known that he was the most prodigious military genius the planet had ever produced.

I spent three months in the log-cabin home of Jim Gillis and his "pard," Dick Stoker, in Jackass Gulch, that serene and reposeful and dreamy and delicious sylvan paradise of which I have already spoken. Every now and then Jim would have an inspiration, and he would stand up before the great log fire, with his back to it and his hands crossed behind him, and

deliver himself of an elaborate impromptu lie—a
fairy tale, an extravagant romance—with Dick
Stoker as the hero of it as a general thing. Jim always soberly pretended that what he was relating
was strictly history, veracious history, not romance.
Dick Stoker, gray-headed and good-natured, would
sit smoking his pipe and listen with a gentle serenity to these monstrous fabrications and never utter
a protest.

In one of my books—*Huckleberry Finn,* I think—
I have used one of Jim's impromptu tales, which he
called "The Tragedy of the Burning Shame." I had
to modify it considerably to make it proper for print,
and this was a great damage. As Jim told it, inventing it as he went along, I think it was one of the most
outrageously funny things I have ever listened to.
How mild it is in the book, and how pale; how extravagant and how gorgeous in its unprintable form!
I used another of Jim's impromptus in a book of
mine called *A Tramp Abroad,* a tale of how the
poor innocent and ignorant woodpeckers[6] tried to fill
up a house with acorns. It is a charming story, a delightful story, and full of happy fancies. Jim stood
before the fire and reeled it off with the easiest facility, inventing its details as he went along and
claiming as usual that it was all straight fact, unassailable fact, history pure and undefiled. I used
another of Jim's inventions in one of my books, the
story of Jim Baker's cat, the remarkable Tom
Quartz.[7] Jim Baker was Dick Stoker, of course;

[6] Blue jays.
[7] In *Roughing It.*

Tom Quartz had never existed; there was no such cat, at least outside of Jim Gillis's imagination.

Once or twice Jim's energetic imagination got him into trouble. A squaw came along one day and tried to sell us some wild fruit that looked like large greengages. Dick Stoker had lived in that cabin eighteen years, and knew that that product was worthless and inedible; but heedlessly and without purpose, he remarked that he had never heard of it before. That was enough for Jim. He launched out with fervent praises of that devilish fruit, and the more he talked about it the warmer and stronger his admiration of it grew. He said that he had eaten it a thousand times; that all one needed to do was to boil it with a little sugar and there was nothing on the American continent that could compare with it for deliciousness. He was only talking to hear himself talk; and so he was brought up standing and for just one moment, or maybe two moments, smitten dumb when Dick interrupted him with the remark that if the fruit was so delicious why didn't he invest in it on the spot? Jim was caught but he wouldn't let on; he had gotten himself into a scrape but he was not the man to back down or confess; he pretended that he was only too happy to have this chance to enjoy once more this precious gift of God. Oh, he was a loyal man to his statements! I think he would have eaten that fruit if he had known it would kill him. He bought the lot, and said airily and complacently that he was glad enough to have that benefaction, and that if Dick and I didn't want to enjoy it with him we could let it alone—he didn't care.

Then there followed a couple of the most delight-

ful hours I have ever spent. Jim took an empty kero-
sene can of about a three-gallon capacity and put it
on the fire and filled it half full of water, and
dumped into it a dozen of those devilish fruits; and
as soon as the water came to a good boil he added a
handful of brown sugar; as the boiling went on he
tested the odious mess from time to time; the unholy
vegetables grew softer and softer, pulpier and pulpier, and now he began to make tests with a table-
spoon. He would dip out a spoonful and taste it,
smack his lips with fictitious satisfaction, remark that
perhaps it needed a little more sugar—so he would
dump in a handful and let the boiling go on a while
longer; handful after handful of sugar went in and
still the tasting went on for two hours, Stoker and
I laughing at him, ridiculing him, deriding him,
blackguarding him all the while, and he retaining
his serenity unruffled.

At last he said the manufacture had reached the
right stage, the stage of perfection. He dipped his
spoon, tasted, smacked his lips, and broke into enthusiasms of grateful joy; then he gave us a taste
apiece. From all that we could discover, those tons
of sugar had not affected that fruit's malignant
sharpness in the least degree. Acid? It was all acid,
vindictive acid, uncompromising acid, with not a
trace of the modifying sweetness which the sugar
ought to have communicated to it and would have
communicated to it if that fruit had been invented
anywhere outside of perdition. We stopped with
that one taste, but that great-hearted Jim, that
dauntless martyr, went on sipping and sipping, and
sipping, and praising and praising, and praising, and

praising, until his teeth and tongue were raw, and Stoker and I nearly dead with gratitude and delight. During the next two days neither food nor drink passed Jim's teeth; so sore were they that they could not endure the touch of anything; even his breath passing over them made him wince; nevertheless he went steadily on voicing his adulations of that brutal mess and praising God. It was an astonishing exhibition of grit, but Jim was like all the other Gillises, he was made of grit.

About once a year he would come down to San Francisco, discard his rough mining costume, buy a fifteen-dollar suit of ready-made slops, and stride up and down Montgomery Street with his hat tipped over one ear and looking as satisfied as a king. The sarcastic stares which the drifting stream of elegant fashion cast upon him did not trouble him; he seemed quite unaware. On one of these occasions Joe Goodman and I and one or two other intimates took Jim up into the Bank Exchange billiard room. It was the resort of the rich and fashionable young swells of San Francisco. The time was ten at night and the twenty tables were all in service, all occupied. We strolled up and down the place to let Jim have a full opportunity to contemplate and enjoy this notable feature of the city.

Every now and then a fashionable young buck dropped a sarcastic remark about Jim and his clothes. We heard these remarks, but hoped that Jim's large satisfaction with himself would prevent his discovering that he was the object of them; but that hope failed; Jim presently began to take notice; then he began to try to catch one of these men in the act of making his remark. He presently succeeded. A large and handsomely dressed young gentleman was the utterer. Jim stepped toward him and came to a standstill, with his chin lifted and his haughty pride exhibiting itself in his attitude and bearing, and said, impressively, "That was for me. You must apologize, or fight."

Half a dozen of the neighboring players heard him say it, and they faced about and rested the butts of their cues on the floor and waited with amused interest for results. Jim's victim laughed ironically, and said, "Oh, is that so? What would happen if I declined?"

"You will get a flogging that will mend your manners."

"Oh, indeed! I wonder if that's so."

Jim's manner remained grave and unruffled. He said, "I challenge you. You must fight me."

"Oh, really! Will you be so good as to name the time?"

"*Now.*"

"How prompt we are! Place?"

"*Here.*"

"This is charming! Weapons?"

"Double-barreled shotguns loaded with slugs; distance, thirty feet."

It was high time to interfere. Goodman took the young fool aside and said, "You don't know your man and you are doing a most dangerous thing. You seem to think he is joking but he is not joking, he is not that kind; he's in earnest; if you decline the duel he will kill you where you stand; you must accept his terms, and you must do it right away for you have no time to waste; take the duel or apologize. You will apologize of course, for two reasons: you insulted him when he was not offending you; that is one reason, the other is that you naturally neither want to kill an unoffending man nor be killed yourself. You will apologize and you will have to let him word the apology; it will be more strong and more uncompromising than any apology that you, even with the most liberal intentions, would be likely to frame."

The man apologized, repeating the words as they fell from Jim's lips—the crowd massed around the pair and listening—and the character of the apology was in strict accordance with Goodman's prediction concerning it.

I mourn for Jim. He was a good and steadfast friend, a manly one, a generous one; an honest and honorable man and endowed with a lovable nature. He instituted no quarrels himself but whenever a quarrel was put upon him he was on deck and ready.

The world loses a good deal by the laws of decorum; gains a good deal, of course, but certainly loses a good deal. I remember a case in point.[8] I started to walk to Boston once with my pastor—pastor and old familiar friend in one. At nine that night, twelve hours out, we had tramped nearly thirty miles

[8] This passage is one of the random pieces that preceded Mark's sustained work on the *Autobiography*. It is difficult to date but was probably written in the 1880's and at one time formed part of a long manuscript—I cannot tell which one. The walk to Boston with Twichell occurred in 1874 and is described in Paine, *Biography*, pp. 527 ff.

and I was nearly dead with fatigue, cold, pain, and lameness; skin mostly gone from my heels, tendons of my legs shortened by a couple of inches, each and every limp a sharp agony. But the Reverend was as fresh as ever; and light-hearted and happy to a degree that was not easy to bear. There were small farmhouses at intervals but the occupants all fled down cellar whenever we hailed or knocked, for the roads were alive with murderous tramps in those days.

By ten at night I had dragged myself another half mile and this, to my unutterable gratitude, brought us to a village—call it Duffield,[9] any name will do. We were soon in the bar of the inn and I dropped at once into a chair behind the big hot stove, full of content, happy to the marrow, and desiring only to be left unmolested. But the Reverend did not care to sit down; he was brimming with unexpended vigors, his jaw was not tired with twelve hours' wagging, he must stir about, he must ask some questions.

The room was about twelve by sixteen, a snug little place—unpainted counter at one end, four or five feet long, three unpainted white-pine shelves behind it with ten or twelve bottles scattered along them, containing liquor and flies; no carpet, no decorations except a lithograph on the wall—horse race in a hailstorm, apparently; hail turns out to be flyspecks. Two men present: No. 1, the old village bummer, seated and hovering over the stove, opposite side from me—expectorating on it occasionally, where he could find a red-hot spot; No. 2 was a young and

[9] A notebook entry made four years after the event shows that they stopped for the night at the village of Ashland.

vigorous man, in a chair tilted back against the white-pine partition; chin buried in his breast; coonskin cap on, its natural tail sticking down past left ear; heels propped on round of chair; breeches rolled to boot tops. Now and then *he* shot at the stove, five feet away, and hit it without breaking up his attitude.

These men had not moved since we entered, nor made utterance except to answer our greeting, in the beginning, with a grunt, courteously meant. The Reverend browsed around, now here, now there, plying me with remarks, which I did not disturb my bliss to respond to; so, at last he was obliged to apply elsewhere. He is an observer. He had observed signs and smelt smells which suggested that although these men seemed so dumb and dead, the one tilted against the wall might possibly be coaxed into a state of semi-interest by some reference to horses:—an ostler, the Reverend guessed, and was right, as transpired later. So he said, "Well, ostler, I suppose you raise some pretty fine breeds of horses around here?"

The young fellow unbent right away; and his face, which was a good face, lighted pleasantly, eagerly in fact. He untilted, planted his feet on the floor, shoved his coon tail around to the rear, spread his broad hands upon his knees, beamed up at the tall Reverend, and turned himself loose:

"Well, now, I tell *you!—pretty* fine ain't the word!—and it don't *begin!*"

Evidently he was as good-hearted a young fellow as ever was, and as guiltless of wish or intent to offend; yet into the chance chinks of that single little short sentence he managed to wattle as much as two yards and a half of the most varied and wonderful profanity! And that sentence did not end his speech —no, it was the mere introduction; straight after it followed the speech—a speech five minutes long, full of enthusiastic horse statistics; poured out with the most fluent facility, as from an inexhaustible crater, and all ablaze from beginning to end with crimson lava jets of desolating and utterly unconscious profanity! It was his native tongue; he had no idea that there was any harm in it.

When the speech ended there was a mighty silence; the Reverend was in a state of stupefaction— dumb, he was, for once. The situation was unique, delicious. The bliss which I had been feeling before was tame to what I was feeling now. Skinned heels were nothing; I could have enjoyed this thing if I had been skinned all over. I did not laugh exteriorly for that would be indecorous. I made no motion, gave no sign; simply sat still and slowly died with joy. The Reverend looked at me appealingly, as much as to say, "Don't desert a friend in heavy trouble—help me out of this." I did nothing—was too near dissolution to be useful—and the ostler turned himself loose once more; once more he oozed eloquent profanity and incredible smut from every pore; and all so naturally and sweetly and innocently that it would have been flattery to call it a sin.

In desperation the Reverend broke in with a question about some other matter—mild, commonplace, less exciting than horse affairs: something about the roads and distances thence to Boston; hoped and believed that this cold topic would furnish no chances for lurid language. A mistake; the ostler sailed into that subject, rained, hailed, blew great guns, and thundered and lightened over it, under it, around it, and through it, with all the profane splendor which had distinguished his horse talk.

The Reverend rushed to the front again, pulled the ostler loose from the roads and got him to tackle the crops. Another failure. He went into the crops with as fresh a zeal as ever and drove his dialectic night cart through it at as rattling a gait and with as fragrant effect as in the beginning. In a sort of pathetic despair the Reverend fled, as a refuge, to the ancient bummer at the stove and uncorked him with a most innocuous remark, a colorless and un-incendiary remark, about my lame and sore condi-tion; whereupon the bummer, a pitying and kindly creature, turned *him*self loose with a perfectly Ve-suvian eruption of charitable dirt and blasphemy concerning the healing properties of "Karosine" ex-ternally applied; appealed to the ostler to confirm the almost miraculous excellence of Karosine for bruises and abrasions; the ostler responded with mephitic enthusiasm; and for five minutes the Rev-erend stood speechless there while the unutterable tides from these two sewers swept over him.

At last a saving thought slipped into his brain. He sauntered to the counter, got a letter out of his pocket, glanced through it, returned it to its en-velope, laid it on the counter, ciphered aimlessly upon it with a pencil; then presently sauntered away and left it there with a sinful pretense of having forgot-ten it. There was a pale joy in his jaded eye when he saw the bait take; saw the ostler loaf toward the counter; saw him take up the envelope and drop his eye on it. There was a pause, and silence! then the ostler broke out with glad surprise:

"What!—you are a preacher?"

(Prodigious and long-continued thunderpeal of improprieties and profanities), "Why didn't you *tell* a body so! *I* didn't know you was anybody!"

And straightway he flew around with loving alacrity, routed the cook out of bed, chambermaid likewise, and in two minutes these people were hard at work in our behalf. Then the delightful and delighted orator seated the Reverend in the place of honor and told him all about the state of church matters in Duffield: a flowing, masterly, good-hearted, right-purposed narrative which was fifteen minutes passing a given point, and was torch-lighted with indelicacies from end to end, which flickered lambent through a misty red hell of profanity rent and torn at four-foot intervals all down the line by sky-cleaving rocket explosions of gorgeous blasphemy! Admirable artist!—all his previous efforts were but lightning-bug-and-glowworm displays compared to this final and supreme conflagration!

As we turned in, in a double-bedded room, the Reverend remarked, with subdued gratefulness:

"Well, as to this thing, there is one comfort, anyway—such as it is: You can't *print* it, Mark."

He was right about that, of course. It was extravagantly funny. But only because those men were innocent of harmful intent. Otherwise it would have been barren of fun, and merely disgusting. Next morning the warm-blooded ostler bounded into the breakfast room, perishing with laughter, and told the grave and respectable landlady and her little daughter how he had found the geese frozen fast in the pond; and his language was just as terrific as it had been the night before. These persons showed great interest in the geese, but none at all in the language—they were used to that and found no offense in it.

◇◇◇◇◇

(November 24, 1906)

I believe that our Heavenly Father invented man because he was disappointed in the monkey. I believe that whenever a human being, of even the highest intelligence and culture, delivers an opinion upon a matter apart from his particular and especial line of interest, training, and experience, it will always be an opinion of so foolish and so valueless a sort that it can be depended upon to suggest to our Heavenly Father that the human being is another disappointment, and that he is no considerable improvement upon the monkey. Congresses and Parliaments are not made up of authors and publishers, but of lawyers, agriculturists, merchants, manufacturers, bankers, and so on. When bills are proposed affecting these great industries, they get prompt and intelligent attention, because there are so many members of the lawmaking bodies who are personally and profoundly interested in these things and ready to rise up and fight for or against them with their best strength and energy. These bills are discussed and explained by men who know all about the interests involved in them; men recognized as being competent to explain and discuss and furnish authoritative information to the ignorant.

As a result, perhaps no important American or English statutes are uncompromisingly and hopelessly idiotic except the copyright statutes of these two countries. The Congresses and the Parliaments are always, and must always remain, in the condition of the British Parliaments of seventy-five and eighty years ago, when they were called upon to legislate upon a matter which was absolutely new to the whole body of them and concerning which they were as strictly and comprehensively ignorant as the unborn child is of theology and copyright.

There were no railroad men in those Parliaments; the members had to inform themselves through the statements made to them by Stephenson, and they considered him a visionary, a half-lunatic, possibly even ass and poet. Through lack of previous knowledge and experience of railway matters, they were unable to understand Stephenson. His explanations, so simple to himself, were but a fog to those well-meaning legislators; so far as they were concerned, he was talking riddles, and riddles which seemed to be meaningless, riddles which seemed also to be dreams and insanities. Still, being gentlemen, and kindly and humane, they listened to Stephenson patiently, benevolently, charitably, until at last, in a burst of irritation, he lost his prudence and proclaimed that he would yet prove to the world that he could drive a steam locomotive over iron rails at the impossible speed of twelve miles an hour! That finished him. After that the lawmakers imposed upon themselves no further polite reserves but called him, frankly, a dreamer, a crank, a lunatic.

Copyright has always had to face what Stephenson faced, bodies of lawmakers absolutely ignorant of the matter they were called upon to legislate about, also absolutely unteachable in the circumstances and bound to remain so—themselves and their successors—until a day when they shall be stockholders in publishing houses and personally interested in finding out something about authorship and the book trade—a day which is not at all likely to arrive during the term of the present geological epoch.

Authors sometimes understand their side of the question but this is rare; none of them understands the publisher's side of it. A man must be both author and publisher, and experienced in the scorching griefs and trials of both industries, before he is competent to go before a Copyright Committee of Parliament or Congress and afford it information of any considerable value. A thousand, possibly ten thousand, valuable speeches have been made in Congresses and Parliaments upon great corporation interests, for the men who made them had been competently equipped by personal suffering and experience to treat those great matters intelligently; but so far as I know, no publisher of great authority has ever sat in a lawmaking body and made a speech in his trade's interest that was worth remembering or that has been remembered. So far as I know, only one author has ever made a memorable speech before a lawmaking body in the interest of his trade—that was Macaulay. I think his speech is called great to this day by both authors and publishers; whereas the speech is so exhaustively ignorant of its subject, and so trivial and jejune in its reasonings, that to the person who has been both author and publisher it ranks as another and formidable evidence, and possibly even proof, that in discarding the monkey and substituting man, our Father in Heaven did the monkey an undeserved injustice.

Consider a simple example. If you could prove that only twenty idiots are born in a century and that each of them, by special genius, was able to make an article of commerce which no one else could make; and which was able to furnish the idiot and his descendants after him an income sufficient for the modest and economical support of half a dozen persons, there is no Congress and no Parliament in all Christendom that would dream of descending to the shabbiness of limiting that trifling income to a term of years, in order that it might be enjoyed thereafter by persons who had no sort of claim upon it. I know that this would happen because all Congresses and Parliaments have a kindly feeling for idiots, and a compassion for them, on account of personal experience and heredity. Neither England nor America has been able to produce in a century any more than twenty authors whose books have been able to outlive the copyright limit of forty-two years, yet the Congresses and the Parliaments stick to the forty-two-year limit greedily, intensely, pathetically, and do seem to believe by some kind of insane reasoning that somebody is in some way benefited by this trivial robbery inflicted upon the families of twenty authors in the course of a hundred years. The most uncompromising and unlimited stupidity can invent nothing stupider than this; not even the monkey can get down to its level.

In a century we have produced two hundred and twenty thousand books; not a bathtub-full of them are still alive and marketable. The case would have been the same if the copyright limit had been a thousand years. It would be entirely safe to make it a thousand years, and it would also be properly respectable and courteous to do it.

When I was in London seven years ago I was haled before the Copyright Committee of the House of Lords, who were considering a bill to add eight entire years to the copyright limit, and make it fifty. One of the ablest men in the House of Lords did the most of the question asking—Lord Thring[10] —but he seemed to me to be a most striking example of how unintelligent a human being can be when he sets out to discuss a matter about which he has had no personal training and no personal experience.

There was a long talk, but I wish to confine myself to a single detail of it. Lord Thring asked me what I thought would be a fair and just copyright limit. I said a million years—that is to say, copyright in perpetuity. The answer seemed to outrage him; it quite plainly irritated him. He asked me if I was not aware of the fact that it had long ago been decided that there could be no property in ideas and that as a book consisted merely of ideas, it was not entitled to rank as property or enjoy the protections extended to property. I said I was aware that somebody, at some time or other, had given birth to that astonishing superstition, and that an ostensibly intelligent human race had accepted it

[10] Paine, in the *Biography,* makes this Lord Thwing. It appears to have been either George Herbert Thring, an authority on copyright, or Sir Henry Thring, later Baron Thring, Parliamentary Counsel.

with enthusiasm, without taking the trouble to examine it and find out that it was an empty inspiration and not entitled to respect. I added that in spite of its being regarded as a fact and also well charged with wisdom, it had not been respected by any Parliament or Congress since Queen Anne's time; that in her day, and the changing of perpetual copyright to a limited copyright of fourteen years, its claim as property was *recognized*; that the retaining of a limit of any kind—of even fourteen years, for instance—was a recognition of the fact that the ideas of which a book consisted were property.

Lord Thring was not affected by these reasonings —certainly he was not convinced. He said that the fact remained that a book, being merely a collocation of ideas, was not in any sense property and that no book was entitled to perpetual existence as property, or would ever receive that grace at the hands of a legislature entrusted with the interests and well-being of the nation.

I said I should be obliged to take issue with that statement, for the reason that perpetual copyright was already existent in England, and had been granted by a Parliament or Parliaments entrusted with the duty of protecting the interests and well-being of the nation. He asked for the evidence of this and I said that the New and Old Testaments had been granted perpetual copyright in England, and that several other religious books had also been granted perpetual copyright in England, and that these perpetual copyrights were not enjoyed by the hungry widows and children of poor authors but were the property of the press of Oxford University, an institution quite well able to live without this charitable favoritism. I was vain of this unanswerable hit, but I concealed it.

With the gentleness and modesty which were born in me, I then went on and pleaded against the assumption that a book is not properly property because it is founded upon ideas and is built of ideas from its cellar to its roof. I said it would not be possible for anybody to mention to me a piece of property of any kind which was not based in the same way and built from cellar to roof out of just that same material, ideas.

Lord Thring suggested real estate. I said there was not a foot of real estate on the globe whose value, if it had any, was not the result of ideas and of nothing except ideas. I could have given him a million instances. I could have said that if a man should take an ignorant and useless dog and train him to be a good setter, or a good shepherd dog, the dog would now be more or less valuable property and would be salable at a more or less profitable figure, and that this acquired value would be merely the result of an idea practically and intelligently applied—the idea of making valuable a dog that had previously possessed no value. I could have said that the smoothing iron, the washtub, the shingle or the slate for a roof, the invention of clothing, and all the improvements that the ages have added, were all the results of men's thinkings and men's application of ideas; that but for these ideas, these properties would not have existed; that in all cases they owe their existence to ideas, and that in this way they become property, and valuable.

I could have said that but for those inspirations called ideas there would be no railways, no telegraphs, no printing press, no phonographs, no telephones—no anything in the whole earth that is called property and has a value. I did say that that holy thing, real estate, that sacred thing which enjoys perpetual copyright everywhere is like all other properties—its value is born of an idea, and every time that that value is increased it is because of the application of further ideas to it and for no other reason.

I said that if by chance there were a company of twenty white men camping in the middle of Africa, it could easily happen that while all of the twenty realized that there was not an acre of ground in the whole vast landscape in view at the time that possessed even the value of a discarded oyster can, it could also happen that there could be one man in that company equipped with ideas, a far-seeing man who could perceive that at some distant day a railway would pass through this region and that this camping ground would infallibly become the site of a prosperous city, of flourishing industries. It could easily happen that that man would be bright enough to gather together the black chiefs of the tribes of that region and buy that whole district for a dozen rifles and a barrel of whisky, and go home and lay the deeds away for the eventual vast profit of his children. It could easily come true that in time that city would be built and that land made valuable beyond imagination, and the man's children rich beyond their wildest dreams, and that this shining result would proceed from that man's idea and from no other source; that if there were any real justice in the world, the idea in a book would rank breast to breast with the ideas which created value for real estate and all other properties in the earth, and then it would be recognized that an author's children are fairly entitled to the results of his ideas as are the children of any brewer in England, or of any owner of houses and lands and perpetual-copyright Bibles.

◇◇◇◇◇

(September 7, 1906)

For good or for evil we continue to educate Europe. We have held the post of instructor for more than a century and a quarter now. We were not elected to it, we merely took it. We are of the Anglo-Saxon race. At the banquet last winter of that organization which calls itself the Ends of the Earth Club, the chairman, a retired regular army officer of high grade, proclaimed in a loud voice, and with fervency, "We are of the Anglo-Saxon race, and when the Anglo-Saxon wants a thing *he just takes it.*"

That utterance was applauded to the echo. There were perhaps seventy-five civilians present and twenty-five military and naval men. It took those people nearly two minutes to work off their stormy admiration of that great sentiment; and meanwhile the inspired prophet who had discharged it—from his liver, or his intestines, or his esophagus, or wherever he had bred it—stood there glowing and beaming and smiling and issuing rays of happiness from every pore, rays that were so intense that they were visible and made him look like the old-time picture in the Almanac of the man who stands discharging signs of the zodiac in every direction, and so absorbed in happiness, so steeped in happiness, that he smiles and smiles and has plainly forgotten that he is painfully and dangerously ruptured and exposed amidships and needs sewing up right away.

The soldier man's great utterance, interpreted by the expression which he put into it, meant in plain English, "The English and the Americans are thieves, highwaymen, pirates, and we are proud to be of the combination."

Out of all the English and Americans present, there was not one with the grace to get up and say he was ashamed of being an Anglo-Saxon, and also ashamed of being a member of the human race since the race must abide under the presence upon it of the Anglo-Saxon taint. I could not perform this office. I could not afford to lose my temper and make a self-righteous exhibition of myself and my superior morals that I might teach this infant class in decency the rudiments of that cult, for they would not be able to grasp it; they would not be able to understand it.

It was an amazing thing to see, that boyishly frank and honest and delighted outburst of enthusiasm over the soldier prophet's mephitic remark. It looked suspiciously like a revelation, a secret feeling of the national heart surprised into expression and exposure by untoward accident, for it was a representative assemblage. All the chief mechanisms that constitute the machine which drives and vitalizes the national civilization were present—lawyers, bankers, merchants, manufacturers, journalists, politicians, soldiers, sailors—they were all there. Apparently it was the United States in banquet assembled, and qualified to speak with authority for the nation and reveal its private morals to the public view.

The initial welcome of that strange sentiment was not an unwary betrayal, to be repented of upon reflection; and this was shown by the fact that whenever during the rest of the evening a speaker found that he was becoming uninteresting and wearisome, he only needed to inject that great Anglo-Saxon moral into the midst of his platitudes to start up that glad storm again. After all, it was only the human race on exhibition. It has always been a peculiarity of the human race that it keeps two sets of morals in stock—the private and real, and the public and artificial.

Our public motto is "In God we trust," and when we see those gracious words on the trade-dollar (worth sixty cents) they always seem to tremble and whimper with pious emotion. That is our public motto. It transpires that our private one is, "When the Anglo-Saxon wants a thing *he just takes it*." Our public morals are touchingly set forth in that stately and yet gentle and kindly motto which indicates that we are a nation of gracious and affectionate multitudinous brothers compacted into one—*"e pluribus unum."* Our private morals find the light in the sacred phrase, "Come, *step* lively!"

We imported our imperialism from monarchical Europe, also our curious notions of patriotism— that is, if we have any principle of patriotism which any person can definitely and intelligibly define. It is but fair then, no doubt, that we should instruct

Europe in return for these and the other kinds of instruction which we have received from that source.

Something more than a century ago we gave Europe the first notions of liberty it had ever had, and thereby largely and happily helped to bring on the French Revolution and claim a share in its beneficent results. We have taught Europe many lessons since. But for us, Europe might never have known the interviewer; but for us certain of the European states might never have experienced the blessing of extravagant imposts; but for us the European Food Trust might never have acquired the art of poisoning the world for cash; but for us her Insurance Trusts might never have found out the best way to work the widow and orphan for profit; but for us the long delayed resumption of Yellow Journalism in Europe might have been postponed for generations to come. Steadily, continuously, persistently, we are Americanizing Europe, and all in good time we shall get the job perfected.

"For ourselves we do thoroughly believe that man, as he lives just here on this tiny earth, is in essence and possibilities the most sublime existence in all the range of non-divine being—the chief love and delight of God."—Chicago *Interior* (Presb.)

Land, it is just for the world the way I feel about it myself, sometimes, even when dry. And when not dry, even those warm words are not nearly warm enough to get up to what I am feeling, when I am holding on to something, and blinking affectionately at myself in the glass, and recollecting that I'm it.

And when I am feeling historical, there is nothing

that ecstatifies me like hunting the Chief Love and Delight of God around and around just here on this tiny earth and watching him perform. I watch him progressing and progressing—always progressing— always mounting higher and higher, sometimes by means of the Inquisition, sometimes by means of the Terror, sometimes by eight hundred years of witch-burning, sometimes by help of a St. Bartholomew's, sometimes by spreading hell and civilization in China, sometimes by preserving and elevating the same at home by a million soldiers and a thousand battle-ships; and when he gets down to today I still look at him spread out over a whole page of the morning paper, grabbing in Congress, grabbing in Albany, grabbing in New York and St. Louis and all around, lynching the innocent, slobbering hypocrisies, reeking, dripping, unsavory, but always recognizable as the same old Most Sublime Existence in all the range of Non-Divine Being, the Chief Love and Delight of God; and then I am more gladder than ever that I am it.

◇◇◇◇◇

(October 2, 1906)

The morning mail brings me a letter from a young woman in New York, in which I find the remark, "You are the blessedest 'accident' I have yet met with in my life." This brings back to my mind a conversation which I had with her a week ago, and I wish to recall some of the details of it because they illustrate a philosophy of mine—or a superstition of mine, if you prefer that word. I have been able to do for her what she regarded as a great service and, frankly speaking, I realized that it was, although it

was a service which had cost me so little in the way
of effort that the time and labor involved did not
entitle it to a compliment. She said:

"You have accomplished this for me and I am not
acquainted with another person who could have done
it. It was a happy accident that I accidentally met
you last April—no, not an accident, there being no
such things as accidents—it was ordered."

"Ordered by whom? Or by what?"

"By the Power that watches over us and commands all events."

"Issuing the orders from day to day?"

"Perhaps so. Yes, I suppose that is the way."

I said: I believe that only one command has ever
been issued and that that command was issued in the
beginning of time, in the first second of time; that
that command resulted in an act, in Adam's first
act—if there was an Adam—and that from that act
sprang another act as a natural and unavoidable
consequence, let us say it was Eve's act—and that
from *that* act proceeded *another* act of one of these
two persons as an unavoidable consequence; and
that now the chain of natural and unavoidable happenings being started, there has never been a break
in it from that day to this. And so, in my belief,
Adam's first act was the origin and cause of the
service which I have been enabled to do for you, and
I am quite sure that if Adam's first act, howsoever
trifling it may have been, had taken a different form,
no matter how trifling a form, the entire chain of
human events for all these thousands of years would
have been changed, in which case it is most unlikely
that you and I would ever have met. Indeed it is

most unlikely that *both* of us would have been born in the same land. The very slightest change in Adam's first act could have resulted in your being an Eskimo and I a Hottentot, and could also have resulted in your being born five centuries ago and in my birth being postponed until century after next.

I am not jesting. I have studied these things a long time and I positively believe that the first circumstance that ever happened in this world was the parent of every circumstance that has happened in this world since; that God ordered that first circumstance and has never ordered another one from that day to this. Plainly, then, I am not able to conceive of such a thing as the thing which we call an *accident* —that is to say, an event without a cause. Each event has its own place in the eternal chain of circumstances, and whether it be big or little it will infallibly cause the *next* event, whether the next event be the breaking of a child's toy or the destruction of a throne. According to this superstition of mine, the breaking of the toy is fully as important an event as the destruction of the throne, since without the breaking of the toy the destruction of the throne would not have happened.

But I like that word "accident," although it is, in my belief, absolutely destitute of meaning. I like it because it is short and handy and because it answers so well and so conveniently, and so briefly, in designating happenings which we should otherwise have to describe as odd, curious, interesting, and so on, and then add some elaboration to help out our meaning. And so for convenience sake, let us say it was an accident that you and I met last April, and that out of that accident grew, in a quite natural way, the linked series of accidents which led up to and made possible the service which I have had the good fortune to render you. Accident is a word which I constantly make use of when I am talking to myself about the chain of incidents which has constituted my life.

I will undertake to go back now and give name and date to some of these accidents. When I was six years old and my brother Henry four, he had the erysipelas, and when he was getting well of it Nature provided him with a new skin. I liked the old one and wished I could have it. I was prodigiously interested in the peeling process. The skin of one of his heels came off and was tough and stiff and resembled a cup, and it hung by only a shred of skin. I wanted it to play with, but, young as I was, I had a good deal of judgment and I knew that I couldn't get it by asking for it—therefore I must think up some more judicious way. When at last I was alone with him for a moment, there was my chance. The time was brief; there were no scissors handy and I pulled that heel-cup loose by force. Henry was hurt by this operation and he cried—cried much louder than was necessary, as it seemed to me, considering how small was his loss and how great my gain; but I was mainly troubled because it attracted attention and brought rebuke for me and punishment.

If I had the kind of memory I would like to have I could recall what the punishment produced in the way of a *next* link in my chain, and could then go on, link by link, all down my seventy years and prove to my perfect satisfaction that nothing has ever happened to me in all that time which could have happened to me if I had let that heel-cup alone. I haven't any idea what the links were that led down to the heel-cup event and produced it, neither can I supply from my memory the long series of events stretching down through the next six years and caused by it— but in my twelfth year another incident happened. My father died and I was taken from school and put in a printing office. I was likely to remain there forever. I had to have an accident in order to get out of it. My elder brother came up from St. Louis and furnished it by providing me an equally unpromising place in a printing office of his own.

Nothing but another accident could get me free and give me another start. Circumstances enabled me to furnish it myself. I ran away from home and was gone a year. A series of accidents—that is to say, circumstances—shipped me to St. Louis, then to New York, then to Philadelphia, then to Muscatine, Iowa, then to Keokuk; and by this time I was twenty-one years old. I was likely to remain in Keokuk forever but another accident, decreed by Adam's first act and thereby made unavoidable, came to my rescue. I had been longing to explore the Amazon River and open its headwaters to a great trade in coca, but I hadn't any money to get to the Amazon with. But for the accident thrown in my way at this time by Adam's first act, I should never have even got started toward the Amazon. That accident was a fifty-dollar bill. I found it in the street on a winter's morning. I advertised it in order to find the owner and then I immediately left for Cincinnati for fear I might succeed if I waited. At Cincinnati I took passage in the *Paul Jones* for New Orleans, on my way to the Amazon. When I had been in New Orleans a couple of days my money was all gone and I had found out that there was no ship leaving for the Amazon that year, nor any likelihood that a ship would be leaving for the Amazon during the next century.

It was imperatively necessary that another accident should come to my help. Exactly at the moment foreordained by Adam's first act it arrived. On the way down the river I had gotten acquainted with one of the pilots of the *Paul Jones*, and I went to him now and begged him to make a pilot of me. It was by accident that I had made his acquaintance. Ordinarily he would not have wanted my society in the pilothouse, and would have enabled me to find it out; but on the day that I entered it one of *his* accidents happened to be due. He was suffering from a malady or a pain of some kind, and was hardly able to stand at the wheel, so he was grateful for my advent. He gave the wheel to me and sat on the high bench and superintended my efforts while I learned how to steer. Thenceforth to New Orleans I steered for him every day all through his watch. If he hadn't had that pain I should not have made his acquaintance and my entire career down to this day would have been changed, and by a new train of accidents I should have drifted into the ministry or the penitentiary or the grave or somewhere, and should not have been heard of again.

When the war broke out three or four years later, I had been a pilot a couple of years or more, and was receiving so sumptuous a wage that I regarded myself as a rich man. I was without occupation now; the river was closed to navigation; it was time for another accident to happen or I should be drifting toward the ministry and the penitentiary again. Of course the accident happened. My elder brother was appointed Secretary of the new Territory of Nevada, and as I had to pay his passage across the continent I went along with him to see if I could find something to do out there on the frontier. By and by I went out to the Humboldt mines. The expedition was a failure. In the middle of '61 I went down to the Esmeralda mines and scored another failure. By and by I found myself shoveling sand in a quartz mill at ten dollars a week and board. I lasted two weeks and was obliged to quit, the labor was so intolerably heavy and my muscles so incompetent.

Once more there was no outlook, and I stood upon the verge of the ministry or the penitentiary— nothing could save me but a new accident. Of course it happened. In those days everybody that had a mining claim wrote descriptions of it and prophecies concerning its future richness, and published them in the Virginia City *Enterprise*, and I had been doing the like with my worthless mining claim. Now then, just as a new accident was imperatively necessary to save me from the ministry and the penitentiary, it happened. Chief Justice Turner came down there and delivered an oration. I was not present, but I knew his subject and I knew what he would say about it and how he would say it, and that into it he would inject all his pet quotations. I knew that he would scatter through it the remark about somebody's lips having been sweetened by "the honey of the bees of

Hymettus," and the remark that, "Whom the gods would destroy they first make mad," and the one which says, "Against the stupid even the gods strive in vain." He had a dozen other pet prettinesses and I knew them all, for I had heard him orate a good many times. He had an exceedingly flowery style and I knew how to imitate it. He could charm an audience an hour on a stretch without ever getting rid of an idea. Every now and then he would wind up an empty sentence with a flourish and say, *"Again,"* and then go on with another emptiness which he pretended was a confirmation of the preceding one. At the end he would say, *"To sum up"*— and then go on and smoothly and eloquently sum up everything he hadn't said, and his audience would go away enchanted.

I didn't hear his speech, as I have already said, but I made a report of it anyway and got in all the pet phrases; and although the burlesque was rather extravagant, it was easily recognizable by the whole Territory as being a smart imitation. It was published in the *Enterprise*, and just in the nick of time to save me. That paper's city editor was going East for three months and by return mail I was offered his place for that interval.

That accident had in it prodigious consequences for me, although I did not suspect it at the time, of course. Like all our other accidents, it happened on the minute, on the second, on the fraction of a second. No accident ever comes late; it always arrives precisely on time. When that one happened I had never been so near the ministry in my life.

I took that berth and during my occupancy of it

I had to go to Carson City, the capital, and report the proceedings of the legislature. Every Sunday I wrote a letter to the paper, in which I made a resumé of the week's legislative work, and in order that it might be readable I put no end of seasoning into it. I signed these letters "Mark Twain."

Signing them in that way was another accident which had been decreed by Adam's first act. It was the cause of my presently drifting out of journalism and into literature. I could go on now and trace everything that has ever happened to me since, in all these forty years, straight back to that accident. Out of it grew, two years later, the accident which gave me a correspondence job to live on when I was discharged from the San Francisco *Morning Call*; out of that correspondence grew the accident of my being sent to the Sandwich Islands for the Sacramento *Union*; out of that accident grew a notoriety which enabled me to mount the lecture platform when I was once more penniless and pointed for the ministry; out of the lecture accident resulted my opportunity to join the *Quaker City* Excursion; out of the excursion grew the accident of an invitation to write *The Innocents Abroad* and become profitably notorious all over America; out of that same accident grew the accident of my stepping into Charley Langdon's stateroom one day when the ship lay at anchor in the Bay of Smyrna and finding on his table a likeness of his sister, whom I was to seek out within the year and marry two years later; out of this happy accident resulted a thousand other happy accidents, link after link, year after year, until the chain reached down to you and your affairs, a week ago, and enabled me to do you a service which you believe could not have been done for you by any other person with whom you are acquainted. To my mind, it is absolutely certain that if ever a link, a single link, a link of the most apparently trifling sort, in the chain that stretches back from me to Adam, had ever been broken, there is no likelihood, nor even a remote possibility, that you and I would ever have looked into each other's faces in this life.

INDEX